Assault on the Deadwood Stage

Also by Robert K. DeArment

Assault on the Deadwood Stage

Acknowledgments

For help in the research required to tell the story of the assault on the Deadwood stage I am indebted to the following good friends:

Sharon Cunningham of Samburg, Tennessee, who passed along material about shotgun messenger Boone May that she had acquired from the May family;

Elnora L. Frye of Laramie, Wyoming, author of the essential research source for a study of criminal activity in early Wyoming, *Atlas of Wyoming Outlaws at the Territorial Penitentiary*, who generously provided a wealth of material and photographs;

Ann Gorzalka of Sheridan, Wyoming, who loaned me copies of photographs she had gathered for her valuable book, *Wyoming's Territorial Sheriffs*;

Robert McCubbin of Santa Fe, New Mexico, who delved into his fabulous collection of Wild West photographs to locate images I could use;

Rick Miller of Harker Heights, Texas, who passed along to me the Deadwood stage holdup material he had unearthed in his research into the Texas gang's activity there for his definitive biography, *Sam Bass & Gang*;

Joan Pennington of Fairfax Station, Virginia, expert cartographer, who converted my crude sketch into a fine map of the Deadwood stage routes;

And, of course, editor-in-chief Charles E. Rankin and all the fine folks at the University of Oklahoma Press with whom I have had the pleasure of working for many years.

forcement officers, backed by the U.S. marshals, set about tackling what was becoming a serious problem.

At one point, in an attempt to beat the road agents, some vehicles were fitted with chilled steel safes and special Yale locks. Two coaches were also constructed with iron plating and other features that made them virtually impregnable.

Among the most formidable opponents of the bandits was Luke Voorhees, a frontiersman who had much experience where gold and its protection were concerned. He arrived in Cheyenne as superintendent of the new stage line set up by Gilmer, Salisbury, & Patrick Company. Under his guidance, a number of other noted individuals joined the fight against the road agents. These included Walter Scott ("Quick Shot") Davis, backed by the likes of Seth Bullock, the first sheriff of Lawrence County.

Here is the real strength of this book. For years we have read about Black Hills road agents and those who fought them, but this is perhaps the first collation of both the good and the bad men. Names familiar in many books or articles are chronicled together with details of their origin, misdeeds, and, where known, their demise. In effect, the sheer volume of information is remarkable.

Well-known characters include the likes of Johnny Slaughter, the son of the city marshal of Cheyenne, an expert and much-respected stage driver who was murdered in a holdup. Similarly, one encounters the legendary James L. ("Whispering") Smith, a famous railroad detective probably more familiar to moviegoers as Alan Ladd in the film *Whispering Smith*, but in his own time a formidable opponent of the road agents.

This volume, in its story of Deadwood and other famous Black Hills cities, provides wide-ranging coverage of the hazards met when entering, establishing, and maintaining communications in a largely lawless region. That they survived and prospered, expanded, and still command our attention, is a tribute to those who fought so hard to bring order out of chaos. I envy those who will be reading *Assault on the Deadwood Stage* for the first time.

JOSEPH G. ROSA
Ruislip, Middlesex, England

and Crook City. Deadwood at that time had only one main street, which weaved like a moving rattlesnake in and out among the tree stumps and potholes left by early arrivals. Hastily constructed frame buildings familiar to most frontier habitats of the time flanked both sides of the street. Brick-built dwellings and business premises were yet to come. The few sidewalks were wooden and did little to keep back the dust of summer and the mud of winter. Communication with Cheyenne could be made by horseback in days, but to move freight and other essentials by wagon could take up to two weeks provided the route was passable.

Several attempts were made to provide a link between the camps and the outside world. Charlie Utter organized the Black Hills Transportation line with his brother Steve, and others engaged in similar ventures. But it was the establishment of stagecoach routes into the Hills and what happened afterward that has attracted the most attention and that has inspired this present study.

The stagecoach is iconic in the annals of the Old West, and invokes the image of a crimson coach balanced on springs attached to a yellow chassis and pulled by six horses or mules. The driver, seated at the front, together with a messenger or shotgun guard, handled the team as it thundered through the scrub and dust of a prairie landscape.

Some years ago, I visited a company in Oklahoma City that reproduced full-size Abbott-Downing Concord stagecoaches. When I asked why, when the stagecoach driver sat on the right side where the brake was, did Americans now drive on the right side of the road instead of the left as they had done until the early years of the twentieth century? I was told, with a smile, that when Henry Ford moved the steering wheel of his car from the center to the left, Americans then drove on the right—but the reproduction stagecoaches remained unchanged!

The establishment of both freight and financial links between Deadwood, Cheyenne, and other cities ensured that the stagecoach and freight wagons became much-needed and valued vehicles.

The stagecoach acted like a magnet to would-be and established road agents anxious to gain wealth without effort and, if need be, by force of arms. Soon passengers were never sure if their journey would be safe or if they would be divested of money and valuables or indeed their lives. In an effort to combat the gangs of road agents, law en-

Foreword

Deadwood, in the Black Hills of South Dakota, is legendary, both for its real and imaginary reputation, which is kept alive by historians and thousands of tourists. It was created at a time in frontier history that witnessed the growth of the West, but it also had a major attraction: there was gold in the Black Hills.

In 1804 Lewis and Clark described the region, which covered an area from the North Platte to the Yellowstone rivers, then westward to the Big Horn Mountains, as the Black Mountains. By the mid-1870s, however, they became known as the Black Hills.

Over the centuries, various tribes of Indians took possession of the Black Hills by force, and later by treaty, and they had little to fear from the whites. But in 1874 when Lieutenant Colonel George Armstrong Custer, at the head of a government survey expedition, confirmed that there was gold in the Hills, it created a gold fever similar to California in the late 1840s and 1850s. By 1875, aware that entering the Black Hills was illegal, and despite military efforts to keep them back, hordes of would-be gold seekers poured into the Hills. Eventually even the army realized it was fighting a losing battle to stop them.

"Wild Bill" Hickok, whose final trail led to Deadwood and his murder on August 2, 1876, helped perpetuate the town's fame. He is believed to have visited the Black Hills in the fall of 1875 or early 1876. Later he went to St. Louis, where he began organizing a large party to travel to the Hills, but another group beat him to it. He then went to Cheyenne, where he joined up with Charlie ("Colorado Charley") Utter and accompanied him to Deadwood.

Deadwood was one of several illegal camps established in the Black Hills in 1876. According to the *Cheyenne Daily Leader* of August 17, 1876, it was laid out on April 28. It was situated in a gulch, a dead-end canyon in which were also located two other camps, Elizabeth City

Illustrations

Contents

Publication of this book is made possible through the
generosity of Edith Kinney Gaylord.

Library of Congress Cataloging-in-Publication Data
DeArment, Robert K., 1925–
Assault on the Deadwood stage : road agents and shotgun messengers /
Robert K. DeArment ; foreword by Joseph G. Rosa.
p. cm.
Includes bibliographical references and index.
ISBN 978-0-8061-4182-4 (hardcover : alk. paper)
1. Deadwood Region (S.D.) — History — 19th century.
2. Outlaws — South Dakota — Deadwood Region — Biography.
3. Brigands and robbers — South Dakota — Deadwood Region — Biography.
4. Peace officers — South Dakota — Deadwood Region — Biography.
5. Stagecoaches — South Dakota — Deadwood Region — History — 19th
century.
6. Frontier and pioneer life — South Dakota — Deadwood Region.
7. Dakota Territory — History, Local.   I. Title.
F659.D2D43   2011
978.3′91 — dc22   2010044189

Assault on the Deadwood Stage

ROAD AGENTS AND SHOTGUN MESSENGERS

ROBERT K. DeARMENT

Foreword by Joseph G. Rosa

UNIVERSITY OF OKLAHOMA PRESS • NORMAN

— I —

1876: THE MOMENTOUS YEAR

We do not believe this or any other country affords such another example of rapid development as what is now known as the "Dead-wood country." Three months ago it was occupied by only a few hardy miners—scarce fifty in number. Now Deadwood, Whitewood, and their tributaries are peopled by more than 7,000.
— *Black Hills Weekly Pioneer*, June 26, 1876

The year 1876 was a most memorable one for Americans. It was the year they celebrated the one hundredth birthday of their nation, highlighted by a great Centennial Exposition in Philadelphia, the first exhibit of its kind ever held in the country. In attendance at its opening on May 10 were President Ulysses S. Grant and wife and Brazilian emperor Don Pedro and lady. Before it closed on November 10, more than ten million visitors had an opportunity to glimpse for the first time some of the wonders of the American future, including Alexander Graham Bell's telephone, the Remington Company's typewriter, Heinz ketchup, and Hires root beer.

A time of national celebration, 1876 was also a year of great internal turmoil. The presidential election of that year, with Republican Rutherford B. Hayes opposed by Democrat Samuel J. Tilden, ended in political chaos. Early returns indicated that Tilden had a substantial lead in the popular vote and seemed assured of the necessary 185 votes for victory in the Electoral College, but Republicans cried foul, claiming that many black voters in Florida, Louisiana, and South Carolina, who overwhelmingly favored Republicans, had been denied access to the polls. They demanded canvassing boards be formed to examine the voting in those states. While investigations proceeded, the issue was fought for months in the halls of Congress, which was divided, with Democrats controlling the House of Representatives and Republicans having a majority in the Senate. Each body put forward a proposal to resolve the problem, but, as might be expected, each proposal favored the candidate of the originators. Finally an electoral commission was formed to decide the issue. While Tilden and Hayes waited, the question of who would occupy the White House for the next four years dragged on. Finally, when the Republican-controlled canvassing boards reported that blacks had indeed been denied voting rights in the three southern states, Tilden conceded, and on March 2, 1877, only the day before the scheduled inauguration, the president of the Senate announced that Hayes had 185 electoral votes, Tilden 184, and Rutherford B. Hayes would become the nineteenth president of the United States.[1]

The year was also momentous in the history of the settling of the American West.

On the first of August Colorado became the thirty-eighth state, laying claim to the title "Centennial State."

Three of the most memorable events in the history of the West occurred in a little over a ten-week period in the summer of that year.

On June 25 George Armstrong Custer, nationally lionized for his military feats in the Civil War and later Indian conflicts, met his doom at the hands of combined Sioux and Northern Cheyenne Indian tribesmen when he led his Seventh Cavalry to disaster at Little Big Horn in Montana Territory. News of what became known as the "Custer Massacre" did not reach the east coast of the country until July 5, dampening the festivities of the day previous.

On August 2 another celebrated American fighting hero died violently when James Butler ("Wild Bill") Hickok was assassinated in a remote Black Hills mining camp called Deadwood.

And on September 7, when a gang led by yet another legendary figure of the American West, Jesse James, attempted to rob the bank at Northfield, Minnesota, aroused citizens of the community resisted with shot and ball and virtually destroyed the outlaw band.

The "Custer Massacre" was a great victory for the Indians mobilized to resist the relentless incursion by whites into their hunting grounds and an area the tribes held sacred, the Black Hills of Dakota Territory, but in the end it led to their defeat, for retaliation by the whites was swift and powerful.

On July 17 a unit of the Fifth U.S. Cavalry engaged a party of Cheyenne Indians near Hat Creek in Nebraska and yet another frontier figure of legendary status, William F. ("Buffalo Bill") Cody, added to his public renown by killing war leader Yellow Hair in what was widely publicized as a "duel" (actually a long-range shooting), waving a trophy of that victory, and proclaiming: "First scalp for Custer!"

In August a vindictive Congress voted to discontinue all subsistence to the Sioux, Northern Cheyenne, and Arapahoe tribes if they did not cease resistance to the white invasion of the Black Hills. Tribal leaders reluctantly agreed, and on September 26 the region of the Black Hills was officially opened to white settlement. Only a month later, on October 27, the Fifth U.S. Infantry under the command of Colonel Nelson Miles defeated a force of 2,000 Sioux at Big Dry River, Montana.

Consequences of the other dramatic events of that summer in the West followed in the fall. Jesse and Frank James had escaped the vengeance of Minnesotans after the botched bank robbery at Northfield, but their closest associates, the three Younger brothers, were shot up and captured. At a trial held in November they were convicted of robbery and murder and sentenced to life terms at the Minnesota penitentiary at Stillwater. And in December Jack McCall, the murderer of "Wild Bill" Hickok, was tried in Yankton, Dakota Territory, convicted, and hanged there on March 1, 1877.

Rumors of extensive gold deposits in the Black Hills had been rife for years in the West, but an expedition led by Custer into the country in 1874 confirmed the reports, and the region became a magnet for American fortune seekers and adventurers. During 1875 camps sprang up in the gulches hidden in the hills, and by the early months of that memorable year of 1876 the population of whites had grown immensely, with dozens of camps established on creeks throughout the region. Several of them on Whitewood Creek grew rapidly, merging into a town whose name would become forever synonymous with the excitement of the Black Hills gold rush: Deadwood City. The Indian war scare of 1876 contributed to the mushrooming growth of Deadwood, as some prospectors from remote camps converged on

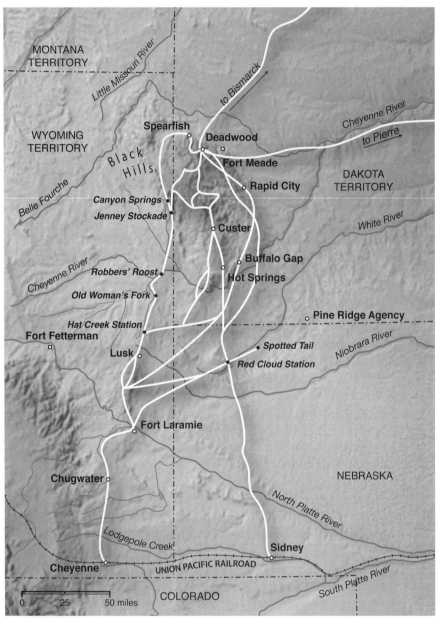

The stage routes leading to Deadwood in the Black Hills. Map by Joan Pennington.

the larger community for safety in numbers. By mid-June the population in the gulch had increased to an estimated 10,000. The name "Deadwood" and a well-deserved reputation for violence became nationally known after the murder of "Wild Bill" in August.

With the continued success of gold extraction from the Black Hills and the extraordinary growth of Deadwood, a need for a stagecoach line servicing this new area became increasingly apparent to western businessmen. Deadwood was situated in a remote location, with nothing but primitive Indian trails and rugged wagon roads leading to it. There were four major routes into the region. Two originated on the Missouri River in Dakota Territory, one from Bismarck, 225 miles to the northwest, and the other from Fort Pierre, 200 miles due eastward.[2]

From the earliest days of western exploration and expansion the Missouri River had been the major artery into the northwest territories, and riverboats transporting passengers and goods still plied its waters. On April 11, 1877, the Northwestern Express, Stage and Transportation Company, headed by Minnesotan R. Blakely, president, and C. W. Richardson, treasurer, began stagecoach service from the river port of Bismarck to Deadwood with twenty-eight Concord coaches, 175 horses, twenty-five drivers, and eight armed guards called "shotgun messengers."[3] One-way fare was $23. Relay stations were established at Little Hart, Dog Tooth, Whitney Springs, Cannon Ball, Grand River, North Moreau, South Moreau, Antelope, Cedar Canyon, Elm Springs, Belle Fourche, Spring Creek, and Crook City. In 1880 the company began operations from Fort Pierre to Deadwood with stops at Willow Creek, Lance Creek, Plum Creek, Mitchell Creek, Medicine Creek, Bad River, Box Elder, Rapid City, Spring Valley Ranch, and Sturgis City. For several years the Northwestern line carried some 5,000 passengers annually.[4] The stage to Bismarck left Deadwood daily, while the Pierre coach departed Deadwood on a triweekly schedule.[5]

But Bismarck and Pierre, anchoring the Missouri River stage routes to the Black Hills, never attained the popularity as gateways to the new bonanza country enjoyed by Cheyenne, Wyoming, and Sidney, Nebraska, towns to the south that connected the Hills to the Union Pacific Railroad, for after 1868 the railroad had supplanted the Missouri as the favored means of east-west transportation.

Only eight years previously the Union Pacific had extended iron rails west across the plains to its historic linkup with the eastbound Central Pacific at Promontory Summit, Utah. The wild sporting crowd attracted to the series of temporary end-of-track camps hastily constructed along the line soon gave these camps the epithet "Hell-on-Wheels." Most of the towns disappeared as the railroad moved on, but two that remained, Cheyenne and Sidney, provided the nearest access by rail to the goldfields of the Black Hills, and the trails leading north from these burgeoning towns became the preferred routes to the new El Dorado. Although Cheyenne was almost 325 miles from Deadwood by available road, about 40 miles more distant than its rival, Sidney,[6] it held certain advantages that led to its initial ascendancy as the major jumping-off point for the Black Hills. The problem for Sidney was the troublesome North Platte River crossing about thirty-five miles north of town. The river was notoriously dangerous when in flood and treacherous when shallow because of quicksand. Pioneers used to say that when the stream lacked water enough to drown a man, it could suck him down below to where the water was. Work on a bridge spanning the river had begun, but by the time construction was completed, Cheyenne had already established a regular stage route to the Hills and captured most of the traffic.[7]

Cheyenne held a certain advantage over its competitors in the contest to provide stagecoach service to the Black Hills. Several years earlier Todd Randall, a trading post operator at the Spotted Tail Indian Agency, situated only about fifty miles from the Black Hills, had secured a contract providing mail delivery from Cheyenne to the agency. No provision for express or passenger service had been made, however. Then in December 1875 the Wyoming Territorial Legislature, recognizing the coming need for such service, passed a bill authorizing the establishment of a daily stage line to carry passengers and express between Cheyenne and the Black Hills. With the outbreak of Indian hostility in 1876, however, many businessmen interested in setting up a line were reluctant to proceed until the Sioux relinquished their title to the Black Hills.[8]

In January 1876 two bold entrepreneurs, Captain W. H. Brown, stationed at the Red Cloud Agency, and his son-in-law, Frank D. Yates, post trader there, subcontracted for the mail service to Spotted Tail. They immediately opened a stage line to Custer City in the Black

Hills by way of the two Indian agencies. Cheyenne newspapers reported that on February 3 the "first coach of the Cheyenne and Black Hills Stage, Mail and Express line, owned by F. D. Yates & Co., stopped in front of the Inter-Ocean hotel at 7 a.m. to pick up passengers."[9] At the reins was J. W. ("Doc") Howard, a former cavalryman.[10]

That initial stage run to Custer City by way of the Red Cloud and Spotted Tail agencies required five days on the road. Two stagecoaches a week started out from Cheyenne the first two weeks, but daily departures were scheduled after that. The coaches were drawn by four horses, and an extra team was added for heavy parts of the route. At the beginning fare prices were flexible, with charges governed by the number of customers.[11]

The daring move by Yates brought quick response from other stage line entrepreneurs. Soon after the Yates coach rolled out of Cheyenne H. E. ("Stuttering") Brown,[12] business scout for Gilmer, Salisbury & Patrick, a company operating stagecoaches throughout the West, arrived in town. On February 12, only nine days after the first coach left Cheyenne for the Black Hills, Brown negotiated a deal to buy out Frank Yates's fledgling stage company.[13]

John Thornton ("Jack") Gilmer, senior member of the purchasing firm, at the age of thirty-five was already a seasoned veteran of transportation in the West. Only fifteen when he left his Illinois home, over the next twenty years he had worked for all the major stage, freighting, and express companies of the West, including Wells, Fargo & Company; Russell, Majors and Waddell; and Ben Holladay's Central, Overland, California and Pike's Peak Express Company. Starting out as a muleskinner, bullwhacker, and stagecoach driver, his energy and business savvy had earned him management positions with several of the companies.[14] As tough as the men he employed, he could handle himself in a fight, but an anecdote told of him indicates he would avoid violence if logic so ordered. Once, after being reprimanded by Gilmer for arriving late, a stage driver challenged his boss to a fistfight. Gilmer eyed the man with disdain. "If I should whip you, it would be no credit to me," he said. "If I should be whipped by you, I would be everlastingly disgraced." Turning on his heel, he walked away.[15]

Forty-one-year-old Monroe Salisbury, a New York native, had partnered Gilmer in several of his mail contracts. An early arrival in

John Thornton ("Jack") Gilmer, senior member of the initial Deadwood stagecoach company. Author's collection.

the Black Hills diggings, Salisbury had acquired part ownership in several mines in the Deadwood area, including the fabulous Homestake mine at Lead. It was he who dispatched "Stuttering" Brown from Salt Lake City to Cheyenne to purchase the infant Yates Stage Line.[16]

Mathewson T. Patrick, the third member of the firm, was forty-two. Born in Pittsburgh, Pennsylvania, he had established a general merchandise and lumber business in Omaha, Nebraska, prior to the Civil War. With the outbreak of hostilities he served as lieutenant colonel of cavalry in the Union army. Later he was an agent for the Sioux, Cheyenne, and Arapahoe Indian tribes for four years. He

Luke Voorhees, superintendent of the Gilmer stage company. Author's collection.

resigned that job to accept the post of U.S. marshal for Utah Territory, a position he held until 1873.[17]

To supervise the new stage line Gilmer hired a man of wide experience in western pursuits. Luke Voorhees, forty-one years old in 1876, was born in New Jersey and raised and educated in Michigan. Heading west at the age of twenty-one, Voorhees participated in the Pike's

Peak, Colorado, and Alder Gulch, Montana, gold rushes; was a member of a group that discovered the Kootenai diggings in Saskatchewan; and was at Virginia City, Nevada, during its turbulent days. He trailed cattle from Texas to Utah and was witness to the driving of the golden spike at Promontory Summit. He arrived in Cheyenne from Salt Lake City on February 17, 1876, and immediately tackled the many tasks required to start up the new enterprise.[18]

As he later wrote, "The excitement being at a white heat about the fabulous gold diggings in the Black Hills," he and his employers were anxious to get the line operating as quickly as possible. The first order of business was the purchase of horses, harness, and coaches. Voorhees dispatched agents to St. Louis to buy 600 well-bred stage horses and mules and transmitted a rush order to J. R. Hill & Company of Concord, New Hampshire, for 100 sets of stage harness. He sent another order to Abbot, Downing & Company of the same town for thirty heavy-duty Concord coaches and specified they were to be brightly painted with shiny red bodies and brilliant yellow wheels and spokes. The coaches were also decorated with elaborate gilt scrollwork and landscape paintings artfully painted on the doors by skilled specialists, making each coach different from the others. To expedite start-up, he had a carload of road-broken horses and all the coaches that could be spared shipped from Salt Lake City by rail. As it happened, a great deal of surplus equipment belonging to Wells, Fargo & Company remained in Utah after completion of the railroad linkup at Promontory Summit, including a number of Concord coaches in good condition. Gilmer and Company snapped up this excess at a cost of $70,000.[19]

The Concord stagecoaches the company purchased were top-of-the-line conveyances for the period. The success of the coaches manufactured by the Abbot-Downing concern was due primarily to the high quality of the workmanship and the innovative use of sturdy leather thoroughbraces to support the coach box rather than steel springs. Pains were taken to provide as much passenger space as possible while keeping the weight of the vehicle at a minimum to spare the horses. Nine passengers rode on three upholstered bench seats within the coach, while six to nine more could strap themselves to the roof and ride atop the vehicle. A "dickey seat" was immediately behind the driver, and behind that was a most uncomfortable seat gener-

ASSAULT ON THE DEADWOOD STAGE

ally referred to as the "China seat" because any Orientals, always objects of appalling discrimination, were assigned to it. If necessary, two more passengers could ride the "boot" with the driver. Hanging from the rear of the coach was a second boot, a leather device designed to hold luggage, but, in theory, at least, a place where shotgun messengers could strap themselves and pop around the corner to surprise highwaymen in front.[20] There is no record of any Deadwood stagecoach messenger ever utilizing this concept. Fares were set at $20 for first class, $15 for second, and $10 for third, payable in U.S. currency or gold dust at $20 an ounce. Later, demand for tickets grew larger than availability, and scalpers took advantage of the situation by purchasing tickets well in advance and selling them to passengers for $10 more than the published price.[21]

Relay stations along the route to Deadwood had to be established and drivers, blacksmiths, and station keepers employed. Said Voorhees: "From April 3, 1876, I was constantly moving over the Black Hills stage line from Cheyenne to Deadwood, back and forth, in getting stations established and built, and in trying to get the right kind of men to look after them."[22]

Because of its mail commitment, Yates & Company had followed a roundabout route to the Black Hills, with mandatory stops at the two Indian agencies, and had proceeded only as far as Custer City, some fifty miles south of Deadwood. Voorhees laid out a new route northward along the trail to Red Canyon station, passing through the canyon to Spring-on-Hill, and continuing on to Spring-on-Right, Pleasant Valley, and into Custer. To begin operations, that was as far as he was prepared to advance.[23]

With great haste Voorhees established stations from Cheyenne northward. When coaches stopped at these stations horse teams had to be unhitched and replacement teams harnessed in their stead. Voorhees dictated that this operation take no longer than seven minutes. Longer periods were permitted at the larger stations, where eating and sometimes lodging accommodations were provided for passengers. Time for the entire trip from Cheyenne to Deadwood was planned for between fifty and sixty hours in good weather, but more than seventy hours was often required when storms turned the rutted roads into treacherous seas of mud. Record time for the run was forty-seven hours.[24]

The first stop was at Pole Creek Ranch,[25] eighteen miles from the point of departure at Cheyenne, followed ten miles farther on by a meal station at Horse Creek Ranch. There followed Chugwater station, managed by H. B. Kelly; John Owens's ranch at Chug Springs;[26] Tom Hawk's station at Eagle's Nest; and Six-Mile and Three-Mile ranches, so designated by their distance from Fort Laramie. Nourishment for passengers was available at Three-Mile (meals 50 cents each).[27]

Following a stop at Fort Laramie, ninety-eight miles from Cheyenne, was Ten-Mile station, only used for emergencies. Then came Government Farm station and Raw Hide Buttes. A few miles beyond a station at Running Water on the Niobrara River, the road branched, with an eastern leg crossing Sage and Horse Head creeks to enter the Black Hills through Red Canyon.[28] At the height of the period of road agent attacks on the stages someone reportedly put up a sign at the entrance to Red Canyon: "Abandon Hope All Ye Who Enter Here."[29]

Hat Creek station at the crossing of Sage Creek, run by Jack Bowman, "one of the most reliable pioneer station masters along the entire Black Hills route,"[30] was an important stop. It had a telegraph and post office, brewery, bakery, butcher and blacksmith shops, and a rough-hewn "hotel" for travelers. Hat Creek station was situated in rough, broken country they called "the breaks," where in the years to come several notorious outlaw gangs, including one that took its name from the location, made their headquarters.

Harding's Ranch on Indian Creek, a meal and telegraph station, was the next stop. Then there was Cheyenne River Ranch, also with telegraph facilities and accommodations for passengers; Red Canyon station; Spring-on-Hill; Spring-in-Right; Pleasant Valley; and at last, 220 miles from Cheyenne, the southernmost Black Hills community of any dimensions, Custer City. Voorhees later extended his road north beyond Custer and set up stations at Twelve-Mile on Spring Creek, Log Cabin House, Mountain City, Reynolds Ranch, Bulldog Ranch,[31] and Whitewood Creek before reaching his final destination at Deadwood.[32]

In June 1877 Voorhees changed the route of his coaches to what was called the Jenney Stockade cutoff. From Hat Creek station the road ran north to "Old Woman's Fork," so named for what appeared to be the ghost of an Indian woman dancing in the moonlight on the nearby rimrock, where a character remembered only as "Sourdough Dick" had charge of the station. Next came May's Ranch on Lance Creek, where the stock tender and station keeper was Jim May, who, with his brother Boone, would soon join the renowned coterie of shotgun messengers defending the stagecoach line against the onslaught of the road agents. Boone May ran the station at the appropriately named Robbers' Roost on the Cheyenne River. Jenney Stockade, fifty-six miles south of Deadwood, was the next stop, where a Mrs. Scott prepared excellent meals for her stagecoach guests. Then came Beaver station and Canyon Springs, a relay station that would be the scene of one of the most memorable stage robberies a few years later. Ten Mile station was the final stop before reaching the booming camp at Deadwood.[33]

On April 3, with great fanfare, the first three Gilmer and Company stages pulled out of Cheyenne. Jack Gilmer himself, reins in hand, was on the boot of the lead coach. From eighteen to twenty passengers were crammed into and atop each coach, and baggage and express parcels were jammed into every available nook and cranny.[34] Drivers were instructed to roll into each station, and especially Deadwood, the final destination, at a gallop, alerting onlookers to the splendor of the brightly painted coaches with their new leather curtains drawn by some of the finest teams of horses in the West.[35]

But soon the outbreak of Indian hostilities necessitated a suspension of operations. Roaming war parties attacked the stages and wounded passengers. Newly established relay stations between Custer City and Fort Laramie were raided, the stock stolen, and the buildings burned. The routes to the Black Hills became extremely dangerous, even for large wagon caravans with heavily armed men defending them. Scott Davis, a formidable fighting man who was destined to play an important role in the short, violent history of the Deadwood stage, was taking a twenty-mule outfit loaded with stage company supplies to the Black Hills when he and his companions were attacked by a large war party near Hat Creek station and fought a battle lasting three hours before the arrival of a troop of cavalry from Raw Hide Buttes.[36]

Jack Gilmer ordered a halt to his stagecoach operation until conditions improved. By mid-June the raids had diminished in Wyoming and Dakota, and stage travel was resumed on the 24th, ironically the day before the "Custer Massacre" in neighboring Montana.[37]

Voorhees suffered another setback in July when a four-horse stage got through to Custer without difficulty, but on the return trip was beset by Indians who killed the driver, stole the horses, and left the passengers to fend for themselves.[38]

On August 2 (the day "Wild Bill" Hickok was murdered in Deadwood) the down coach driven by C. H. Cameron and carrying four passengers was attacked near Indian Creek. Cameron put the whip to his team, and for twelve miles a running gunfight ensued. Finally the driver swung off the road, and he and his passengers — one had been shot in the cheek and two others had bullets rip their clothes and hats — took to the brush, leaving the coach and horses to their attackers. After dark they made their way to Hat Creek station. Soldiers sent to the scene the following day found the horses gone, the harness cut to shreds, the mail scattered, and the roof of the coach crushed in.[39]

Despite all this turmoil, Luke Voorhees, determined to extend the service all the way to Deadwood, continued to set up relay stations beyond Custer. The horses he acquired to stock these stations, like those on the Cheyenne-to-Custer route, were some of the finest horses in the West and were highly coveted by the Indians. As a protection against raids by war parties, Voorhees ordered construction of heavily walled corrals with ponderous gates and hefty padlocks. By September he had established a route north beyond Custer to Hill City, Sheridan, Camp Crook, and across the headwaters of Box Elder, Elk, and Bear Butte creeks. On the 25th of that month, the day before the Black Hills were officially opened to white settlement, the first stagecoach from Cheyenne, proudly driven by Dave Dickey, rolled into Deadwood and pulled up at the stage office to the cheers of the local residents.[40]

The trip from Cheyenne had taken six and a half days, but the time would be shortened in the coming months as the road was improved and more relay stations were added. By February 11, 1877, only four and a half days were required for the journey, with three-a-week departures. By March 24 Deadwood-bound coaches left Cheyenne on a daily basis, as proclaimed in ads appearing in the Cheyenne papers:[41]

CHEYENNE AND BLACK HILLS STAGE CO.
Coaches Leaving Every Day. We Are Running Six-Horse Coaches Through to Deadwood! Via Custer, Battle Creek, Rapid, Golden, Gayville And All Mining Camps in the Hills. The U.S. mail carried free. We have first-class eating stations, and the division agents take all pains to secure the comfort of passengers. The route is well protected, having three military posts on the road, leaving only 45 miles between military camps, insuring safety over the entire route.

In that same month of March 1877, Gilmer and Salisbury bought controlling shares in the Western Stage Company, which had begun running stages to the Black Hills from Sidney, following the construction of a toll bridge over the Platte River. In April they began daily passenger service from Sidney, thus relieving some of the congestion they were experiencing at Cheyenne.[42] The trail from Sidney to the Black Hills led almost due north. Stations were established approximately fifteen miles apart at "Water Hole," Greenwood, Court House Rock, Camp Clarke at the Platte River bridge, Red Willow, Snake Creek, Point of Rocks, Running Water on the Niobrara River, Red Cloud Indian Agency, and Carney's station. At a point nine miles beyond Carney's and three miles below the territorial line the trail forked. One branch led northwest to Custer City and the southern mining camps. The other swung to the northeast, skirted the southern hills, and, heading north again, went on to Deadwood. The total length of the route was listed as 267 miles.[43]

By July 1877 the company managers could proudly report that having spent $200,000 in establishing stations and stocking the lines into Deadwood, employing 100 men with a monthly payroll of $7,000, and feeding 600 head of horses 5,000 pounds of grain a day, regular passenger service over 600 miles of route was now available. In the first six months of that year they had carried over 3,000 passengers, $1,500,000 in gold, and more than 5,000 express packages.[44]

Stage lines into the Black Hills from Bismarck and Fort Pierre never attained the success of the Gilmer, Salisbury & Patrick Company, which first opened the stagecoach door to Deadwood and offered two routes to the railroad and the outside world. In addition to lucrative passenger and mail service provided by the company, the owners obtained an exclusive contract to transport the golden treasure of the Black Hills to the railroad by means of their coaches.[45]

While Gilmer and company had made access to the great new boom camp in the Black Hills by stagecoach available for passengers, only a masochist would actually enjoy a journey by nineteenth-century stagecoach. Winter travel, as noted in the *Omaha Herald*, was especially uncomfortable. It urged passengers

> to avoid tight boots in cold weather; to walk when the driver told them to, both to ease the coach and warm themselves; to avoid liquor, which made people freeze all the quicker; to put up with the food at the stations; to avoid pipes and cigars in the coach, and if they chewed to spit to leeward; if they did drink to buy their liquor before they started as that available at the stage stations was not of the best quality, and to pass the bottle around in a friendly fashion; not to shoot, which scared the horses; not to swear or discuss politics or religion; not to grease their hair, as traveling was dusty; and, above all, not to "imagine for a moment that you are going on a picnic; expect annoyance, discomfort and some hardship."[46]

Passengers were often crammed into the coaches so tightly that some actually preferred a precarious perch on top where, braving the wind and the weather, they had to hang on to avoid being tossed off as the stage bounced over rough stretches of road. A story that went around was illustrative of problems arising from the close proximity within the coach:

> In the early days when the Deadwood-Cheyenne Stage was in operation, on one trip the passengers included an impeccably dressed, stout, and rather pompous Britisher. . . . Seated across from him in the stage was a sweet-faced, cherubic, innocent blonde in her early twenties dressed in most conservative garb. The day was hot and dusty; the windows in the coach were closed. A sudden jolt in the stagecoach caused the Englishman audibly to break wind. To cover his embarrassment, the Englishman said, "I say, the air is a bit fixed, what?" Which brought forth an immediate retort from the demure young thing: "It sure is and you're the son-of-a-bitch that fixed it."[47]

But any "annoyance, discomfort and hardship" passengers experienced on ordinary stagecoach trips would pale in comparison to what stage travelers going through the Wyoming and Dakota wilderness to and from the Black Hills would face in the coming months when highway robbers, or "road agents" as they were called, converged on the routes and the assault on the Deadwood stage began.

— 2 —

ROAD AGENTS FROM TEXAS

History does not record a more foul and dastardly murder than was perpetrated by highwaymen on the night of the 25th instant, when John Slaughter was shot dead. . . . When we consider that this affair happened within two and a half miles of this place, a city boasting of three or four thousand, and within a stone's throw of several miners' cabins, we are surprised at the boldness of the attack, and we inadvertently offer up a prayer for the speedy extermination of the vile perpetrators of such horrid deeds.
— Letter from Deadwood in the *Cheyenne Daily Sun*,
April 5, 1877

In the fall of 1876 a party of cowboys rode into the Black Hills with money from the sale of a herd of cattle they had driven all the way from Texas burning a hole in their pockets. The longhorns had belonged to ranchers back in the Lone Star State, but the cowpunchers, hired to drive the herd to the northern markets, were larcenous of heart, and, after disposal of the cattle, proceeded to spend the proceeds on a riotous spree in the deadfalls of wild and raucous Deadwood.

Leader of the bunch was twenty-eight-year-old Joel Collins. At just under six feet in height, taller than the average male of the time, Collins, with his jet-black hair and beard, was a fine figure of a man. Many considered him handsome. An experienced trail boss, he had driven cattle to market for several Texas ranchers in the early 1870s, and had also engaged in the sporting life, partnering the notorious frontier gambler and gunman "Rowdy Joe" Lowe in the management of a San Antonio saloon. No stranger to violence, he had killed a man six years earlier, stood trial, and won a jury's acquittal.[1]

At San Antonio some time in late 1875 or early 1876 Collins met a twenty-four-year-old footloose racehorse gambler named Sam Bass. The two hit it off from the start, and when Collins contracted to drive another herd north, he signed Bass on as a partner.

Unlike Collins, young Bass did not strike most observers as good-looking. An uncomplimentary description was provided by one who knew him personally:

> He was about five feet eight inches in height, dark sallow complexion, dark hair, and brown or hazel colored eyes. He had a thinly scattered black beard, which habitually appeared about a week old. He was stooped in his shoulders, and wore a downcast look, more a look of embarrassment than of villainy. He rarely spoke, except under the influence of whiskey, and when he did his words were drawled out with a shrill, nasal twang that was devoid of melody and exhibited a total absence of refinement. He was dull in all but trickery.[2]

Born in Indiana in 1851, Bass lost his mother before he was ten and his father three years later. He was eighteen when he left home to make his fortune in Texas. For several years he worked at odd jobs on farms and ranches before acquiring a lightning-fast racehorse named Jenny and becoming a familiar sporting figure in north Texas race courses with his celebrated "Denton Mare."

Two others believed to have joined Collins and Bass in the northward cattle drive were Bill Potts and Jack Davis.

Potts was an experienced trail hand, having worked on several drives to Kansas, where he had gotten himself crossways with the law on occasion and consequently sometimes used the alias Bill Heffridge or Bill Heffery. A native of Pennsylvania, he was about thirty years old, of average height and weight, with light brown hair and beard and distinguishing tattoos on his hand and arm.[3]

Davis, from Arkansas, was about the same age but a larger man, standing six feet tall and weighing 190 pounds. Stoop-shouldered, with curly hair, he was described as a man who talked and drank a

In a photo believed taken a few months before they headed north for Deadwood and short-lived road agent careers in the Black Hills, Joel Collins and Sam Bass are seen with pals John E. Gardner and Joe Collins. Bass is standing at left beside Gardner. Joel, with a smirk, points a pistol at his brother, who by his look sees no humor in it. Courtesy Robert G. McCubbin Collection.

great deal.[4] Some historians believe he was a veteran of the gambling dens of Virginia City who served time in a Nevada prison for participating in the holdup of a Central Pacific train.[5]

Once these fellows decided to keep the $8,000 derived from the sale of the cattle herd and carouse in Deadwood, a lurid chapter in western criminality and violence was opened.

Collins reportedly invested $3,500 of the cattle sale cash in a building that he converted into a dance hall described as "a dive of the very lowest grade, and the resort of the very worst and most dangerous characters in the Black Hills."[6] He staffed the establishment with members of the Deadwood demimonde, from whom he and others of the Texas crowd chose paramours. As one of their early chroniclers put it, Collins "had a 'gay girl' to solace his hours, and Sam [Bass] and Jack Davis had to have one each, too."[7] The names of the Bass and Davis consorts have been lost in the mist of history, but the bed partner of Joel Collins is remembered as Maude, a woman who, although never legally married to her lover, assumed his last name, a common custom among women of that class.[8]

With the help of their Cyprians, the Texas drovers soon depleted their funds with their program of debauchery and began looking for new ways to acquire money. For the criminally inclined, robbery of the Deadwood stage seemed like the logical next move. They saw the coaches arriving from Cheyenne with passengers carrying thick wallets of money for investment in the booming Black Hills. And leaving Deadwood were stages with gold dust–laden folks who had struck it rich already. Also to be highly coveted were the treasure coaches conveying boxes of gold from the Black Hills mines to government mints via the railroad.

Once committed to a stage-robbing enterprise, the Texas cowboys needed other men with similar criminal ambitions, but possessing better knowledge of the country. Deadwood was full of such men, and Collins had no trouble enlisting "Reddy" McKimie, Jim Berry, Tom Nixon, and Frank Towle.

Robert McKimie,[9] tagged with the nickname "Reddy" because of his red hair, was an even-featured young man of twenty-one years, but with a smart-aleck look about him. His birth about 1855 was the result of the seduction of Rose McKimie of Rainsboro, Ohio, by a man named Charles Richards, who promptly disappeared. Raised by

Bandit Robert ("Reddy") McKimie killed stagecoach driver Johnny Slaughter. From *The Life and Adventures of Robert McKimie, Alias "Little Reddy," from Texas*, by J. W. Bridwell, author's collection.

a sister of his mother, McKimie enlisted in the army at age fourteen. According to Seth Bullock, sheriff at Deadwood, who had much experience tracking McKimie in later years, the young man deserted the army about 1873 and "joined a gang who were depredating along the stage route in Utah, murdering and robbing."[10] Captured and sentenced to fifteen years in the Utah penitentiary for killing a man, he escaped after a year with a convict named Jack Williamson. During the escape a guard was killed, but "Reddy" always blamed William-son for the deed.[11] McKimie next turned up in Cheyenne, where he worked for a time as a handyman at the Inter-Ocean Hotel before joining the rush to the Black Hills.[12] With his experience in road agentry, he fitted well into the stagecoach robbing plans of the Texans and was welcomed.

Jim Berry was also a redhead. His sandy, reddish hair, beard, and mustache were touched with gray, for, having been born in Mis-souri in 1837, he was considerably older than the others. Blue-eyed and florid of complexion, he stood five feet nine or ten inches and weighed 180 pounds. He had been a member of "Bloody Bill" Ander-son's notorious guerrilla band during the Civil War and brought to the Collins gang considerable experience as a fighting man. Unlike the others, who were all single, he was married and had six chil-dren, but had left his family in Missouri to seek his fortune in the Black Hills.[13]

What little is known about Tom Nixon's appearance appeared in a reward poster published jointly a year later by the Pinkerton National Detective Agency and the Union Pacific Railroad. A reward of $500 was offered for the arrest and detention of "Tom Nixon, alias Tom Barnes, five feet seven or eight inches high, 145 to 150 lbs. weight, 25 years of age, blue-gray eyes, light hair and whiskers; beard not heavy or long; mustache older and longer than beard. He is a blacksmith, and worked at that trade in the Black Hills last summer."[14]

The mystery man of the lot was James F. ("Frank") Towle. Prac-tically nothing is known of his background or appearance, but in the coming months Towle would be a member of three different Black Hills stage-robbing bands, and his eventual demise would be one of the memorable stories of the period of Deadwood stage assault.

By March 1877 the Cheyenne and Black Hills Stage Company was proudly announcing in the pages of the *Cheyenne Daily Leader* that the company was now running "huge six-horse coaches, carrying eighteen passengers" out of the city every morning. "Fast horses, easy coaches, first-class eating stations and quick time," it boasted, "are the advantages possessed by this, the only stage line in the Black Hills."

But even as the company's proud advertisement appeared in the Cheyenne papers, an event was transpiring on the Deadwood route that would be a foretaste of a problem consuming owners, managers, and employees of the concern for months to come.

On Monday, March 25, 1877, the northbound coach was halted in a robbery attempt at Whitewood Canyon, about two and a half miles from its Deadwood destination. The honor (or dishonor) for this, the first of many assaults on the Deadwood stages, would go to Joel Collins and his Texas gang.

The driver of the stage was Johnny Slaughter, who had grown to manhood in "The Magic City of the Plains," as Cheyenne was billing itself, and was very popular in that city. He was the son of western pioneer John N. Slaughter, an early arrival in the town who had quickly been appointed justice of the peace. Although in the following years the elder Slaughter held a number of important offices, including his current position as city marshal, he always was called "Judge."[15]

Seated beside young Slaughter on the box was passenger Walter Iler, a distillery representative from Omaha. When masked and armed men suddenly appeared in Whitewood Canyon shouting orders to halt, they startled Johnny Slaughter's six-horse team, and the horses shied and jerked the coach forward. Almost instantly the shotgun in the hands of "Reddy" McKimie roared, and a load of buckshot tore into the chest of the young driver. Pellets struck Iler in the arm and hand, and both men tumbled to the ground. With no restraining hand on the reins, the horses reared and bolted, as a volley of shots from the road agents further frightened them. They galloped down the road with the coach careening behind and continued on for half a mile before the entangled harness brought them to a halt. The highwaymen, evidently unnerved also by the unexpected turn of events, melted away.[16]

When news of the attempted robbery and the murder of their driver reached Deadwood, Isaac Gray, the stage company agent stationed there, immediately wired Luke Voorhees at the Cheyenne headquarters: "Deadwood, March 25: Road agents attempted to rob the coach about 2 1/2 miles from here to-night. They killed Johnny Slaughter and wounded Mr. Iler. We start after body now. Notify Johnny's father. Gray."[17]

Subsequent wires provided additional details. Slaughter had been hit by fourteen buckshot pellets, which killed him instantly. (It was reported that the shots formed an almost perfect circle just above Slaughter's heart.[18]) In addition to the deadly fire killing the driver and inflicting a flesh wound on passenger Iler, a bullet had passed through the coat of a passenger named Smith without hurting him.

Before leaving Deadwood with a posse in search of the outlaws, Lawrence County Sheriff Seth Bullock had announced that a reward of $500 would be offered for their apprehension, dead or alive.[19]

The following day Bullock arrested Frank Towle on suspicion, but later released him for lack of evidence.[20]

Well-attended funeral services for Johnny Slaughter were held at the Grand Central Hotel in Deadwood on March 27, with the Reverend L. P. Norcross of the Congressional Church presiding.[21] The next morning a special stage departed for Cheyenne with the body of the murdered driver. It was met at Fort Laramie by John N. Slaughter, who took charge of his son's remains and brought the body back to Cheyenne for additional funeral services and burial. Six dappled grays, provided by Luke Voorhees and matching the team Johnny was driving when he was killed, drew the hearse to Lakeview Cemetery. Following were more than forty carriages, the longest funeral procession seen in the town up to that time.[22]

Citizens of Cheyenne, the hometown of Johnny Slaughter and his highly respected father, the city marshal, were outraged by the murder of the popular young stagecoach driver. A March 29 letter from a Deadwood resident to Edward A. Slack, owner and editor of the *Cheyenne Daily Sun*,[23] is evidence that the citizens of the Dakota mining town also shared the sense of outrage at the needless death and murderous audacity of the road agents as well. "History," he said,

> does not record a more foul and dastardly murder than was perpetrated by highwaymen on the night of the 25th instant, when John Slaughter was shot dead. . . . We could scarcely find a parallel instance of cowardly, cold-blooded murder. The shooting and instant death of the driver, together with the murderous fire upon the unsuspecting passengers, commenced simultaneously with the demand to surrender. . . . To murder every one on board the stage seemed to be the object of these devils in human form, and had it not been for the stage team taking fright and running away, in all probability the ten passengers would have shared a like fate with the driver. When we consider

that this affair happened within two and a half miles of this place, a city boasting of three or four thousand, and within a stone's throw of several miners' cabins, we are surprised at the boldness of the attack, and we inadvertently offer up a prayer for the speedy extermination of the vile perpetrators of such horrid deeds.

The writer went on to extol the virtues of the slain young man who, he said, many in Deadwood had "learned to admire and respect" for his "noble traits of character. . . . Always courteous and obliging, he had made himself popular with the mass of people."[24]

For some weeks after the attack on the Deadwood coach and the widely lamented killing of Johnny Slaughter there were no more attempts on the Deadwood stages by the Texas gang or any other band of road agents. The reason for this may have been that some of the outlaws shared the revulsion at the wanton and unnecessary murder of the popular driver felt by the residents of Cheyenne and Deadwood. Joel Collins and others of the Texas band are said to have denounced "Reddy" McKimie severely for his hotheadedness and banished him from the gang. Whatever their feelings in the matter, it is true that McKimie moved on and participated in no more of that gang's activities.

The dearth of assaults on the coaches may also have been the result of the unusually wet spring and early summer of 1877 that made portions of the road impassable at times, causing delays or cancellations of the stage schedules. When the coaches did roll, they often carried heavily armed passengers determined to resist any robbery attempt as three competitive gang members learned on the evening of June 1.

Some eight and a half miles north of Hat Creek a bandit on horseback confronted a coach driver named Drake and ordered him to stop, firing a pistol to show he meant business. Drake pulled up as two other road agents, brandishing weapons, stepped out of the brush. But the would-be robbers were dumfounded to see an array of gun muzzles appear suddenly from the windows of the coach. In no uncertain terms a voice from inside ordered them to skedaddle. They skedaddled.[25]

The Texas gang can be credited (or charged) with the initial robbery assault on the Deadwood stage, and although it had proved

TERRITORY OF DAKOTA

A Proclamation.

Five Hundred Dollars Reward.

EXECUTIVE OFFICE,
Yankton, Dakota, April 13, 1877.

WHEREAS, It has been represented to me that on the night of the 25th of March last, some person or persons unknown, attacked the stage of the Cheyenne and Black Hills Stage Company, near Deadwood, in the county of Lawrence, in this Territory, killing John Slaughter, the driver; and

WHEREAS, The person or persons committing the said murder have fled, or so concealed themselves that the officers of the law have been unable to make arrests and bring them to justice; Now, therefore,

I, JOHN L. PENNINGTON,

Governor of the Territory of Dakota,

By virtue of the authority vested in me by the Laws of the said Territory, do offer a reward of

FIVE HUNDRED DOLLARS,

for the apprehension and delivery to the Sheriff of Lawrence County, or the confinement in any jail or prison, so that he, the said Sheriff of Lawrence County, may get them, of the person or persons who killed the said John Slaughter.

Done at Yankton, the Capital of the said Territory, this, the 13th day of April, in the year of our Lord one thousand eight hundred and seventy-seven.

JOHN L. PENNINGTON.

By the Governor:

GEO. H. HAND,

Governor's proclamation offering a reward for the killers of Johnny Slaughter. Courtesy Robert G. McCubbin Collection.

fruitless, resulting only in an atrocious death, the attempt still precipitated the organization of a number of other road agent gangs that were soon in operation on the Black Hills stage routes with hopes of greater success.

Because the rash of stage attacks that began in June 1877 and continued through the next year were perpetrated by several different outlaw gangs, it is impossible to determine exactly how many or which ones were the work of the Texas outfit. Sam Bass on his deathbed would confess to seven attempted stage robberies in the Black Hills.[26]

Thomas Hogg, a Denton, Texas, attorney who knew Bass personally and wrote the first history of the notorious outlaw in 1878, described some of the gang's Black Hills stagecoach robberies. According to Hogg, the gang concentrated on the coaches operating between Deadwood and the outlying mining towns, and their ventures proved to be a succession of frustrating disappointments.

One of their first robberies was of a stage that they stopped about ten miles from Deadwood, an endeavor that netted them the grand total of $11.

Latching on to a rumor that a government paymaster with a thick wad of money was slated to be on a certain stage, they waylaid the vehicle and with leveled weapons loudly demanded that the driver raise his hands. He cheerfully complied, saying, "Boys, I've got nothing for you this time; there's a dozen peaches in the stage that you are welcome to, if acceptable." They took the peaches, but found neither paymaster nor money, for they had picked on the wrong stage.

They stopped another stage and went through the pockets of its four passengers, only to collect a total of $30, causing Jack Davis to explode: "You are the darndest set of paupers I ever saw. What are you traveling for if you don't carry any more money than that? Why, darn it, we fellows will starve if you don't get to doing better!"

To which a passenger responded: "Well, it seems you are going to starve us. Why, you've left me without enough money to buy my breakfast. Now, come, lend us a dollar apiece to get our breakfast with. We're hungry now, and what's a fellow to do without his breakfast?" That plea made sense to Sam Bass, said Hogg, and he gave them a dollar apiece.

Robbery of another coach with a single passenger netted only $3 and a gold watch. A week later they tried again. The lone passenger on this stage coughed up $6, which they relieved him of and sent him on his way with "some very sarcastic remarks about his being so thriftless as not to have accumulated more money at his age."[27]

The Hogg account is full of inaccuracies — the attack on the Deadwood coach in which Johnny Slaughter was killed took place in August 1877, he said, rather than its actual date of March 25 — and it contains many direct quotations that had to be of his own invention, but it would seem that his portrayal of the deplorable incompetence of the Texas gang in their Black Hills stage robbery attempts is right on target.

Despite the ineptitude of the road agents, the Wyoming authorities viewed the assaults on the Deadwood stages with great concern, as evidenced by the following notice that appeared in the *Black Hills Times* of September 1, 1877: "We offer two hundred dollars for the arrest and conviction, or dead body, if killed resisting arrest, of any of the men who were implicated in robbing the coach and the passengers on the Cheyenne and Black Hills Stage road within the last sixty days." It was signed by Erasmus Nagle and Alexander H. Swan, Laramie County commissioners.

After six months of highway robbery failure, Collins and his followers were running out of money. In late August Collins disposed of his Deadwood dive and led his original Texas cohorts — Sam Bass, Jack Davis, and Bill Potts — out of town in a search for better pickings elsewhere. Two others who had joined the gang after it arrived in the Black Hills, Jim Berry and Tom Nixon, tagged along. Before a month had passed the Collins gang would make front-page headlines across the country with a sensational train robbery, but within a year four of the six would be shot dead.

The other two members of the Texas gang remained in the Black Hills. "Reddy" McKimie had already moved on to another gang; Frank Towle followed his lead. Towle, too, would come to a particularly violent end before the era of Deadwood stagecoach robberies was over.

— 3 —

THE RISE OF THE HAT CREEK GANG

There is a nest of these vile marauders in the vicinity of the Cheyenne river, and the authorities must make an effort to bring the miscreants to justice [or] the road will acquire a very bad reputation. It should, therefore, be the business of the people on both sides of this route to rid the country at once of such monsters. Hemp is the proper and unfailing remedy.

— *Cheyenne Daily Leader*, June 28, 1877

The attack on the Deadwood coach and the murder of the popular driver Johnny Slaughter convinced Superintendent Luke Voorhees of the Gilmer stagecoach line that he needed to employ guards to ride the stages and protect his passengers, their belongings, and the treasure coming out of the Black Hills. From a country abounding in experienced fighting men he enlisted a company of the nerviest and most respected. These "shotgun messengers," armed with hand-guns and rifles as well as the scatterguns that gave them their name, would be on the very front line of the war about to be waged against the road agents.

Scott Davis, who because of his swiftness with weapons came to be called "Quick Shot," was made captain of the outfit. Stocky and strongly built, at five feet nine inches in height, Scott Davis was a little taller than the average-size man of his time. Also, as he was to prove, he was smart, determined, and utterly fearless. Frank Root, an old-time driver on the trail, described him as "a splendid scout, and one of the self-appointed undertakers of many of the lawless characters."[1]

An army man stationed at Fort Laramie during this period called Davis "the Slade of this line . . . , a man of powerful physique, dauntless nerve and wonderful endurance, with an eye like an instantaneous camera, and a trigger finger that could follow the lightning flash of his eye."[2]

Scott Davis was born on October 2, 1851, on a farm near Kinsman in Trumbull County, Ohio. The fourth child of James and Sarah Davis, he was christened Walter after his paternal grandfather, Walter Davis, born in Ireland circa 1779 and living near his son James during the boy's early years. Never happy with the name Walter, young Davis shed it when he grew to manhood and always went by his middle name, Scott. A brother named William Wilson, one year his elder, also disliked his given name and took the name Ross.[3]

During their early years the brothers seem to have been shunted back and forth between the Davis farm in Ohio and the homestead of relatives Ruben W. Hazen and his wife, Harriet, near Fremont, Dodge County, Nebraska.[4] Scott helped work the farm for a few years before leaving home in the early 1870s to head farther west. He worked at freighting and construction jobs in Colorado, Utah, Idaho, and Texas before signing on as an express messenger for the Northwestern Express, Stage and Transportation Company. In 1876 he joined the rush to the Black Hills and in April of that year took a job with the Gilmer stage company. One year later his brother Ross joined him at Deadwood and also took employment as a stagecoach guard.[5]

One of Scott Davis's messengers rivaled his captain as a terror for road agents. Daniel Boone May (like Davis, always referred to by his middle name, Boone), a native of Bourbon County, Kansas, came to the Black Hills in 1876 at the age of twenty-four with two brothers, William, four years older, and James, three years younger.[6] Initially the brothers established a ranch on Lance Creek and set up stage stations there and at Robbers' Roost on the Cheyenne River, with "Jim" May managing the former and Boone the latter. "Bill" May, meanwhile, devoted most of his energies to prospecting for Black Hills gold, an endeavor that eventually brought him great financial gain. But all three brothers were tough and gun-handy, and Luke Voorhees soon recruited them into the ranks of his force of shotgun messengers.[7]

The stagecoach approaching Deadwood in the Black Hills. Courtesy Denver Public Library, Western History Collection.

In that role Boone May quickly became renowned. By 1879 a Deadwood freighter named Rolf Johnson would note in his diary that he had met on the road a striking-looking fellow, "tall and well developed, well dressed, with a long linen duster on, a red silk handkerchief knotted around his throat, a cartridge belt and ivory handled six-shooter strapped to his waist." Only later did Johnson realize he had been talking to Boone May, whom he described as "the most noted scout, detective, Indian fighter, and shooting man of the Black Hills. He is at present employed as 'shotgun messenger' or guard for the Sidney and Deadwood stage line. He has had more fights with Indians, road agents and desperadoes, captured more stage robbers and horse thieves, and killed more men than any other man in the Black Hills."[8]

One Black Hills historian called Boone May "one of the best pistol shots in the Rocky Mountain regions" and said brother Jim was "a

ASSAULT ON THE DEADWOOD STAGE

twin in courage if not in birth."[9] Another writer described Boone as "one scary man, possibly the fastest gun in the Black Hills and along the Deadwood-Cheyenne stage road."[10] A decade after lawmen and Luke Voorhees's shotgun messengers had won their battle with outlaws on the Deadwood trail an article in the *New York Sun* would credit Boone May with being a "terror to the road agents [and] to him more than any other man is due the credit of clearing the country of stage robbers."[11]

Another noteworthy messenger was Jesse Brown. A little older than the Davis and May brothers, Brown was a thirty-two-year-old frontier veteran when he joined the Black Hills rush in 1876. Born on August 24, 1844, in Washington County, Tennessee, and raised on a farm in Missouri, he decided at the outbreak of the Civil War that he wanted no part of that fight and headed west. He whacked bulls; drove freight wagons; fought Indians in Colorado, Wyoming, and Montana; and rose to the position of assistant wagon master before joining the rush to the Black Hills in 1876.[12] Of him Captain Scott Davis said, "Jesse Brown was a true-blue friend, known as the man that was in the right place at the right time. We fought a good many Indian fights together and road agent fights and I always found him Johnny-on-the-spot."[13]

Galen E. ("Gale") Hill, a Missourian born in 1850 and a first cousin of the May brothers,[14] had also worked the western trails as a freighter before becoming a shotgun messenger for the Gilmer outfit. In 1873, when he was only twenty, he was reputed to have bossed a freight outfit for Joe Small out of Cheyenne. In addition to riding shotgun on the Deadwood stages he saw service as a deputy sheriff and constable at Deadwood. Inspector John B. Furay of the Post Office Department found him to be "a gentleman in his instincts and deportment."[15] His fellow messenger Jesse Brown, impressed by Hill's genial personality, called him "a likeable fellow, always cheerful and jolly." But Brown was quick to add that Gale Hill did not lack for sand: "There was no yellow in his makeup, he was game from first to last, and deserves to be classed with the heroes of the west. He was the right man in the right place. Necessity demanded men of his stripe at the time when the Black Hills were being settled and was [*sic*] overrun with outlaws, thieves and murderers. Galen came to the front as one to combat this class of law violators, and he did it with all his might."[16] Gale Hill, road agents were to learn, was also a very hard man to kill.

Others employed over the next five years to ride shotgun for the Gilmer concern included William Brewer; Dick Bullock, called by some "Deadwood Dick"; John Cochran, later a deputy sheriff based at Deadwood; Eugene Decker; Charley Hayes; John Lafferty; Bill Linn, of whom it was said he "lacked only five inches of being seven feet tall and could strike terror to road agents just by standing up"; Robert McReynolds; M. M. Moore; William Rafferty; Billy Sample; C. A. Skinner; Eugene S. Smith; James ("Whispering") Smith; Clark B. Stocking; and perhaps for one trip only a tall, slim native of Illinois who in later years would become a legendary figure of the frontier West—Wyatt Earp.[17] Nerm Seebold, Joe Slattery, Johnny Hunter, and Joe Goss were employed as messengers on the road to Fort Pierre.[18] Paul Blum worked the Bismarck route.[19]

One of the first organized gangs of road agents the shotgun messengers ran up against came to be called the Hat Creek outfit, because of its regular rendezvous not far from that stage station. Members of this gang were a mixed bag, composed of hardened frontier desperadoes like "Reddy" McKimie, who hooked up with the Hat Creek bunch after being tossed out of the Joel Collins Texas gang, and young men hardly out of their teens like Jim Wall and Clark Pelton. Their leader was a thirty-two-year-old former sailor with piercing eyes from the maritime province of Nova Scotia, Canada, named Duncan Ellis ("Dunc") Blackburn.

Born and raised in the great port city of Halifax, Blackburn quite naturally took to the sea at an early age. But in 1869, after several years as a sailor, he turned his gaze to the setting sun and headed for the American West to seek his fortune. After laboring for wages as a teamster for eighteen months, he made enough money to buy his own wagons and bull teams and contracted to supply Fort Laramie and other military posts with hay and wood. Tiring of the arduous freighting life, he turned to horse thievery. Often arrested, he proved to be a slippery jailbird. He was said to have been thrice incarcerated in Utah jails and prisons and to have made his escape every time.[20] In July 1876 he joined the rush to the new bonanza in the Black Hills, where he scratched out a precarious existence by trading in horses.[21]

ASSAULT ON THE DEADWOOD STAGE

For a time he worked at the Gilmer stage company's Hat Creek station.[22] A livelihood derived from these efforts did not satisfy his ambitions, and he again chose the outlaw life, taking up stagecoach robbery. At five feet eight inches and 165 pounds, with gray-blue eyes and dark hair, he was described as "a well-built man with a very good countenance."[23] He had a certain charm that attracted both men and women. Martha ("Calamity Jane") Canary was one of the female denizens of Deadwood who reportedly became "enamored" with him.[24] There is little doubt that he possessed natural leadership ability, for he quickly assumed command of the new road agent band.

One of those accepting his leadership was a seasoned desperado who only a few years earlier had led his own gang of horse thieves. Wyoming lawmen had found Jack Watkins a troublesome bur under the saddle for years. When Watkins teamed up with Dunc Blackburn, the two veteran outlaws formed the nucleus of a formidable gang. Edgar Beecher Bronson called them "the two most desperate bandit-leaders in the country."[25]

Jack Watkins arrived in Wyoming with the Union Pacific Railroad in 1868 and two years later was one of thirty-two men and one woman enumerated by a U.S. census taker in the widely scattered settlements of Albany County. His name, he said, was John W. Watkins. He was twenty-eight, had been born in Arkansas, and was a hunter by trade.[26] A year later, however, he told the editor of the *Laramie Daily Sentinel* his name was Andrew J. Watkins (but everyone called him "Jack") and had come to Wyoming in 1856 from Nashville, Tennessee, where he had been born thirty-three years earlier.[27] Like many westerners who resented questions about their past and refused to answer inquiries or obfuscated their replies, Watkins seems to have chosen the latter option.

Supplying meat for the Overland Stage stations, he gained early fame as a hunter. A Laramie editor commented that he had "chased the antelope over the Plains for half a generation. Few in all the west can compare with him as a good shot with rifle or revolver, or as a successful hunter."[28]

All during the winter of 1867–68 Wyoming pioneer Jesse S. Hoy bunked in Cheyenne with Watkins, who had already acquired a reputation as a fast and deadly accurate gunman. Cheyenne was a wild town in those days, and Hoy felt fortunate to have the friendship and protection of the expert gun-wielder. "Jack was a fighting man without being a bully," remembered Hoy.

> Owing to his superiority . . . he attracted the attention of men generally, and was an object of jealousy, fear, admiration or hate. . . . He slept with his right arm above his head with a six-shooter in his hand. So lightly did he sleep, that a rat running across the room brought him to a sitting position with the gun automatically leveled in the direction of the noise. When in a saloon . . . he usually stood with his back to the wall, ready for officers or town toughs, who all envied his attainments.[29]

Sheriff Seth Bullock of Deadwood, who chased members of the Hat Creek gang during the period of their ascendancy, was quoted in an 1878 newspaper as saying Watkins was particularly skilled in the art of pistol-fanning. Members of the gang, Bullock declared,

> made a specialty of shooting from the hip, and by continued practice became very expert. The modus operandi was to place the right hand holding the "gun" firmly against the hip, and strike the hammer back rapidly with the left hand. For this reason self-cockers were scarcely ever used by the gang. The advantage of this plan was that the arm could be drawn and fired very quickly, and without attracting attention like the arms-length motion. It also enabled them to aim at the middle of a man's body, where the shots were almost certain to prove fatal. By turning slowly they could direct their shots to different points, and empty every barrel in an almost incredible short space of time. Bullock says that Jack Watkins, a member of the gang, became very expert in this manner of firing, and could put every ball from a six-shot navy revolver into a space four inches square, at long range. This is what we should call a two-legged Gatling gun arrangement.[30]

Another early Wyoming resident, cattleman Ed Lemmon, recalled that Watkins participated in the bloody riot at Bear River, Wyoming, in November 1868. Employed as a "commissary man" by a railroad subcontracting firm, Watkins led a gang of railroad men against an opposing force headed by Thomas Smith, who, as "Bear River Tom," would gain later fame as town marshal of wild and woolly Kit Carson,

Colorado, and Abilene, Kansas. Lemmon said the battle "was the largest killing during U.P. construction," and Watkins "was "unquestionably the best and quickest shot" of that time. Lemmon, a boy of ten at the time, was so impressed by Watkins that he later ranked him on a level with such six-gun luminaries as James Butler ("Wild Bill") Hickok, Bill Tilghman, Texas Ranger Captain Bill McDonald, William B. ("Bat") Masterson, Jim Bridger, and Kit Carson.[31]

By 1871 Watkins had abandoned the pursuit of wild game for the pursuit of wild games on the owl-hoot trail. He stole horses and hurrahed Wyoming towns with drunken sprees. On one of his riotous benders in Cheyenne the tough, no-nonsense sheriff of Albany County, Nathaniel K. Boswell, although out of his jurisdiction, pinned on a deputy U.S. marshal's badge hastily bestowed by a federal judge, and collared and jailed the desperado.[32]

Later that year, seeing a Laramie newspaper report that the town had been invaded by a gang of horse thieves, members of "Jack Watkins gang,"[33] another sheriff, William Miles Hawley of Carbon County, came to Laramie carrying four warrants for the outlaw's arrest. On October 23 Watkins was jailed on $5,000 bail. The editor of the *Laramie Daily Sentinel* remarked: "This Watkins is wholly devoid of principle, and his acts show a malignant and abandoned heart. He is a very desperate character and it will be difficult to keep him confined."[34]

On November 13 a jury acquitted Watkins of three of the charges against him but convicted him on the fourth, "assault with intent to commit bodily harm on the person of William Brower with a knife on August 15, 1871," and he was sentenced to a month in jail and a $100 fine.[35] The *Sentinel* editor interviewed him in his cell and found him to be "a good specimen of the frontiersman" exhibiting "wild, reckless bravado."[36]

Following his jail release Watkins avoided law trouble for several years. Then in early 1875 he attended a dance near James M. Sherrod's ranch on the Little Laramie River. Sherrod later described what happened when a fight broke out:

> Guns began to pop all over the place. . . . It was pretty lively around there when the notorious Jack Watkins took a hand. His gun misfired three times in succession, something it had never

done before, Jack said, and the fellow he was shooting at, or someone else in the crowd, got Jack in the hip. He got outside somehow and made for my stable and hid in my haystack. When he didn't show up in the morning the boys were all afraid to check out the stack—for Jack was a dead shot, and everyone thought his gun might not misfire again.

Finally I went out. He was just crawling out of the stack. I said, "Hello, Jack, you're not dead yet, are you?" "No," he replied, "but I'm pretty well used up."

I took him up to the house and dressed his wound and kept him there until he recovered, which didn't take long.

Sherrod said he believed someone had tampered with Watkins's gun, hoping to get him killed.[37]

On May 24, 1875, shortly after this incident, Watkins and a member of his "gang," twenty-one-year-old Richard Rogers, alias Sam Jackson, rode into Laramie. Rogers was a former telegraph operator and, like future Watkins cohort Dunc Blackburn, was a native of Canada.[38] The purpose of their visit was to obtain a court document regarding possession of a horse. Spotting them in the courthouse, Albany County Sheriff J. R. Brophy and his deputy, Larry Fee, took the opportunity to arrest Watkins for an earlier offense. Both Watkins and Rogers immediately drew pistols and opened fire. A bullet creased Brophy's abdomen and struck Fee in the leg, dropping him to the floor. While Brophy struggled with Rogers, Watkins ran from the building, leaped upon his horse, and galloped out of town as the sheriff and courthouse personnel hustled Rogers into a cell.[39]

Nathaniel Boswell, now Laramie city marshal, heard the shots and rushed to the scene. Organizing a posse, he rode off in pursuit of Watkins. At one point in the chase Boswell got within gunshot of the fleeing fugitive and dropped him from the saddle with a long shot, but Watkins, not badly hurt, held on to the reins, climbed back on his horse, and made his escape. The posse returned empty-handed.[40]

On August 14, 1875, Richard Rogers was tried and convicted of assault with intent to kill and sentenced to three years in the territorial prison. A year later he was convicted on a second charge of larceny. On July 31, 1876, Governor John M. Thayer pardoned him for the first offense and eight months later issued another pardon for the second offense. Rogers walked out of the Laramie prison to

Albany County, Wyoming, courthouse, scene of a Jack Watkins shootout and a Bill Bevins conviction. Courtesy Ann Gorzalka, *Wyoming's Territorial Sheriffs.*

freedom after serving one year, seven months, and seventeen days, and disappeared from the pages of history.[41]

Following the courthouse shooting Jack Watkins became a fugitive with a $500 reward offered for his capture.[42] Laramie City Marshal Boswell was particularly interested in nabbing the troublemaker for crimes committed in years past. As the Laramie representative of the Rocky Mountain Detective Association, he received a wire in August 1875 from Dave Cook, chief of the association, informing him that Watkins had reportedly been sighted near Denver. Boswell left immediately, as the *Sentinel* put it, to join Cook and "help bag the desperado."[43]

Cook and Boswell chased all the leads they could turn up in Colorado, but finally gave up the search after getting a reliable tip that their quarry had left for New Mexico "with a drove of horses," probably not his own.[44]

From time to time over the next few years the elusive fugitive was reported working with various outlaw gangs. In August 1876 a paper in Golden, Colorado, reported that he was riding with the notorious

Prison photo of William ("Bill") Bevins, who had a long history as a desperado before turning to road agency. Courtesy Elnora L. Frye, *Atlas of Wyoming Outlaws at the Territorial Penitentiary.*

outlaw, William F. ("Persimmon Bill") Chambers,[45] but by June 1877 he had thrown in with Dunc Blackburn's outfit.

Another hard case who joined Blackburn's Hat Creek gang at that time was William "Bill" Bevins, a craggy-faced, balding thirty-nine year-old with a wealth of exciting adventures on the frontier. Blevins was tight-mouthed about his origins, but he probably came from Ohio; his mother was living there in 1877.[46]

Frank Grouard, a noted frontiersman and U.S. Army scout, came to know the future road agent at Helena, Montana, in 1866, when Bevins was at the peak of his celebrity as a successful prospector and reckless gambler. "He owned the best claim in the gulch and was supposed to be worth a million dollars," remembered Grouard. One night he got on a hot streak in a Helena gambling hall and won

$120,000, but disgruntled losers in the game attacked him with guns and knives and almost took his life. "He got shot and cut eighteen times and was pretty well used up when he got through with it," recalled Grouard, who saw Bevins often that summer as he slowly recovered from his wounds. "He was a regular gambler, and one of the 'leading men' of Helena at that time. This was before the vigilante committee was organized, and that was how he came to go away from there. He got broke at last; lost all his money."[47]

One jump ahead of the Montana vigilantes, Bevins went to Colorado. There he and an accomplice named Williams took to stealing cavalry horses and mules. In April 1869 they were pursued and captured by another famous scout, William F. ("Buffalo Bill") Cody, who locked them up for a night in the jail of Denver City Marshal Dave Cook.

The next day Cody and three other scouts started for Fort Lyon with their prisoners and the stolen stock, camping that night on Cherry Creek, seventeen miles from Denver. During the early morning hours Bevins made a daring escape attempt. Grabbing his shoes, he jumped over the fire and ran off in his stocking feet. Awakening, Cody sent a shot after him, but missed. "Williams attempted to follow him," Cody recalled, "and as he did so, I whirled around and knocked him down with my revolver. [Scout Bill Green] started after Bevins, firing at him on the run; but the prisoner made his escape into the brush. In his flight, unfortunately for him and luckily for us, he dropped one of his shoes."

They could hear Bevins breaking through the brush, but seeing it was useless to try to trail him on foot in the dark, the scouts waited until morning. At daylight Cody and Green saddled two of the fastest horses and struck out on Bevins's trail, which was clearly visible in the snow. Said Cody:

> He had got an hour and a half the start of us. His tracks led in the direction of the mountains and the South Platte River, and as the country through which he was passing was covered with prickly pears, we knew that he could not escape stepping on them with his one bare foot, and hence we were likely to overtake him in a short time. We could see, however, from the long jumps he was taking, that he was making excellent time, but we frequently noticed, after we had gone some distance, that the

prickly pears and stones along his route were cutting his bare foot, as nearly every track of it was spotted with blood.

We had run our horses some twelve miles when we saw Bevins crossing a ridge about two miles ahead. Urging our horses up to their utmost speed, we reached the ridge just as he was descending the divide toward the South Platte, which stream was very deep and swift at this point. It became evident that if he should cross it ahead of us, he would have a good chance of making his escape. So pushing our steeds as fast as possible, we rapidly gained on him, and when within a hundred yards of him I cried to him to halt or I would shoot. Knowing I was a good shot, he stopped, and coolly sitting down, waited till we came up. . . .

Bevins' run was the most remarkable feat of the kind ever known either of a white man or an Indian. A man who could run bare-footed in the snow eighteen miles through a prickly pear patch was certainly a "tough one," and that's the kind of person Bill Bevins was. . . . I considered him as game a man as I ever met.[48]

In consideration of Bevins's damaged foot, the scouts let him ride one of the horses for the trip back to camp, while Cody and Green took turns walking and riding the other mount. As they resumed their journey to Fort Lyon Bevins's foot swelled to "enormous size." Cody said it "must have pained him terribly but not a word of complaint escaped him." From Fort Lyon the scouts took their prisoner to Boggs's ranch on Picket Wire Creek, where they turned him over to the civil authorities, who locked him up in a log jail to await his trial.

But as soon as his foot healed the elusive outlaw escaped again, made a remarkable run of eight miles, had his horse shot from under him, was caught again, and again escaped.[49]

"Buffalo Bill" Cody never saw Bevins again, but closely followed in the newspapers the later career of the desperate outlaw he had come to admire for his courage and fortitude.

The other famous scout, Frank Grouard, ran into Blevins again at the Red Cloud Indian Agency in Nebraska in 1876. Blevins was dead broke and driving a stagecoach to make a living. As Grouard related the tale, somehow Bevins learned that a trader named Robert Foote,[50] who kept a store at Fort Halleck on the Overland Trail and freighted between the fort and Laramie, Wyoming, often carried a large amount of money on his trips. Enlisting the aid of two other toughs, identified by Grouard as Herman Leslie and George Hastings, Bevins went to Laramie with larceny and perhaps murder on his mind. Grouard put it bluntly: "[Bevins] went over to the Laramie Plains and jumped an old man named Robert Foote, and I think he tried to kill him for the money he was supposed to have."[51]

The records show that on August 13, 1876, Bevins and a companion, twenty-seven-year-old Herman Lessman (not Leslie), attacked and wounded Foote, but he survived. Two brothers named Lee tracked and captured Lessman at Fort Fetterman, Wyoming. A Carbon County, Wyoming, jury convicted him of assault with intent to kill on September 24, 1876, and he was sentenced to two and a half years in the territorial prison.[52] Bevins, arrested and tried on the same charge, was convicted on February 7, 1877, in the Albany County court on a change in venue and given an eight-year sentence. He was confined in the Albany County jail at Laramie, pending an appeal hearing filed by his lawyers.[53]

Other inmates of the hoosegow at the time included a petty crook named Charles Bond; three Laramie Cyprians, Elizabeth ("Pawnee Liz") Stevens, Julia Coyle, and Mary Frank; and a seventeen-year-old kid with sharp gray eyes, recently arrived in the West from his Ohio home.[54]

The youngster, Clark Pelton by name, fancied himself an expert with guns and had come to the Great Plains in the fall of 1876 with the romantic notion that he could become a great antelope hunter. Working from a cabin in the Laramie Mountains he did well for a while, but winter brought a scarcity of game and dampened the ambitions of the youthful nimrod. A couple of acquaintances, small-time stock thieves Ellen Card and Charles Henry, convinced him that he could do better with a running iron, and the impressionable greenhorn turned rustler. But the law soon caught up with him, and he was tossed into the jail at Laramie to await trial.[55]

Despite Pelton's inept initial step into outlawry, his cell mate, old warhorse Bill Bevins, saw potential in the young man and took him under his wing. He enlisted Pelton, the three women, and Bond in an escape attempt from the flimsy Albany County jail. With the aid of a knife blade one of the inmates had secreted, they cut a hole from

Young Clark Pelton was indoctrinated into outlawry by Bill Bevins.
Author's collection.

Pawnee Liz's cell to the outside and on the night of April 3, 1877,
made their break. There was no chivalry in evidence as the men went
first. Bevins, Pelton, and Bond successfully squirmed through the
narrow opening. Mary Frank, the slimmest of the women, made it
also, but Pawnee Liz Stevens with her ample hips got wedged in, and
Julia Coyle never got a chance for freedom. Officers quickly apprehended Mary Frank, but the three men got away. Bevins and his
protégé Pelton stole two horses belonging to a man named Don
Cameron and rode hard north, finally holing up near Hat Creek
station on the Deadwood trail. After giving up his pursuit, Sheriff
Daniel Nottage posted a reward notice: $100 for Bevins, $50 for
Pelton, or $150 for the two.[56]

ASSAULT ON THE DEADWOOD STAGE

Over the next two months Bevins and Pelton ran a two-man robbery campaign, concentrating on lone travelers on the road leading into and out of Deadwood. A traveler stopped by them on Sunday, April 22, near Custer City, was relieved of three ounces of gold dust. The victim said the highwaymen, believed to be Bevins and Pelton, were masked, and one carried a rifle and the other a pistol. The taller man, wielding the rifle, was disguised with part of an old shirt in which eyeholes had been cut, but a gust of wind blew the mask from his face, and the traveler recognized Bill Bevins. An old hand at this business, Bevins went about his work "in a cool and collected manner," while his neophyte cohort (Pelton) "shook and shivered so" the robbery victim was fearful his revolver would discharge accidentally.[57]

The heavy rainfall that spring made the roads impassable in many sections, resulting in stage run cancellations. It was therefore an unprofitable period for road agents. So Bill Bevins, the old horse thief, reverted to his earlier occupation.

About mid-May William Lykins, Laramie County stock inspector for the Wyoming Stock Growers Association, while en route to the Red Cloud Indian Agency to check out a report of stolen horses there, met near the Running Water crossing two men riding large gray mounts. They "excited his suspicions by their conduct and remarks," but he rode on. Stopping at the next ranch, he was told that the two were horse thieves belonging to the Bill Bevins gang. By chance Brigadier General George Crook, on his way to Fort Laramie, was camped nearby with a detail of soldiers. Lykins called on the general and asked his assistance in tracking down the suspected horse thieves. General Crook assigned two men to the task. When at dawn a few days later Lykins and the soldiers came on the suspects driving a herd of horses, they opened fire, dropping the mount of one of them and, they believed, striking the other man in the head. The shooting stampeded the horses, and in the confusion the thieves escaped, but Lykins and the soldiers managed to round up twelve of the herd, including the two valuable grays, recently reported stolen from a ranch, and ten animals belonging to Arapahoe Indians at the agency. The local ranchmen, Lykins reported, were convinced that Bevins was operating in the area with two confederates, one of whom was Clark Pelton, the other unknown.[58]

It was probably the unknown horse thief who was shot in the head by Lykins and his military companions, because only a week or so later the Bevins-Pelton duo struck again. A Cheyenne freighter named F. M. Darling, on a return trip from Deadwood, together with three companions who had joined him on the road, was camped on the night of June 3 near the mouth of Red Canyon. Darling was rudely awakened during the night by a masked man who "shoved a cocked revolver under his nose" and demanded all his valuables. His companion, also wearing a mask and brandishing a pistol, stood nearby. Darling handed over $14 in gold dust, his watch and chain, his rifle, and his pistol. The first robber, who was undoubtedly Bevins, returned the watch, saying he knew Darling, having done business with him in Cheyenne, and had always been fairly treated. This magnanimous gesture did not prevent the outlaws from stripping Darling's wagon of all provisions, leaving their victim with nothing to eat until he reached the next ranch. They also went through the property of the other three travelers "like a dose of salts."[59]

Two weeks later, at 8:30 on the morning of June 14, the bandit pair made their first attempt to rob a stagecoach and its treasure box. Their target was the southbound coach from Deadwood containing four passengers, three men and a woman. C. A. Skinner, the shotgun messenger, sat beside the driver. As the stage passed through a narrow ravine about twenty-five miles north of Hat Creek, Bevins and Pelton, their faces blackened as disguises, leaped out in the road just ahead. One raised a rifle to his shoulder, fixed the driver in his sights, and ordered him to stop. When the driver reined the horses to a halt, the other robber leveled a revolver at Skinner and shouted at him to throw down the treasure box. The messenger reached behind him, pulled out a padlocked box, and dropped it to the ground. The two bandits, delighted with their easy success, did not take the time to rob the passengers, but told the driver to move on. Moments after the stagecoach rattled away they smashed open the box, only to find that the wily messenger had tossed them an empty. Another box containing gold dust from the Black Hills mines was still in its place behind messenger Skinner as the coach rapidly disappeared in the distance.[60]

Dismayed by this latest stagecoach assault and convinced that local law enforcement officers could not put a stop to the rash of road robberies, editor Edward A. Slack of the *Cheyenne Daily Sun* suggested that the Wyoming authorities

> place the matter of the detection and arrest of these outlaws in the hands of the Rocky Mountain Detective Association, who have been so successful is this class of business. Where the perpetrator of a crime is known, then it is well to offer a reward, but in the case of these road agents there should be a regular force of men employed to ferret out the gang, if there is one, and bring the outfit to speedy punishment.
>
> The pursuers should operate upon some well devised system and be directed by a man of shrewdness and ability. There are ranchmen along the route who know more than they dare disclose, and who live in constant fear of these desperadoes, and whose assistance might be obtained if they were certain that they would be protected.[61]

Ironically, the aspiring road agent team of Bevins and Pelton, displeased by this latest foray because of its meager return, was also seeking help. Aware that another road agent gang, the seasoned outlaw outfit of Dunc Blackburn, Jack Watkins, and "Reddy" McKimie, was operating from a Horse Head Creek hideout not far away,[62] they made contact and offered their services. Calculating, perhaps, that in greater numbers lay greater success, Blackburn took them on.

The gang had another new member, a twenty-two-year-old curly-headed teamster from St. Paul, Minnesota, named James Wall, whose handsome face was marred only by an ugly two-inch scar on his forehead.[63] Little is known about this fellow's earlier activities, but a Deadwood denizen named Harry Young claimed he and Wall had worked as teamsters together for about two years.

About midnight on a dark spring night Young was a passenger on a stage bound from Deadwood to Custer City. His companions he identified as "a dance-hall girl, a Jew, and four other men, one of whom everybody called 'Telegraphy,' he having constructed the telegraph line from Fort Laramie to Deadwood." They were dozing as the driver eased his team up a steep grade in the road. Young said:

> The stage came to a sudden stop, awakening the occupants, when a loud voice commanded: "Hands up!" a shotgun point-

ing in one door and two six-shooters in the other. This same voice, accompanied by a great deal of profanity, ordered us to get out with our hands up and stand in line. . . . The dance-hall girl became hysterical and screeched. They paid no attention to her. My position was in the middle of the line with a road agent standing at each end and one standing at the horses' heads, with his gun pointed at the driver. The fourth one, with his six-shooter in his left hand, performed the gentlemanly act of collecting our toll. This man, having no disguise, I readily recognized. . . . His name was Jim Wall. My first thought was, "Will he rob me?" I had on my person five hundred dollars in greenbacks and at that particular time the loss of it would have caused me considerable embarrassment. The Jew begged piteously, asserting that he was dead broke, and if they would not kill him when he arrived in Cheyenne he would send them five hundred dollars to any place they might designate.

Wall laughed at the Jew and leisurely started feeling around his waist, and found a money belt (which the Jew afterward claimed contained fifteen hundred dollars). The Jew then collapsed, falling on the ground as dead. Wall then went through his pockets, relieving them of what small change they contained. The next on line was Telegraphy. Wall, knowing him and also knowing that [he] was a hard whisky drinker, remarked "Telegraphy, you are not making this trip without a bottle of whisky."

Telegraphy . . . replied: "There is a bottle under the cushion of the rear seat."

Wall ordered one of his men to get it, while he himself went through Telegraphy's clothes. . . .

Wall looked at me for a moment and playfully tapping me under the chin with his six-shooter, remarked in a low tone, "I see, old pal, you are also caught in the net." But he did not molest me. Passing on to the last two men, he quickly relieved them of their cash and valuables. He did not rob the girl.[64]

Since Jim Wall and Pelton were the youngest members of the outfit, both were tagged with the nickname "Kid" by the older men, which led to later confusion about their identities by robbery victims and newspapers. Pelton had started to use the alias "Billy Webster," and "Kid" Webster and "Kid" Wall were often misidentified.[65]

Before doubling the gang's strength from three to six members, Blackburn, Watkins, and McKimie had gone through their own humiliating experience on the road. The night of June 1 they stopped a coach just north of Hat Creek station, but when a bunch of determined-looking passengers poured out of the coach brandishing pistols, the road agents beat a hasty retreat. The tale was related by a newspaper editor with dripping sarcasm:

> We flatter ourselves that we are not especially vindictive, but we cannot help saying that it would please us to see those passengers come into town naked and penniless. They allowed three of the worst men in this country to ride away unharmed, after having threatened the lives of the timid fellows on the coach, when they should have shot them down like dogs. We care not who these passengers are, but denounce them for their cowardice and hold them up to the contempt of all brave men.[66]

But now emboldened by their increase in numbers, the Blackburn gang pulled off three stagecoach robberies on successive nights in late June 1877. On Monday, the 25th, they stopped the down coach from Deadwood six miles south of the Cheyenne River crossing. The driver, "Huck" Plum, said later that he was unarmed and, not wishing to share the fate of poor Johnny Slaughter, "pulled up gracefully."

While one bandit covered him with "an ugly-looking double-barreled shotgun," another demanded to know where the messenger was.

"I ain't got none tonight, boys," Plum replied.

"Pony up the treasure-box, then," said the road agent, "and if you make a movement or shout, you're a dead man."

Plum explained that he could not do that as the company had double-locked the treasure boxes and riveted them to the front boot of most of the coaches, including this one. The robber demanded Plum's monkey wrench, but was told he had none. A hatchet was found, however, with which the road agents labored for almost an hour to crack open the box. They finally broke one lock, but were unsuccessful with the other. Disgusted, they asked Plum how much money the box contained. When he said $900, "they told him he ought to quit working for a company that did not carry more money than that."

The robbers then turned their attention to the five passengers in the coach, who, although all armed with six-shooters, remained quiet throughout the affair. They "were scared almost to death,"

Plum said. Even after the robbery was over, "their teeth chattered for forty miles."

The robbers, one of whom was armed with a Sharp's rifle and revolver and the other with a shotgun and revolver, ordered them out of the coach, disarmed them, and stripped them of valuables. Garrett Crystal, a freighter, was relieved of $700 in cash and a gold watch and chain. Alex Francis lost $300, and a miner named Irwin coughed up $198. F. B. Reed of Denver reluctantly contributed $120 and a gold ring to the haul. In all, the robbers collected about $1,400 in money and jewelry.

Surprisingly, before the bandits told Plum to drive on, they returned the weapons taken from the passengers after emptying their contents in a salvo fired into the sky.[67]

About eleven o'clock the next evening, Tuesday, the 26th, the Deadwood coach, with Cy Hawley at the reins, slowly traversed a rocky ravine some two miles south of the Cheyenne River and about four miles north of the previous robbery. A shotgun messenger named Roberts occupied the box with Hawley, and another messenger, W. H. ("Scotty") Jenks, rode inside with the seven passengers. A heavy rainstorm had recently passed, and the road was slick. No sooner had one of the passengers remarked, "Boys, this is a bully place for road agents," than all heard the cry "Stop that team, God damn you!"[68]

Mounted bandits brandishing rifles suddenly appeared on either side of the stage. Although Hawley thought he counted eight men in the attacking party, the Blackburn gang had only six members. To the startled driver, it must have seemed like an army of outlaws was assaulting him. Both messengers, Roberts and Jenks, had their guns in readiness when the attack came, they reported later, but "finding the assailing parties had them covered with their rifles, they saw all attempts at defense were useless, and would have led, more than likely, to the assassination of the entire party."[69]

The coach came to a stop as the bandits shouted orders for everyone to throw up their hands. One of the passengers jacked a round into his Spencer rifle and in his haste to shoot one of the robbers he later described as "a big ugly looking fellow" triggered off a wild shot that ripped through the roof of the coach. Almost instantly an answering shot from "Reddy" McKimie's rifle struck driver Hawley in the side. McKimie, as he had proved with the murder of Johnny

Slaughter, was as hair-triggered as his weapons. Other gang members gave stern warnings to the passengers in the coach that another shot would trigger a massacre and they would all die. There were no more attempts to resist. Roberts handed over his shotgun, and Jenks and the quick-shooting passenger got out of the coach and surrendered their weapons. The two messengers were then permitted to lower Hawley to the ground and tend to his wound, which did not appear to be life threatening.

"I never saw a lot of men more cool or self-possessed," a passenger later wrote in his account of the robbery. He said the robbers were all masked. One had a shotgun and a handgun; the others carried Sharp's rifles and packed pistols.[70]

While "the captain" (Blackburn) tackled the treasure boxes, the others ordered the passengers out of the coach. M. Pierce, J. S. Sutherland, H. H. Gove, Levi Chambone, J. H. Holliday,[71] George McDonald, and J. M. Mattison were lined up and searched. "Greenbacks, coin, gold dust and watches changed hands," a newspaper reported, "in a very lively time."[72] Pierce was relieved of a $375 gold watch, Mattison lost his timepiece worth $250, and a watch valued at $400 was taken from another unidentified passenger. In all, the passengers lost about $400 in cash. One managed to secrete $60 in the lining of his hat and escaped with it.

Blackburn, meanwhile, was hard at work on the two treasure boxes. Vigorously wielding a hatchet, he managed to rip open the Custer City box, a wooden, iron strap-bound affair, only to find it contained only a few ore specimens. "By God," he swore, venting his rage on the Black Hills town that could not produce better wealth, "I'm going to burn that town. It ain't worth a damn anyhow."[73]

He then turned to the boiler-iron Deadwood box, riveted to the frame of the coach at the bottom of the boot, attacking the iron strap surrounding it with the hatchet and a chisel. He snapped open the strap, but after an hour's toil could not break the lock on the box. At one point in his frustration he suggested they turn the coach around and take it back to the last station to obtain better tools with which to work, an idea that was quickly rebuffed by his fellows. Finally Blackburn demanded the fulminate exploding powder messenger Roberts was believed to be transporting. Roberts turned it over, and the bandit went back to work on the treasure-box lock. He filled the keyhole with powder, lit a paper fuse, and blew the lock off, sending shrapnel flying over the heads of the entire party.

Inside were sacks of gold dust and stacks of currency. The jubilant Blackburn pulled out the packages, "making playful remarks all the while: 'By George, this is a daisy! — Twenty-five dollars — God damn! Well, that's good whisky money. — Hello. Check here for $500 — we'll put that back; we don't want any checks.' "[74] The box had yielded about forty pounds of gold worth nearly $8,000, as well as greenbacks totaling some $4,000.[75] The bandits did not molest the U.S. mail, but did break open the "way packet" and went through the letters, strewing debris along the road.

One of the messengers asked for the return of a valuable pocket-pistol taken from him, and the outlaws, after firing off its chambers and relieving him of additional ammunition, obligingly gave it back. As an expression of their generosity, they also handed messengers Jenks and Roberts $10 each. They apologized to Hawley for his injury, saying it was an accident, and awarded him $20 for his trouble. By this time the robbers had been at work for two hours, but seemed in no hurry to leave. One told the passengers: "We are waiting for the up coach; going to take that in while we are about it."[76] But the storm had delayed the coach from Cheyenne, and the gang finally tired of waiting.

Before departing, in a last display of bravado, they advised their victims that their next robbery would be performed at a point three miles north of where they stood and gave assurance that they only wanted money and, if not interfered with, would harm no one.[77]

Several of the band — including Bill Bevins, known by some of them from his days around Cheyenne and Laramie — had been recognized by their victims.[78] Another, the obvious leader, was Dunc Blackburn. "Both," said a paper recounting the affair, "are dangerous and murderous villains. These robberies cannot possibly be prevented or the highwaymen dispersed, except by actual capture or by providing the stage companies with an adequate mounted escort." "Scotty" Jenks on his return to Deadwood was urged to send down some "fighting men" to "make it interesting. . . . It is too late to stop the downward bound Deadwood stage by telegraph. . . . It will come through tonight [and] its robbery is almost a foregone conclusion."[79]

Commented the *Cheyenne Daily Leader*: "It is very evident that there is a nest of these vile marauders in the vicinity of the Cheyenne river, and the authorities must make an effort to bring the miscreants to justice. If such acts are long tolerated the road will acquire a very bad reputation. It should, therefore, be the business of the people on both sides of this route to rid the country at once of such monsters. Hemp is the proper and unfailing remedy."[80]

True to their promise, the Blackburn gang pulled off their third consecutive stagecoach robbery on the next night, Wednesday, June 27, stopping the Deadwood stage near the Cheyenne River again. A passenger on that coach named J. W. Minor was a printer employed by the *Omaha Republican* and later wrote a firsthand description of the robbery, which was published in his paper and subsequently reprinted in newspapers throughout the country.

He said that no messengers were on this trip, but the stagecoach was not entirely undefended. The driver, whose name Minor did not mention, was armed with a rifle, and two passengers carried "small revolvers." Seated on the boot beside the driver was a young man in the employ of the telegraph company named Pat Keeley. Passengers within the coach were Dr. J. M. Edwards of Deadwood; John (or Charles) Wilson of Montana; W. L. G. Soule, a salesman; Mrs. W. G. Tonn of Deadwood and her infant son; Miss Mary M. Boggy (or Bogy) of Deadwood; and J. W. Minor, the Omaha printer.[81]

In anticipation of the promised third robbery, some of the passengers had taken precautions. Before leaving Deadwood most had turned in their dust and currency to the stage company and obtained drafts that they could exchange upon reaching Cheyenne. Wilson, who had not done this, later changed his mind and, when they passed the up coach, sent back $180 in gold dust to Deadwood. "Three of the men had their watches with them," said Minor. "Mine was concealed in my baggage in the back boot. We had just about money enough to pay our expenses to Cheyenne."[82] Mrs. Tonn, however, was carrying considerable cash, amounting to between $1,500 and $1,700. The wife of the owner of a Deadwood general store, she had with her the entire year's profits from her husband's store, which she planned to deposit in a bank.[83] The afternoon was passed, the writer said, in a kind of "road agent love feast" — that is, some of the passengers who had been robbed by highwaymen in Montana, Arizona, California, etc., told their experiences. It had the effect of preparing us for the approaching event. The shades of evening drew about us, and the coach rolled rapidly toward the ambuscade of the highwaymen. It was a wild country that we passed through. Foot hills all about us, deep and narrow gulches in the road, not a house or human being in sight for miles. . . . I was very weary from long traveling, and I soon dropped away into a light "stage coach" nap. I tried hard to keep awake, for I knew we were within a few miles of the Cheyenne river, but I couldn't. I had slept about half an hour, when I awoke and found the coach standing still. I heard voices outside, and in the first moments of my awakening . . . , I put my head out of the window.

"Take in that head, or I'll put a bullet through it. Don't make such a break as that again."

I got all of myself inside the coach in the quickest time possible. I knew then we were in the hands of the highwaymen of the Black Hills. . . . The captain of the gang was on our side of the coach; his three men on the other. The driver and Keeler [*sic*] were "covered" with guns, and were told to "put up their hands," which they didn't hesitate to do. . . .

The captain then made the driver reach down for his gun, bring it up muzzle foremost and then throw it out upon the ground. The driver and Keeler were then made to descend from their seats.

The Custer box was taken out, broken open, and nothing of value found therein. The work of removing the Deadwood box from the coach was then commenced. The driver and Keeler were made to do the work. All the tools they had to do the work with were the stage wrench and a broken stage bolt. The stage was stopped at about 8:30 p.m. and after they had worked about an hour one of the gang said, "These fellows are d——d fools, boys. I have been in the penitentiary half a dozen times with more iron than that about me and I got out every time."[84] So he lent a helping hand and in half an hour afterward the box was out of the boot and on the ground.

While the removal of the box was progressing we were busy secreting what valuables and cash we had. Mrs. Tonn stowed her property away in a safe place. One passenger cut a seat open slightly and hid his watch so that he wasn't able to find it himself until daylight. Another passenger hid his watch on the floor of the coach, and he too could not find it until morning. Two or three of us stowed away what little cash we had reserved for expenses in the upper lining of the coach, but unfortunately the nervousness of one of the passengers caused two packages of the money to fall out of the open window, where it was lost.

The robbers were obviously in high spirits. They told Mr. Keeler that they got $13,000 the night before.[85] They sent word by the driver to Luke Voorhees of Cheyenne, superintendent of the stage line, that he must send them up a pair of good scales. They had been dividing the gold dust with a spoon, supposed to hold about six ounces, and they couldn't make a fair divide, so they wanted the gold scales. They told the driver that he needn't be afraid. They didn't propose to bust him so long as he made no "break." What they wanted was the company's treasure. If he (the driver) was discharged they would not only take care of him, but they would kill the driver who took his place. They wanted Jack Gilmer to come up the road, they said, so that they could make him get out and walk a ways. They didn't fear the soldiers they heard were coming up the road. They were fighting for big money; soldiers for a few dollars per month; there were fourteen of them, and in a fight any one of them would take his chances with the fourteen rather than with the soldiers. They didn't want to disturb the mails as it was against the law. All they wanted was gold dust and currency. Drafts, etc., they would put back in the boxes and leave them in the road where the next up-coach could get them and take them back to Deadwood. . . .

After the box was taken off, one of the men who had been watching the road back of the coach came up and said, "Now, let's rob the women." The captain emphatically said "no" to that proposition and told the driver to drive on. As he did so he said, "Our gang has divided up. There are two gangs farther down. Three miles from here you may meet the second detachment. If not, eight miles below you will probably meet the third gang. If you (addressing the driver) drive slow, and have no one outside with you, you may pass them all, as they may see that we have detained the treasure-box." So we drove on, and were not further molested that night.[86]

The story of the holdup as related by passenger W. L. G. Soule on arrival of the coach in Cheyenne was similar. Soule added that the robbers had said "they did not intend to harm drivers, but would kill messengers if they offered to resist, and if any of their men were hurt they would kill the passengers. They said that the shooting of the driver the night before was not intentional as the shot was intended for Roberts, the messenger." Mrs. Tonn, he said, was "perfectly cool and collected" throughout the affair, and Miss Boggy, although somewhat nervous at first, "after the first flush of excitement, was as cool as anyone."[87]

The high spirits and sense of humor of the gang members were best revealed by their audacious demand for Luke Voorhees to provide them a pair of scales so they could better divide their loot. This was followed a few weeks later by another message to Voorhees from the gang and reported in the *Leader* under the head "The Height of Impudence." The outlaw gang had received the scales, they said, and thanked the stagecoach boss for his generosity and helpfulness. Now, they added, "if he would be so kind as to renew the shipment of gold dust, temporarily stopped, their happiness would be complete." Voorhees was at a loss to understand the meaning of this communication until W. F. Bartlett, his Deadwood agent, advised him that in a subsequent holdup a pair of gold scales had been stolen from a passenger on a northbound coach, and was apparently being used by the road agents for the very purpose they described.[88]

The three robberies in a row made the pages of newspapers all over the country. At least one in a headline referred to "THE DAILY ROBBERY OF THE DEADWOOD COACH."[89] Although the editor of the *Laramie Daily Sentinel* seemed proud of the notoriety the robberies had brought his region, commenting that "we are beating the famous days of Dick Turpin and Claude Duval,"[90] most folks at either end of the Deadwood Trail were angered by this series of robberies and the bombast emanating from the Hat Creek outlaws. Their newspapers reflected that outrage.

Said the *Cheyenne Daily Leader* under the headline, "HANKERING FOR HEMP": "If there is power in the land to stop this devilish work and hang these hellhounds, we call upon all in authority—military or civil—to use immediate and potent means. Other wise the people must rise and summarily end the career of road agents and horse thieves, after which inefficient officials will be deposed."[91]

ASSAULT ON THE DEADWOOD STAGE

Although witness accounts all agreed that the highwaymen had deliberately refrained from opening and looting the U.S. mail pouches carried by the stages, Herman Glafcke, editor of the *Cheyenne Daily Leader*,[92] editorialized only two days later that the U.S. government should enter into the road agent fray to protect the mails. "It is surprising," he said,

> that neither the Government of the United States, through its officials of the U.S. Marshalls [*sic*] office, nor the County Commissioners, through the officials of the Sheriff's office, have made any effort whatever to pursue and capture the highwaymen who have waylaid and stopped the U.S. mails . . . and interrupted travel on the public highway of Laramie county, and robbed the people traveling in the coaches of the Stage Company, as well as the treasure boxes of the company.
>
> Does it not come within the sphere of duties of the United States and county officials to proceed at once to the place where these crimes against the United States and this Territory have been committed? Do they wait for orders to do this duty? And who is to give these orders? We remember a few years ago, when a U.S. mail coach was stopped and robbed in Utah, the government officials, assisted by Mormon deputy sheriffs, had the robbers in irons within three days after the crime was committed. But here in Wyoming where the same crime has been perpetrated three days in succession, not a county or government official, so far as can be learned, has made the slightest effort to bring the criminals to justice.
>
> It is high time that our officials should wake up, and assist the stage company in preserving its property from the depredations of highwaymen, and to keep the best route to the Black Hills open and secure to public travel. If we cannot guarantee safety to life and property on the route, the travel will be diverted to other channels.[93]

Glafcke was a leading figure in the history of early Cheyenne. In addition to owning and editing the *Leader*, he served as mayor and postmaster of the burgeoning town. The possible loss for his city of the lucrative Black Hills commerce worried him, of course, but as postmaster he was now concerned about the protection of the U.S. mail, which actually had gone unmolested to that point. It would be another year before road agent gangs began the plundering of the mails, and when that happened the Post Office Department was quick to react.

The rash of robberies in June 1877 prompted the editor of the *Black Hills Weekly Pioneer* of Deadwood to comment that the stagecoach assaults were

> coming too thick and fast. It is making it a matter of public concern. Black Hills stage robbers are public enemies, and becoming more troublesome than the Indians were when they were doing their bloodiest work. . . . Our people are in no disposition to adopt half-way measures, should they move as a community in ridding the country of these desperate characters. They should be hunted down like escaped convicts doomed to death, and, when captured, and their guilt fully established, they should be hung until dead, and their bodies left to hang in the wilderness near the scenes of the robberies in which they participated. Something of this kind must and will be done. . . . The first stage robber captured will be hung, and so will the last one . . . , and some of them are now nearer eternity than they suppose.[94]

Military officials got the message. On the morning of June 29 a detachment of twenty Third Cavalry troopers led by Second Lieutenant Bainbridge Reynolds rode out of Fort Laramie in search of the gang.[95] They were unsuccessful, but the mere presence of a force of armed military men in the vicinity kept the road agents quiet for a time.

— 4 —

THE DEMISE OF THE HAT CREEK GANG

I'll tell you one thing, Bullock — I am going to "crease" you if I ever get the chance.
> — Robert ("Reddy") McKimie to Sheriff Seth Bullock

On June 29, 1877, the same day cavalrymen left Fort Laramie to hunt for members of the Hat Creek gang, Jack Gilmer of the stagecoach company was interviewed by a newspaper reporter in Deadwood. For some time past, since the decision was made for the stages to carry treasure, Gilmer said, he had anticipated just the kind of robberies as had recently occurred. This kind of criminal activity was to be expected when a stage line operated at great distances over a country so sparsely settled. Temptations were too great for desperate men to resist. He called the robberies "little incidents" that occur quite naturally when so much treasure is shipped and the times of the shipments are common knowledge. He was pleased that troops had been deployed to patrol the road in the neighborhood of Hat Creek, an indication that the government was showing a disposition to protect the route from repetitions of what had happened in recent days. He downplayed the losses in the raids as reported in the press, saying the value of treasure and passenger valuables stolen totaled no more than $3,000, and assured everyone his stages would continue to operate, carrying passengers and treasure as usual. He was confident they would arrive safely at their destinations.[1]

What Gilmer did not know was that the notorious Hat Creek gang was in the process of self-destruction at that very time. With a troop of cavalry combing the breaks of Hat Creek in search of them, members of the gang thought it wise to clear out of there for a time. The proceeds of their robberies were also burning holes in their pockets, and they were itching to celebrate the Fourth of July and their successes in a town. They rode west to South Pass City, Wyoming, camped on the outskirts, and sent McKimie and Pelton in to buy supplies. When the two returned, a female hanger-on with the gang took McKimie aside and informed him she had overheard Bevins plotting to murder McKimie and Pelton, take their money, and split it with the others. McKimie and the woman conspired to beat the others to the double cross. They pushed whisky on everyone until they got drunk and passed out. Then they took the horses and guns and all the loot they could find, said to have totaled about $11,000,[2] and rode to Point of Rocks, where they disposed of the horses and hardware and entrained for St. Louis. There McKimie gave the woman $1,000 and left her to her own devices while he pursued his own.[3]

When the other gang members awoke from their alcoholic slumbers and found they had been robbed and left without weapons or mounts, Bevins went berserk. Picking up a pair of ne'er-do-wells in South Pass City named James Barker and Frank P. Warmoth, he raised hell in Lawn's Saloon and other of the town's dives, and then moved on to Atlantic City and Lander City. Everywhere he sought information about the missing pair, a little redheaded man and "a woman dressed like a man." On a tip that his quarry might be on the Sweetwater stage, he even stopped that vehicle and searched it without success. "By God, I'll find them," Bevins was quoted as growling. "They have the swag." Some jumped to the erroneous conclusion that those sought were Jack Watkins, long a notorious outlaw in the district, and "Calamity Jane," well known for her propensity to wear male attire.[4]

Bevins's unusual behavior caught the attention of Sheriff John W. Dykins of Sweetwater County, who dispatched one of his deputies, Ervin F. Cheney, to look into the matter. The deputy, accompanied by a noted civilian scout named McCabe and two Second Cavalry sergeants, Carpenter and Pottiger, from nearby Camp Brown, approached Bevins with drawn revolvers as he ate his dinner in a Lander City restaurant and arrested him as a suspicious character. Bevins offered no resistance. They searched him and found a watch that had been taken from J. H. Holliday in the robbery of June 26.[5]

When Sheriff Dykins realized he had the notorious Bill Bevins in custody, he had the army hold him at Camp Brown and wired Sheriff Dan Nottage of Albany County. Nottage, he knew, badly wanted the convicted felon who had escaped from the Laramie jail three months earlier. The Albany County sheriff and several deputies went to Camp Brown, and, taking no chances, slapped a new Leininger Patent shackle[6] on the prisoner, and conveyed him directly to the penitentiary at Laramie, where he entered a cell to serve out his eight-year sentence for shooting Robert Foote.[7]

As for the other gang members, crafty old Jack Watkins, evidently convinced that he had played his luck to its limit in Wyoming, simply disappeared and was not seen in those parts again, while Dunc Blackburn, Clark Pelton, and Jim Wall slipped back to the Cheyenne-Deadwood road.

On July 21 Blackburn and young Pelton, who was still using the go-by "Kid Webster," were spotted at Fort Laramie.[8] The next day Cheyenne resident Charles B. Hayes, who held a special appointment as deputy U.S. marshal, learned that the outlaws were at the Six-Mile Ranch on the Deadwood Road. Enlisting the aid of Adolph Cuny, one of the owners of the ranch and a deputy sheriff, and Robert Sprague as a posseman, Hayes set out to collar the two brigands.

Arriving at the ranch, Hayes gave instructions. Cuny was to enter the front door while Sprague stood guard outside. Hayes himself would come in through the rear door. Cuny and Hayes burst into the room with leveled rifles to find a man they recognized as Blackburn seated at a table engaged in a card game with three other men. They stood him against the bar and searched him for weapons. They looked hard at the other men at the table, but since neither knew Pelton by sight, did not approach or disarm them. Cuny asked John Bowman, the ranch manager, if he knew the whereabouts of Blackburn's companion and received an equivocal answer. Pressured by the posseman, Bowman finally said the man he sought was outside. Before going to look, Hayes admonished Cuny to keep a sharp eye on all of them, especially Blackburn, and if anyone moved, to shoot to kill.

Sometime after Hayes left the room Blackburn made a desperate attempt to reach two guns that were behind the bar, but Cuny pointed the muzzle of his rifle at his head and ordered him to sit down or he would "blow his brains out." While Cuny's attention was entirely on

Blackburn, one of the men at the table, who was indeed Clark Pelton, slipped into the adjacent dining room. Returning with a Winchester rifle in hand, he crept up behind Cuny and commanded him to drop his gun. Startled, Cuny whirled and triggered off a round. He missed, but Pelton did not; his bullet struck Cuny in the chest, killing him instantly.

Hearing the shots, Deputy Hayes and Sprague ran back to the building, but by the time they got there everyone had vanished. They searched the other rooms and the grounds without finding either Blackburn or Pelton, who had secreted themselves in the icehouse. The other men from the ranch, who were clearly in league with the outlaws, misdirected Hayes, telling him that the fugitives had fled in the direction of Deer Creek. Obviously in need of assistance, Hayes left Sprague in charge at Six-Mile, while he went to Fort Laramie and wired Sheriff T. J. Carr of the developments. He then returned to Six-Mile with Captain Joseph Lawson and twenty troopers of Company F, Third Cavalry, but Blackburn and Pelton had long since ridden off.[9]

On July 23 Deputy Hayes wrote a letter to Sheriff Carr relating in detail the events at Six-Mile Ranch. He said on his return he had arrested Joe Walters and Joe Nye, two men who had been in the saloon at the time of the shooting, as well as Jack Bowman, for refusing to assist the lawmen in the discharge of their duties. "In my telegram of last night I stated that the men I arrested were 'Dunk' [sic] McDonald and Billy Webster," he said. "Webster is the man who shot Cuny. The other man's name is 'Dunk' Blackburn and not McDonald." He included physical descriptions of Blackburn and Webster.[10]

For the next five days the two outlaws remained out of sight, but on July 27 rancher Henry Chase spotted them some twenty-five miles northwest of Cheyenne and sent a messenger with the news to Sheriff Carr. One of Carr's deputies, Tom Talbot, knew Blackburn well, having unsuccessfully tried to arrest him earlier. Sheriff Carr dispatched him to investigate. Stopping at Fort D. A. Russell, Talbot enlisted a squad of sharpshooters led by Sergeant Major Gomey. They rode almost to Yellowstone National Park in search of their quarry, but finally returned empty-handed.[11]

No one reported seeing the hunted pair until August 17, when a freighter named Frank Whitney ran into them near his camp at

Old Woman's Fork on the Deadwood Trail. Whitney and Blackburn knew each other from years earlier when Whitney was a boy in Cheyenne. "Mr. Whitney says both of the desperadoes were armed to the teeth and Blackburn acted as spokesman," taking the opportunity to send word to the Cheyenne authorities through Whitney that he had not committed two murders that had been attributed to him. It had not been his gun that killed Johnny Slaughter as had been often reported, he said, and he could prove he was not even at the scene. He asked Whitney to convey that message especially to Johnny's father, Marshal Slaughter, and his brother-in-law, Peter Hama. He said "he did not know who killed young Slaughter and that if he did, he would take that person's life the first time an opportunity offered." Furthermore, he denied having killed Adolph Cuny, as had been reported. Clark Pelton, listening to the conversation, immediately interjected: "No, Blackburn didn't shoot Cuny. Here is the rifle that did it, and I am the man that fired it."[12]

On August 23 highwaymen stopped the Sidney stage near Buffalo Gap. One of the passengers was Ed Cook, superintendent of the northern division of the line, who was on his way south to pay off some of his employees. In anticipation of a possible holdup Cook had stuffed his greenbacks down the large bore of an old outdated shotgun he had obtained just for that purpose. When the passengers were lined up and searched, the robbers berated Cook for being fool enough to arm himself with such a worthless weapon and threw it into the bushes, where it remained until the superintendent returned the next day and retrieved it and his money. Another passenger, obeying an order to keep his hands in the air, held $500 in his raised and clenched fists, and in the darkness his deception went unnoticed. The take in this robbery amounted to a grand total of $12, although almost $1,000 was missed by the road agents.[13]

The outlaws who bungled this holdup were recognized and identified by Cook as Dunc Blackburn, Jim Wall, "Webster" (Clark Pelton), "Hartwell" ("Laughing Sam" Hartman), and two gimpy criminals known as "Lame Bradley" and "Lame Johnny."[14]

A newspaper reporter wrote in September that Blackburn and a companion "had just returned from a trip to the Missouri River, where they were attacked and chased many miles, losing their arms, and riding away amid a shower of bullets." He said that on September 22 they robbed a coach on the Sidney route and then came over to the Cheyenne road.[15]

None of this was ever confirmed, but on September 26, 1877, Blackburn and Pelton did attempt another robbery of the Deadwood stage. Their target was the southbound coach carrying a new, supposedly robber-proof "salamander safe," and guarded by two soldiers from Jenney Stockade and two shotgun messengers, Scott ("Quick Shot") Davis and John Denny. A few days later in an interview with a *Cheyenne Daily Leader* reporter, messenger Davis gave a clear and concise account of what happened that night:

> The coach had crossed the Cheyenne River and passed the two most noted spots where coaches were previously attacked. I was on the rear boot with the other messenger, Denny, the two soldiers whom we took on at Jenney's stockade were inside the coach, while Division Agent Alex Benham, the driver and a stock-tender who was on his way down the road to take charge of a station, were on top of the coach.
>
> We entered a shallow swale, with the horses on a walk, when a sudden command to halt was heard, followed by two shots. Denny and I jumped to the ground and cocked our shotguns, when the robbers ordered everybody to get down and leave their arms on the coach. The soldiers sprang out, leaving their guns inside, and ran away, one of them putting his hands over his face and yelling with fright. The stock-tender, being unarmed, ran away with them, while Benham and the driver took hold of the horses. While this was going on I was looking for the robbers, and soon discovered them lying on the ground in sheltered positions so that I could only see their heads as they raised up a little occasionally. I at once opened fire, discharging one barrel of my shotgun, when one of the soldiers ran against me and knocked it out of my hands. I then seized my Henry rifle and fired in all ten shots, when a cartridge got stuck in the breech and I could shoot no more. The fellows returned my fire, emptying two or three six-shooters and firing about 20 shots, but did not hit me until my weapon failed, when I got up to get another, and was immediately knocked down by a ball which struck me in the left leg just below the hip, passed through it an into the right leg of my pants, when it fell into my boot.

The soldiers and stock-tender then came running back to the coach, crying, "We give up, we give up," and the robbers walked up and looked us over. They wore heavy black masks. Both knew me and called me by name. They took Benham for a passenger, searched him, taking his "bull-dog" revolver, which he had in a side pocket. They then gathered up all of our arms, saying they needed them. They inquired if the safe was on the coach and took a look at it, but did not try to open it. They said they thought they were tackling a regular passenger coach, expecting to get a few hundred dollars. They took a silver watch from Denny, but I cursed and ridiculed them until they gave it back to him. I asked them to give me back my arms, but they refused, saying they would select what they wanted and leave the others at the foot of a lone tree near the road.

The stage was stopped about 10 p.m. and they kept us over an hour. They took all the ammunition they could find, taking our belts from our persons.[16]

An early erroneous report of the robbery in the *Cheyenne Daily Sun* stated that, although it was not known for certain how many robbers participated in the holdup, "at least five men were seen." One of the robbers, said the story, "very much resembled 'Dunk' [*sic*] Blackburn, one of the Cuny murderers."[17]

The next day the *Sun* also carried a lengthy account based on an interview with Scott Davis, who had arrived in town by stagecoach on the morning of September 28 and went at once to the Inter-Ocean Hotel. Unable to walk upstairs unassisted because of his wound, he was helped by H. A. Iddings of the stage company; G. L. Holt, a friend; and George M. Bradley, a reporter for the *Sun*, who got the interview.

Although Davis's account of the robbery as reported in the *Sun* generally followed the *Leader* story, details differed in many respects. In the *Leader* recital Davis was quoted as saying he fired only one barrel of his shotgun before the weapon was knocked from his hands by a fleeing soldier. In the *Sun* account he fired both barrels and "then dropped the scatter gun, seized his revolver and fired." One of the bandits he was shooting at, the story went on,

keeled over, apparently dead, and Benham . . . exclaimed, "Scott, you've settled him!" But such was not the case. The rascal was either stunned by the close call of the bullet, or was simply feigning death. . . . The robber rose to his feet and fired three or four shots at him in rapid succession, to the music of which the other robber . . . kept time by practicing on his devoted anatomy. . . . It was a perilous time for Mr. Davis. . . . He emptied his revolver at the fellows, and then seized his Winchester rifle [not a Henry rifle as reported in the *Leader*]. . . . He fired three shots, and at the fourth attempt the thing missed fire [*sic*]. As he was in the act of striking the gun against the wheel of the coach to settle the cartridges, one of the robbers plugged him in the leg, and he fell.

In the *Sun* version Davis, after being shot, had a twenty-minute conversation with the man who winged him, during which the fellow apologized for the deed, to which Davis is said to have replied: "You need not worry about me; I'm not squealing any. I tried my best to kill you."

A doctor described Davis's injury as a flesh wound, "the ball entering the left thigh, in the lower portion of the upper third, on the external lateral surface, passing upward and backward, making its exit the posterior surface about six or eight inches above the point of entrance."

The reporter concluded his story: "Too much praise cannot be awarded [Davis] for the part he took in the transaction. If he had received the assistance he had reason to expect, we would have been able to give full particulars of the death of a couple of road agents."[18]

Although no money had been stolen from the "salamander safe," two road agents had managed to rob a coach guarded by two shotgun messengers and two soldiers. Luke Voorhees of the stage company, chagrined by the incident, offered a reward of $1,000 for the arrest of these two brigands and $200 for their bodies.[19] The *Laramie Daily Sentinel* remarked: "There are men in Deadwood who will undertake to clean out all the Stage robbers in Wyoming and Dakota for $1,000 a head. Give them a chance."[20]

Blackburn and Pelton may have taken pleasure from the little escapade, but they would come to rue the day they aroused the ire of "Quick Shot" Davis, who proved to be a formidable adversary indeed. Malcolm Campbell, a Wyoming sheriff, said that "on being held up and wounded, [Davis] swore to the thieves that he would follow them and kill them to the last man. On his recovery he carried out his threat fully, and became a terror to the criminals of Dakota from that time on." He did not "carry out his threat fully," for he did not hunt down and kill Dunc Blackburn and Clark Pelton, but he did, as Campbell said, become a terror to road agents from that day on.[21]

Dunc Blackburn and Clark Pelton, after their contretemps with Scott Davis, teamed up again with Jim Wall, who had taken as a partner Samuel S. ("Laughing Sam") Hartman, a notorious frontier reprobate.

"Laughing Sam," described as a "dour uncompromising individual, quick to take offense and the quicker to retaliate," seldom cracked a smile, and his sobriquet can be attributed to the wry humor of his frontier associates.[22] Born in 1846 or 1847, probably in Iowa, Hartman's formative years were spent in Kansas, where the family had moved just prior to the Civil War. He was exposed to violence at an early age; his father, James B. Hartman, active with the antislavery guerrillas called Jayhawkers, enlisted his teenage son in conducting destructive, murderous raids into Missouri.[23] The behavior of the elder Hartman so outraged some citizens of Atchison, Kansas, that four of them drew straws to see who would execute him. A man named James McEwan drew the short straw and promptly "filled Hartman with buckshot from his head to his heels, but strange to say, the fellow did not die for months afterward."[24]

Young Sam signed up for a three-year enlistment in the Seventh Cavalry, Kansas Volunteers in April 1862, but deserted soon thereafter. He then headed west for the Rocky Mountain region, where he hunted buffalo and took jobs as a muleskinner and bullwhacker hauling into the army forts. He laid rails for a time on the westward-building Union Pacific Railroad when construction resumed after the Civil War. But due to a violent nature he never kept a job long. In the frontier towns of Abilene and Wichita in Kansas and Las Animas, Colorado, he gained an unsavory reputation for drunken rows and lawlessness. He was said to have had several gun battles, exchanging bullets at Custer City with a man named Ed Milligan and getting wounded in a "Sidney shooting sociable." Dark haired with a heavy mustache, he was not a bad-looking man, but his features were somewhat marred by embedded powder from the discharge of a pistol close to his face during one of his brawls.[25]

Like many another frontier drifter he headed for the Black Hills in the rush of 1876. He operated a faro game at Deadwood, consorted with the demimonde, and quickly acquired a reputation as a blackguard and a cheat in a camp swarming with disreputable characters.

After negotiating a night's entertainment, payable in $20 of gold dust, with a harlot remembered only by her nickname "Tid Bit,"[26] Hartman paid the doxy off in the morning "with brass filings and black sand." As the story goes, when "Tid Bit" found she had been deceived, she complained to "Calamity Jane," who threw down on "Laughing Sam" with a pair of "big, ivory-handled six-shooters" and made him compensate "Tid Bit" with genuine U.S. gold coins.[27]

Another difficulty with a prostitute almost cost Hartman his life on August 22, 1876. He and Harry ("Sam") Young, bartender in the Number 10 Saloon, where earlier that month the famous "Wild Bill" Hickok had been assassinated, vied for the primary affections of a female "denizen of the badlands." Hartman narrowly escaped Hickok's fate when Young, seeing a figure in the dim light of the saloon wearing Hartman's distinctive coat and hat, shot the man dead. Instead of "Laughing Sam," the victim of Young's accurate fire turned out to be Myer ("Bummer Dan") Baum.[28]

Evidently Hartman himself had never killed another man, but "parties who are well acquainted with 'Laughing Sam' assure us," Edward A. Slack of the *Cheyenne Daily Sun* reminded his readers, "that he is a desperate fellow who would not hesitate to take life in order to accomplish any object he might have in view."[29]

Thinking the grass might be more luxuriant at another pasture, the four road agents, Blackburn, Pelton, Wall, and Hartman, moved over to the Deadwood-Sidney route. On the night of October 2 near Buffalo Gap they stopped the northbound coach, which contained only one passenger, a man named Ketchum from New York, and the division superintendent, Ed Cook. The robbers wore no masks and were identified by Cook. Passengers had become so wary of road agent attacks that they carried very little cash with them, and the take in this robbery amounted to only $7, a check, and the victims' revolvers. It was a great disappointment to the robbers and led to the dissolution of this new band.[30]

Pelton and Hartman, having decided that further Deadwood stage operations presented risks greater than any possible rewards, took their leave. They crossed the Missouri and settled down near Harlan, Iowa, where, using the aliases S. S. Houston (Hartman) and William Clark (Pelton), they took jobs on a farm at $18 a month. They thought they had left their outlaw life behind them, but within weeks fate intervened.

A neighbor of their employer, just returned from the Black Hills, happened to see "Laughing Sam" working in a field and recognized him as a man who, only weeks earlier, had held a pistol to his head and robbed him. Advised of this discovery by the neighbor, Shelby County Sheriff John Long arrested Sam as well as "Kid," whom he suspected of being Hartman's criminal confederate. The two suspects were taken to Omaha and jailed on October 5, 1877. At a preliminary hearing the next morning they appeared in chains before U.S. Commissioner Watson B. Smith to answer charges that they had committed highway robbery on the Sioux Indian Reservation in Dakota Territory.[31] After hearing testimony from robbery victims brought from Dakota identifying items in the possession of the accused as property stolen from them, Commissioner Smith ruled on October 15 that Hartman and "Kid" should be bound over for trial in Dakota. The two remained in jail at Omaha until November, when federal marshals took them to Rapid City for trial. The *Black Hills Journal* of Rapid City greeted the return of the notorious outlaw "Laughing Sam," while withholding comment, almost ignoring, the arrival of "Kid" Pelton, a relative unknown. "Samuel Young, alias Sam Hartwell, alias 'Laughing Sam,'" it said, was ensconced in the county jail. "The mysterious man of many aliases and that somewhat celebrated knight of the road is now counting the links embraced in the sturdy chain that encircles his ankles."[32]

A question of jurisdiction in Hartman's case arose, and on January 4, 1878, he was returned to Omaha and jailed there for one night, but the next day U.S. Marshal John B. Raymond turned the prisoner around and took him back to Rapid City by way of Yankton. "He was in good spirits although in irons," said the *Omaha Daily Herald*, "and the Marshal says he behaved himself excellently." Arriving back in Rapid City on January 16, Marshal Raymond gave his prisoner over to the custody of Sheriff Frank Moulton, who locked him up in the Pennington County jail, where Sam would cool his heels for the next nine months.[33]

At his trial Hartman's attorney, W. H. Parker, entered a not guilty plea to charges of highway robbery committed on Indian land and theft of U.S. property, but the evidence against the defendant was overwhelming, and the jury brought in a guilty verdict after only an hour's deliberation. On October 16, 1878, "Laughing Sam" was sentenced to a prison term of nine years and eight months and two weeks later entered the House of Corrections at Detroit, Michigan. The editors of both the *Cheyenne Daily Leader* and the *Omaha Daily Bee* could not resist tying the man's nickname to the verdict: "He don't laugh now," remarked the *Leader*, and "This is no laughing matter for Samuel but he will have to grin and bear it," said the *Bee*.[34]

Better advised by his attorneys, Pelton pleaded guilty to horse theft and at a trial at Rapid City received a sentence of one year in prison and a $1,000 fine to cover the costs of catching and prosecuting him. On June 15, 1878, he entered the prison at Stillwater, Minnesota. Before the year was up he petitioned the court to remit the heavy fine and costs as he was destitute and unable to pay the amount. His request was granted, but immediately upon his release on May 21, 1879, Laramie County Sheriff George Draper slapped cuffs on Pelton and brought him back to Wyoming to stand trial for the murder of Adolph Cuny. A reporter for the *Daily Sun* interviewed him on his arrival in Cheyenne and found him wearing "an expression of flinty indifference" without a sign of remorse. His year in prison had "reduced him in flesh and bleached his complexion," and he no longer was the "ruddy, sun-burnt, brawny faced desperado" who had gunned down Adolph Cuny.[35]

Tried in district court in December 1879, Pelton was prosecuted by County Attorney J. W. Fisher and Charles N. Potter. The defense was ably conducted by Judge W. H. Miller and A. Worth Spates. Judge William W. Peck presided. After taking testimony from Charles Hayes and two others, none of whom could swear to seeing Pelton gun down Cuny, the prosecution rested its case. The only witness for the defense of any real relevance was the defendant himself, who testified that he was asleep in another room of the Six-Mile Ranch when the fracas started. "I arose from bed," he said, "and walked to the barroom entrance; saw Cuny with his rifle covering Blackburn, who, as soon as he saw me, turned his rifle upon me and fired instantly, the ball striking near my head in the door post and the flash of the gun nearly blinded me for an instant." He said he returned the fire in self-defense. "I fired on Cuny because I thought I would be mortally wounded unless I did; Cuny was a much larger man than myself; he had a large rifle and could easily have killed me."[36]

After closing arguments and Judge Peck's charge, the jury deliberated several hours before finding the defendant guilty of manslaughter and fixing a sentence of four years imprisonment.[37]

Blackburn and Wall had continued their road agent operations after the departure of Pelton and Hartman. Returning to the Deadwood-Cheyenne road, on October 9, 1877, they struck both the northbound and southbound stages. The down coach proved to be a complete waste of time. There was only one passenger, a woman, whom they did not bother, and the stage carried no treasure. They told the driver, however, "that they were determined to attack the next treasure coach, and that they were after Boone May, the messenger, and would kill him, if possible."[38]

George Chapman was the driver on the up coach, which Blackburn and Wall, wearing masks, halted soon after. Sitting with Chapman on the box was Jack H. Bowman, the station-keeper at Hat Creek, who later gave an account of the affair.

The night was dark, but when Blackburn called out an order to pull up, Bowman, for whom the outlaw had once worked, recognized his voice. Chapman did not rein in his team fast enough to suit the bandits, and Bowman said he could hear "the gun locks click." When the stage finally came to a halt, said Bowman, Blackburn and Wall appeared out of the black and approached the two men on the box with rifles pointed. But the tense confrontation quickly turned into a meeting of old pals. "I laughed at Dunc and he recognized me," said Bowman.

> They pulled off their masks, and passed up a flask of whisky, and then wanted to know if they [the passengers] had any money. I said "No," but told them I had some. They replied, "O, ——, we don't want your money." Dunc asked me what was being said in town about the frequent robberies, and who was getting the credit for it, and when I replied they were, Dunc said, "O, I suppose so." I told them that soldiers were on the road, which made both of them laugh and drew from Wall the remark, "I wish they would put a company of cavalry on our trail, we could make some money out of their horses."

Before they left, empty-handed, Blackburn remarked to Chapman: "Well, George, I will never ask you to put the brakes [on] again, we are going to quit the road; business is too —— bad."[39]

That month Sheriff Seth Bullock of Deadwood came close to capturing or killing Blackburn and Wall on two different occasions. On October 16, acting on a tip that the two road agents were hiding out in a dense thicket near Crook City, Bullock and three deputies approached the site just as darkness set in.

> The sheriff and his men cautiously advanced upon the roost and were about to charge upon it, when the accidental discharge of a gun gave warning to the robbers, who rapidly fled. A volley was fired by the officers, necessarily at random, but, as subsequently proved, with good effect. Shots were returned by the robbers until they reached their horses, when they galloped away, unsuccessfully pursued by the sheriff's posse. On Thursday last [October 18] the robbers appeared at a ranch on the Sidney road and demanded food, which was furnished, and where Blackburn displayed two ugly gun-shot wounds in his arm. These, he said, were the work of Bullock, whom he would kill inside of twenty-four hours, a threat which he has not carried into execution.[40]

Believing that Blackburn and Wall would have to go into Crook City for food and medical assistance, Sheriff Bullock and his three deputies[41] each night thereafter set up a "still hunt" on the road leading into town in the hope the wanted men would walk into the trap. About midnight on October 23 the two outlaws emerged from the brush onto the road, but when Bullock shouted an order to halt, they turned and ran. The officers fired a number of shots at the fleeing pair before they got away, and believed they wounded Wall.[42]

Aware that Jim Wall's brother ran a dance hall in Deadwood and suspecting that the two fugitives might come out of hiding to seek shelter and aid there, Bullock ordered surveillance of the place, but his quarry failed to show up. Blackburn never was able to carry out his threat on Bullock's life, and the sheriff was unsuccessful in his efforts to land the desperado and his pal Jim Wall.[43]

Sheriff Bullock and his deputies in November did arrest four men on suspicion of highway robbery. They gave their names as "Tony Pastor," Finn Davis, A. B. Van Camp, and Lawrence Woodhall. According to the story from Deadwood, the suspects were "cornered" in a saloon, and as the officers entered, "the robbers made a motion to draw their pistols, but they were too late, as the officers already had them covered with six-shooters." Editor Slack of the *Cheyenne Daily Sun* was dubious about this arrest, however, remarking that "it hardly seems probable that a party of four men following the occupation of highwaymen would dare to go into Deadwood and meet in a public house. . . . Bullock, after several unsuccessful attempts to capture Blackburn, Wall and Webster, has given it up for a bad job, and tried some easier ones." Slack took an extra jab at the Dakota lawman, who in an election only days earlier had lost his sheriff's job to John Manning, adding that those arrested were possibly "some chaps who voted for Manning."[44] Slack, it seems, was correct in his hunch that those arrested were innocent, for evidence incriminating them was not produced, and they were quickly released.

Meanwhile, Blackburn and Wall, after their gunshot wounds had sufficiently healed, stole eight stage company horses from the Lance Creek station. Scott Davis, who had also gone through a recovery period after being shot through the legs in the September 26 holdup, requested and received permission from his stage company employers to track the outlaws and their stolen ponies. He set out with an army detail of a noncommissioned officer and four troopers from Fort Laramie. They ran into a winter storm and a two-foot snowfall that blanketed the area, covering the tracks of their quarry. But Davis, following a strong hunch that the two outlaws were headed west, continued to lead his party in that direction. He went to Fort Fetterman and old Fort Caspar, past Independence Rock and Devil's Gate to Split Rock in the Sweetwater Valley. At every stop he inquired if anyone had seen two men driving a herd of eight horses.

He was following fresh tracks in the snow, which he believed were left by Blackburn and Wall and their stolen horses, when another heavy snow again covered the tracks. Discouraged by this latest setback, the soldiers gave up the chase and returned to their post.[45] Davis continued on alone. So determined was he to catch the thieves, and knowing that every moment counted, he ignored basic western protocol, leaving his exhausted mount at a ranch and taking a replacement without even consulting the owner. He went through South Pass and crossed the Continental Divide, pushing on to Atlantic City.

Heavy snow in the higher elevations made trailing impossible, so Davis left his horse at South Pass City and, taking only his saddle and guns, boarded a train for Green River. A telegram awaited him there from a friend advising that two men and a herd of horses had passed Sandy station headed for the Alkali stage ranch.

Enlisting two reliable Green River deputies, Charles Brown and "Pawnee Charlie" Gorsuch, to help him, Davis threw his saddle on a rented horse, and the three men set out for Alkali ranch about nine o'clock that night. After four hours of hard riding they reached the ranch and awakened the man in charge, one "Broncho Jim." When questioned, "Broncho Jim" in a booming voice vehemently denied having seen any strangers with a horse herd, but his wife blurted out, "You know very well that those men are sleeping in the haystack."

That was all Scott Davis needed to hear. Heading straight to a corral haymow barely visible in the dim moonlight, he discerned two men starting to get up, evidently having their sleep disturbed by the loud talking of "Broncho Jim." Davis called out to them to come out with their hands up, but they came up shooting. Davis and his "Charlie" deputies returned the fire. The two men ran from the haymow. One went down, a bullet through both legs, while the other vanished into the night. Davis approached the downed man, who vainly tried to move his damaged legs and complained: "You have put a pair of shackles on me that I can't get off." He gave his name as Thomas Woodby and steadfastly refused to acknowledge that he was James Wall, although Davis had recognized him immediately. After his wounds were treated Charlie Brown took the prisoner in charge and left with him on the first stage for Green River.

In the morning Scott Davis and "Pawnee Charlie" Gorsuch rounded up the stolen horses. They then examined the haystack where the outlaws had holed up and found the pistol that Blackburn had taken from Davis during the stagecoach robbery of September 26. This removed any doubts Davis may have harbored that he had found the men he sought and his arduous trek over 375 miles of freezing, snow-covered wilderness had not been in vain. He had captured one of the men he wanted, but the other, Blackburn, was still on the loose.

Blackburn had fled without coat or hat. In the act of pulling on his boots when the shooting started, he only got one on before he had to run. He carried the other boot with him, but it had a bullet hole through it. Davis knew Blackburn could not last long in that condition out on the wintry prairie; he had to head for habitation. Green River offered the only hope for the fugitive. So Davis went back to Green River, spread the word to everyone to be on the watch for the wanted man, and waited.

As expected, about eight o'clock that night Blackburn showed up. Bareheaded and coatless, his feet wrapped in a pair of underdrawers, he entered Barrett's store "for the purpose," as one paper put it, "of replenishing his wardrobe." An alert citizen, J. R. Morgan, notified the officers, who kept a watch on the store. Blackburn emerged from Barrett's wearing a new hat, overcoat, and rubber shoes and went immediately into Pete Appel's restaurant for some badly needed food. The officers let him fill his stomach, and then "Pawnee Charlie" Gorsuch stepped up and placed him under arrest.

The weary and half-frozen man put up no resistance. Calm and collected as always, Blackburn merely said, "I'd stand you off if I had a gun, but I hid it outside of town." Word of the capture of "the notorious desperado and road agent, 'Dunk' [*sic*] Blackburn, who has for so many months past been a terror on the various Black Hills routes," was telegraphed to the *Leader*, which hailed the news under the headline, "STAGE STOPPERS STOPPED."[46]

When the officers searched Blackburn they found three buckskin money sacks containing about $150 in cash, some odd coins, a watch, and a penknife. The prisoner readily admitted his true identity, but backed up his companion's claim that his name was Thomas Woodby and not James Wall. Blackburn said he had only partnered with "Woodby" for two weeks.

The next day Scott Davis loaded the recovered horses in a car attached to the rear of a Union Pacific passenger train and returned east to Cheyenne with his two prisoners. He had wired Luke Voorhees the day and hour of his arrival, and Sheriff Jeff Carr and his deputies were waiting at the depot with a spring wagon to meet him. A crowd of about 200 had also gathered "to catch a glimpse of the desperadoes" and, as Voorhees explained, "to get a look at a man who had nerve enough to capture two road agents." The man of the hour in Cheyenne, said the *Cheyenne Daily Sun*, was definitely "the gallant and daring Scott Davis."

As soon as it was ascertained which car contained the prisoners a rush was made to enter, and the people succeeded admirably in their design so long as there was standing room in the coach. Sheriff Carr . . . , after allowing the excited spectators to gaze on the captured individuals a few minutes, cleared the car to make room for the transfer of the men to the light spring wagon. . . . Blackburn, heavily ironed hand and foot came out first and was placed in the vehicle. The next and most difficult task was that of removing Wall, who is wounded, and was lying on a stretcher, unable to walk or even sit up. After considerable difficulty he was taken on the "shutter," head first, out the car and placed in the back part of the wagon. By this time the number of spectators had largely increased [and] it was with great difficulty that the officers were enabled to start for the jail with the captives. . . .

By the time their destination was reached an immense crowd of people were surging around the front door of the court house, and filling the large hall. . . . Whenever [Blackburn] saw a familiar face he . . . called out the name of the party and extended his hand in a familiar manner. Wall . . . was also engaged in conversation by several persons who knew him in better days.[47]

Carr took Blackburn, manacled and encumbered by "a new patent contrivance designed for the same purpose as ball and chain, but much superior to that article," to the county jail and locked him up. No shackles were needed for Wall, who, with bullet holes through both legs, was not going to run anywhere for some time. Lying on a rude stretcher and covered by a blanket, he joined his comrade in an adjoining cell.[48]

That evening a reporter for the *Cheyenne Daily Leader* called at the jail and, with the sheriff's permission, interviewed the notorious road agents.

The man who had been identified as James Wall by Scott Davis and others still adamantly declared that his name was Thomas Woodby and refused to tell the reporter anything beyond that. "I don't want to talk," he said, "and now that they call me a liar when I deny that I am Wall, I won't answer any questions."

Blackburn proved much more talkative, answering the reporter's questions in a slow, deliberate manner, which seemed to be his normal style of speech. Although appearing friendly and good-humored, it was obvious to the newsman that Blackburn was assuming "an air of bravado" while "trying hard to resign himself to his fate." He denied ever having robbed a stagecoach, employing the usual excuse of arrested criminals that he was being singled out for persecution. "He said that people 'got down on him' and gave him a hard name, and then the sheriffs and soldiers commenced chasing him, but he didn't know what they wanted him for."

Although his name had been frequently mentioned in the press as a suspect in the murders of both Johnny Slaughter and Adolph Cuny, he was adamant in his insistence that he had never murdered anyone. He could prove, he said, that at the time of the Slaughter shooting he was attending a performance in the Bella Union Theater in Deadwood. He added that he would like to see Marshal Slaughter and proclaim his innocence to him personally, as he had the highest regard for both Johnny and his father. He admitted being present at the Six-Mile Ranch when Cuny was killed, but insisted it was Webster (Pelton) who fired the fatal shot and not him. While fully aware that many believed him guilty of these crimes, he said he was confident he could prove his innocence when brought to trial, if he was successful in getting needed witnesses to appear.[49]

Early in December Blackburn and Wall, who had finally admitted his true identity, were arraigned in district court. On December 8 they surprised everyone by changing their pleas of "not guilty" to "guilty" on all counts in the indictments.

Blackburn was convicted on five counts charged by the territory: robbery, assault to kill and murder, grand larceny, and setting at liberty a prisoner in lawful custody. He was also convicted of the federal crime of highway robbery. He was sentenced to a total of ten years in prison.

Wall was found guilty on territorial charges of robbery and assault to kill and federal charges of grand larceny and highway robbery. The judge imposed a sentence of eight years in prison.[50]

Commented the *Sun*: "Wall, who is still suffering from his recent wounds, had to be brought into court on a stretcher, and of course could not stand up when sentence was pronounced by Judge Fisher. His companion took the sentence of Judge Fisher without a word to offer in remonstrance, which to Dunc Blackburn, the dauntless leader of road agents and highwaymen, was the doom to eight [*sic*] years imprisonment in the penitentiary at Laramie City. But Blackburn has

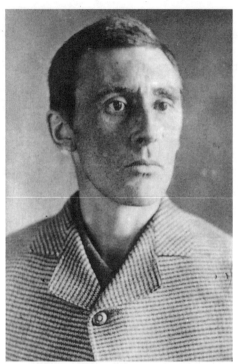

Harassed by Sheriff Seth Bullock, gang leader Duncan Blackburn was finally run down and captured by Scott Davis and had to pose for this prison photo. Courtesy Elnora L. Frye, *Atlas of Wyoming Outlaws at the Territorial Penitentiary.*

become a desperate man, and hence the indifference, real or assumed, which he manifested yesterday."[51]

While the trial of Blackburn and Wall held the attention of folks in Cheyenne, Editor Glafcke of the *Leader* took the opportunity to toss a bomb in the direction of the Bismarck stage line. In an editorial headlined "DASTARDLY CONSPIRACY" he leveled the sensational charge that Superintendent Gidley of the rival stagecoach company had entered into an agreement with the Blackburn road agents to confine their criminal activities to attacks on the Cheyenne and Sidney stages. Glafcke said the source for this serious indictment was Blackburn himself, and quoted the gang leader as declaring, "They put up for us, you bet." It was alleged that the superintendent,

James ("Kid") Wall stuck close to the charismatic Dunc Blackburn and ended up with painful bullet wounds, a prison cell, and a prison mug shot. Courtesy Elnora L. Frye, *Atlas of Wyoming Outlaws at the Territorial Penitentiary.*

while riding in a special coach, met Blackburn and Wall and held over an hour's counsel with the two. . . . Blackburn has confessed this to an intimate friend in this city. Indeed, he told his captor, Scott Davis, that the Bismarck men had given him and his partner passes over their stage line and also a pass over certain railroads. He also admitted to Davis that in consideration of favors received and offered that they would not molest the Bismarck route.

We understand very well that these are serious charges, but we believe that Blackburn tells only half the truth when he says that Gridley [*sic*] "put up for us." When the whole truth is known it will be that this respectable scoundrel was in league with the road agents, and paid them to make raids upon the Cheyenne and Sidney routes. Consequently [Blackburn and Wall] cared but little whether they got much booty, but delighted in sending out high-sounding threats for the purpose of spreading terror along these lines and thus injuring travel in order that the Bismarck route might receive the bulk of the business — both in carrying gold and passengers — and eventually get the exclusive mail contract. It was simply villainous.[52]

Whether there was any truth to the charge that executives of the Northwestern Stage Company had conspired with outlaws, the attack on Gidley was probably precipitated by a growing concern in Wyoming that the Bismarck line might supplant Cheyenne in capturing the lucrative Deadwood gold shipment business. In 1877 a huge bullion shipment worth $350,000 went out from Deadwood on the Bismarck road. The stage, holding a two-compartment, 800-pound safe with a combination lock, was guarded by thirteen heavily armed men, some stationed in the coach, others as outriders in front, behind, and on the flanks. The stage reached Bismarck safely, but later reports had it that road agents planning a holdup at Green River had changed their minds after seeing the size of the protective shield. This great show of force was effective, but very expensive, and gold shipments were soon reverted back to the south.[53]

Dunc Blackburn, that "desperate man," while awaiting transfer from the jail to the Wyoming Territorial Penitentiary at Laramie, displayed that desperation in a last bold bid for freedom. He and three other prisoners — a soldier named James Collins, serving a ten-day sentence for disorderly conduct; Jesse J. Williams, an accused thief; and W. L. Baker, the slayer of a trooper at Fort D. A. Russell — attacked Sheriff Carr and tried to break out. They were unsuccessful. All it got for Blackburn was an additional year tacked on his sentence for stealing Sheriff Carr's pistol in the escape attempt.[54]

On Christmas Day, 1877, Deputy Sheriff Martin loaded Blackburn, Wall, and prisoners Williams, Collins, and Harry Rusten on the caboose of a closely guarded Union Pacific pay car and escorted them to Laramie, where the doors of the prison slammed shut upon them.[55]

Scott Davis, the man primarily responsible for the incarceration of Blackburn and Wall, was meanwhile receiving well-deserved accolades. A resolution passed in the Wyoming Territorial Legislature acknowledged "the indefatigable exertions and signal bravery displayed by Mr. Scott Davis in his recent capture of the notorious 'road agents,' Dunk [*sic*] Blackburn and Wall," and thanked him for "bringing these marauders to justice." On January 12, 1878, the Laramie County commissioners authorized the payment of reward moneys totaling $400 to Davis for the apprehensions.[56]

So, by the end of 1878 the depredations of the Hat Creek gang that had played havoc with stage travel on the Deadwood trails for many months that year were at an end. Five members of the gang, Captain Dunc Blackburn, Jim Wall, Bill Bevins, Clark Pelton, and "Laughing Sam" Hartmen, were locked up in penitentiaries, and Jack Watkins had quit the country, apparently for good.

But what of the other gang member, "Reddy" McKimie, who had ducked out with a sackful of loot, leaving his comrades holding an empty bag?

After splitting with the "woman dressed like a man" at St. Louis, "Little Reddy" went to Texas, perhaps with the thought of tying up again with Sam Bass and the remnants of the Joel Collins gang, but remained there only a short time before entraining again. This time he went far to the east—to Philadelphia—where he exchanged the gold dust he carried for currency. He then returned to his hometown of Rainsboro, Ohio, where he soon became "well known for his lavish expenditure of money, fast driving, and everything that goes toward the makeup of a sporting character." He invested an estimated $7,000 of his ill-gotten, twice-stolen gains in a farm and a dry goods store in Rainsboro. He paraded the streets in a fine carriage drawn by a beautiful matched pair of "fast steppers." Deflecting questions about the source of his wealth with evasive answers, he soon acquired a bevy of sycophantic hangers-on who were more than ready to help him spend it. Completely overwhelmed by this fellow back from the West with pockets bulging, a young woman named Clara Ferguson quickly accepted his proposal of marriage. The future looked bright for "Little Reddy from Texas," who had evidently abandoned the outlaw life.[57]

And then serendipity struck. At Ogallala, Nebraska, a little—five feet six inch, 140 pound—supply store merchant named Millard F. Leech with ambitions as a detective and bounty hunter stepped into the picture. Born on November 24, 1850, on a farm near Tionesta, Pennsylvania, Leech in his teens clerked in a hotel in Meadville and learned telegraphy and engineering. Moving to Tennessee, he took employment as an engineer on the Nashville and Lebanon Railroad and broke into the law enforcement business chasing moonshiners in the Tennessee mountains. Later in Omaha he worked as a telegraph operator for the Union Pacific and traded with the Sioux. His interest in detective work continued, and he boasted that his investigative work led to the 1874 arrest of Mormon leader John D. Lee, charged with multiple murders in the Mountain Meadows Massacre of 1857, and his subsequent execution.[58] Leech was hot on the trail of the Joel Collins Texas gang when he got a tip that one of its members had slipped back to his home in Hillsboro, Ohio. Hurrying to Hillsboro, Leech soon heard about the big-spending redheaded returnee from the West who was making waves at Rainsboro, only ten miles down the road. The detective got a look at Robert McKimie and decided he matched the description of the diminutive redhead who rode with the Collins gang in the Black Hills. Having no arrest authority, Leech simply alerted Seth Bullock of Deadwood of his discovery.[59]

Bullock had been defeated in his bid for reelection as sheriff of Lawrence County, Dakota, but, having organized the Black Hills Detective Agency in affiliation with Dave Cook's Rocky Mountain Detective Association, headquartered in Denver, he was still on the prowl for bad men. Having once arrested McKimie in Deadwood as a suspected horse thief, he knew him well. Bullock went by stage to Cheyenne, where he obtained a requisition for McKimie's extradition to Wyoming from Governor John M. Thayer, and, accompanied by a deputy U.S. marshal named Lyle, set out on the long rail trip through six states and territories to Ohio.

On Tuesday, January 14, 1878, Bullock found McKimie in his Rainsboro, Ohio, store, placed him under arrest, locked him up in the Highland County jail, and immediately wired Luke Voorhees: "I arrested McKenna [sic], alias Reddy, to day. He has $7,000 worth of real estate here, which I will try and secure. Think you or Salisbury ought to be here. I await your instructions. He acknowledges being one of the gang."[60] The next day, after interrogating McKimie further, Bullock sent another telegram to the stage company boss: "Reddy owns up to having secured sixty-five hundred in dust. Have your bank telegraph Citizens' National to go on attachment bonds. This done you need not come."[61]

ASSAULT ON THE DEADWOOD STAGE

Sheriff Seth Bullock of Lawrence County, Dakota, had gun battles with Blackburn and Wall and went all the way to Ohio after McKimie. From *The Life and Adventures of Robert McKimie, Alias "Little Reddy," from Texas*, by J. W. Bridwell, author's collection.

Bullock, however, soon found himself embroiled in a legal imbroglio. McKimie had employed the best legal counsel to be found in the region, the Sloane and Hough law firm, to represent him. The lawyers quickly obtained a writ of habeas corpus and at a hearing held the night of the 15th in the chambers of a Judge Steel, gained their client's release on the grounds that the arrest had been illegal since Bullock had failed to submit his requisition to the Ohio governor and obtain a proper warrant. Bullock hurried to the state capital at Columbus and hired attorney George B. Gardner to represent Wyoming in the case. Acting on his counsel's advice, he had a warrant issued based on his sworn affidavit, charging McKimie with highway robbery. Returning to Highland County, he rearrested McKimie and had him locked up in Sheriff W. C. Newell's jail. Lawyers for the accused argued vainly that the wording of the legal papers was faulty and failed for the second time to gain their client's release.[62]

Bullock, meanwhile, found himself a persona non grata in Highland County. According to the *Laramie Daily Sentinel* the Dakota sheriff "was looked upon as an escaped Bengal Tiger and followed about the streets (at a respectable distance) by a crowd of curious people." It seems McKimie's friends had a notion that once Bullock took control of McKimie, he would hang him to a telegraph pole without benefit of judge or jury. The prisoner himself, while always appearing in court "fashionably attired" and not looking much like a stage robber, still had "a peculiar expression in his eyes [betraying] the bad character of the man." To his cell visitors he displayed "much bravado" and bragged that he expected "to get 'the drop' on Seth Bullock" some day.[63]

While the wheels of justice ground slowly, "Reddy" McKimie planned his escape. Someone had smuggled a pair of guns into his cell, and on the night of February 11, 1878, he saw his opportunity. With both lawmen, Newell and Bullock, out of town, the sheriff on county business elsewhere and Bullock on a trip to nearby Tecumseh, Michigan, to visit relatives, he saw his opportunity. The sheriff's elderly father was acting as jailer while the regular turnkey ate dinner with his family. When the senior Newell opened the cell door to allow a porter to enter with a scuttle of coal, McKimie suddenly leaped at them with a pistol in his hand, yelling, "Get out of the way!" He fired two shots, certainly meant to scare the two men rather than harm them, for even at that close range he hit neither. McKimie burst out of the building and ran into the darkened streets as the old man grabbed a loaded shotgun and fired a load of buckshot in his direction. Some of the pellets found their mark, as evidenced by the discovery the next morning of McKimie's blood-stained and riddled cigar case, but the elusive outlaw made his escape.[64]

Notified of the escape by wire, Sheriff Newell returned to town at once and announced that a reward of $100 would be offered for the escapee's capture. A telegram also brought Bullock hurrying back. On the 14th he wired Luke Voorhees from Chillicothe, Ohio: "McKenna [*sic*], alias Reddy, has escaped jail at Hillsboro. I am on his trail and hope to capture him. I have done everything possible to do and have all the officers of the state on the lookout for the scoundrel. I think he is pretty badly shot in the arm."[65] Voorhees authorized Bullock to add another $500 to the reward amount already offered by Newell. Bullock, Newell, and Deputy U.S. Marshals Lyle and James W. Doggett led search parties through the countryside but found no trace of the escapee, who had been well hidden by friends and relatives. With the aid of these same people he attempted to change his appearance, dying his red hair black and fashioning a mustache from hair cut from his chin whiskers.[66]

Finally venturing out from his hiding place, McKimie, carrying some $600 in cash, caught an eastbound train and by prearrangement met his wife in Richmond, Virginia. The couple traveled through the South, sojourning in Raleigh, North Carolina; Charleston, South Carolina; and Savannah, Georgia. Upon learning that no official extradition agreement existed between the United States and the Bahaman government, McKimie booked passage to Nassau. There he and his wife remained until they ran out of money and began piling up debts. He was thrown into prison for nonpayment of bills and served forty-one days. With the help of the American consul, he got a "working passage" aboard a steamer to New York. Returning to Ohio, he resumed his criminal career, laying plans to rob a bank.[67]

In November 1878 John T. Norris, a detective who had been working on the McKimie case, traced the outlaw to a deserted cabin three miles from Rainsboro. When word of the location of the hideout leaked out, an army of citizens determined to capture or kill the desperado descended on the place. McKimie put up a furious battle before submitting to capture. With two "large six shot navy revolvers, eight inch barrel," in his hands, and another smaller pistol in his hip pocket, he stood off the crowd until downed by bullets. One shot struck him in the left breast near the nipple, but he did not surrender until another bullet hit him in the right cheek at the side of nose, passed through his cheek, and came out near the jawbone.[68]

The citizens turned McKimie over to Sheriff Newell, who put him back in the cell from which he had escaped nine months earlier. Newell notified Seth Bullock of the capture, and the Deadwood detective made the long trip to Ohio again, fully expecting to bring the road agent and accused murderer of Johnny Slaughter back to the

Black Hills with him. But on arrival at Hillsboro he found that the Ohio governor had revoked his original requisition for McKimie, and he had no legal authority to take custody of the prisoner.[69]

While the state of Ohio and the territory of Wyoming argued over which would get the opportunity of bringing McKimie to trial, Bullock visited the outlaw in his cell, where he was recuperating from his wounds. A reporter for the local newspaper recorded a remarkable exchange that took place between the veteran lawman and the tough lawbreaker.

"How would you like to go to with me, Bob?" Bullock asked.

"Oh, first-rate. I am in a pretty tight place here, and they are going to give me a 'lifer' if they can."

"Well, that's perhaps worse than you would get at Cheyenne. They won't give you over five years out there, I guess."

"I would just as soon leave go as not; but I'll tell you one thing, Bullock — I am going to 'crease' you if I ever get the chance."

"All right. If you ever get the chance, I expect you to; but you know damned well that I ain't afraid of you."

"That's so. But if we ever come together on anything like equal chances, one or the other has got to die."

"I'll take my chances, and you better look out that I don't 'get the drop' on you first."[70]

As it happened, Bullock and McKimie never had their gun duel. The last of the Hat Creek gang was put away, as far as we know, when McKimie was tried in Ohio for offenses committed in that state. J. T. Norris, a special detective at Hillsboro, in a letter to T. J. Carr, explained the extent of the charges against McKimie in the Buckeye State:

> We have five cases of burglary and the same number of cases of grand larceny against Reddy. These were committed in three different counties. We propose to try him and his confederates in each case. The evidence is conclusive without a doubt. Part of the property in some of the cases is recovered and identified. Besides this, four of his "pals" have squealed, and one of them confessed while on his way to the penitentiary to serve ten years.
>
> We expect to try Reddy on each separate case; our statute in Ohio provides that a prisoner may be tried on all indictments

separately, and receive a separate sentence on each, if convicted. The sentences are served out in the order in which they are pronounced. One sentence is commenced as soon as the previous one ends.

The laws of Ohio sentence burglars from one to ten years, and those convicted of grand larceny from three to fifteen years. On this basis Reddy will probably get twenty-five years for five cases of burglary and thirty-eight and one-half years for five cases of grand larceny, making a sum total of sixty-three and one-half years. He is now twenty-five years old. He will therefore have to serve until he is eighty-eight and one-half years old in order to fill the requirements of the law. . . . We propose to settle Reddy's hash right here in Ohio, and do it effectively, too.[71]

McKimie was tried for his various crimes and convicted in Ohio, but his sentence was not as severe as predicted by Detective Norris. He received a sentence of fifteen years in the state penitentiary, and was released May 17, 1890, after eleven years behind bars.[72]

He, nor anyone else, ever stood trial for the murder of Johnny Slaughter.

— 5 —

THE VIOLENT PASSING OF "LAME JOHNNY" AND "CURLY" GRIMES

*There were two fellows named Frank Harris and "Lame Johnny" . . .
who had been leading away some halters with horses in them. And the
boys followed them also and one of them, Lame Johnny, got so badly
strangled with a rope while the stage stopped to rest, as he was being
conveyed to jail, that he only lived a few minutes.*
 — Post Office Department Inspector John B. Furay

Two quite noticeable physical abnormalities distinguished Cornelius
Donahue as an outlaw in the Black Hills, a noticeable limp that
quickly earned him the epithet "Lame Johnny," and a mouth described as "enormous." His great oral cavity prompted a western wit
to post this epitaph over his grave:

> Lame Johnny.
> Stranger, pass gently o'er this sod.
> If he opens his mouth, you're gone, by God.[1]

The large mouth was evidently an accident of heredity, but accounts
disagreed on the cause of his lameness. According to A. M. Willard and
Jesse Brown, two lawmen who knew him and presumably got the story
from him, his disability was the result of a childhood accident, a fall
from a horse, that left him with a deformed foot.[2] But a contemporary
newspaper reported that while depredating in Texas he "was severely
wounded, being shot through both limbs, making him a cripple for
life, from which he derived the soubriquet [*sic*] of 'Lame Johnny.' "[3]

Although one respected Black Hills historian averred that Donahue came to Deadwood as an "honest man,"[4] "Lame Johnny" reportedly had a history of lawbreaking before joining the rush to the Black Hills country.

Born on October 6, 1854, in Philadelphia, he had a first-rate education, attending that city's Stephen Girard College from the age of eight until his eighteenth birthday. School records indicate he was an outstanding student, attaining in his final year the highest awards for his conduct and academic achievements.[5] But driven by an adventurous and reckless spirit and a love of horses, the young man after graduation from school left Pennsylvania to become a cowboy on the plains of Texas. There his cattlemen employers soon noticed that he was adept at recovering horses stolen from the ranches by Indians. That he returned from raids on the Indian herds with more head of stock than had been lost also did not go unnoticed (or unappreciated). But the young man soon fell into the trap often experienced by stealers of Indian ponies; he began to run off the stock of neighboring ranchers as well. Condemned as a common horse thief, he found it necessary to get out of Texas.[6] There were unconfirmed newspaper reports that he committed "several murders" in Texas and escaped the state one jump ahead of a vigilance committee.[7]

When he first appeared in the Black Hills in 1876 he was going by the alias of John A. Hurley. Using that name, he worked at a number of jobs in the fast-growing camp, including bookkeeper for the large Homestake Mining Company. Personable and industrious, he had many friends and supporters. In 1877 he even acted for a short period as a deputy sheriff in Custer County. It appeared that, as John Hurley, he had changed the direction of his life and would continue to prosper as a respectable citizen.

But then a newcomer to the camp from Texas recognized Hurley as Cornelius Donahue, the fugitive from the Lone Star State, and spread the information all over town. Since horse thieves were as despised in Dakota Territory as they were in Texas, "Lame Johnny" now found himself shunned by his former friends. Thoroughly embittered, he quit the Deadwood scene and reverted to outlawry.

In July 1877 a spate of holdups pulled off within days of each other and miles apart on stagecoach routes into Deadwood from Fort

Pierre, Sidney, and Cheyenne was conclusive evidence that several different gangs were in operation.

A young prospector with a placer mine near Lead City named John ("White Eye") Anderson was a passenger on a northbound stage that was held up early that month just north of Hat Creek station. His account of the episode indicates that some of the road agents, at least, could display a surprising degree of generosity. "I had to make a trip to Hat Creek Station to collect some money," recalled Anderson.

> I went by stagecoach and collected the money alright, then waited for the next stage to Lead City which arrived at Hat Creek about 7:00 that evening. It was well-loaded with passengers and when we were held up on the road about two hours later, I began to think it was goodbye to the two hundred dollars I had collected at Hat Creek.
>
> The holdup occurred where the road was rough and rocky, with scrubby brush and timber where the stage was going around a rocky point in the road. The road agents all wore masks and had one man in front with a shotgun, one behind and one on each side of the coach. The moon was shining, with clouds flitting by. We all had to get off on the right side with our hands up. I was the last one in the row. One of them went through and searched each of us while another one put all the stuff they got into a gunny sack. When they came to me the moon was shining and the bandit flipped the brim of my broadbrimmed hat and looked in my face. He unbuckled my six-shooter belt and put my gun in the sack. Then he went through my pockets, but took nothing out of them.

For the remainder of the journey passengers in the coach talked excitedly of their experience, but Anderson, who intimates in his account that he had recognized at least one of the robbers, said nothing. About four days after returning to his claim, he came back from his mine to his cabin to find a flour sack with his six-shooter, a belt full of cartridges, and a note: "We thank you for keeping your mouth shut."[8]

The stage to Sidney was stopped about midnight on July 10 near French Creek by five masked bandits who found to their dismay that no passengers, potential robbery victims, were aboard and the treasure box was empty. After questioning the driver about when the northbound coach would be along, they told him to proceed. Of course the driver warned those on the Deadwood-bound stage when he met them down the road that they would probably be held up, so the driver of that stage stopped at French Creek station and stayed overnight. George Caruthers, one of the passengers, said he and the others set up an ambush for the robbers, but although during the night figures were seen skulking about, no hostile move was made on the station, and in the morning the skulkers had disappeared.[9]

Two nights later four masked road agents stopped the Deadwood-to-Sidney stage, driven by a man named McClellan and carrying three passengers, three miles beyond Battle Creek. The bandits ordered the passengers out of the coach, and two searched them while the others stood guard with weapons leveled. Three gold watches and several other articles of jewelry were taken. The brigands opened and ransacked the baggage, removing a number of articles, including a complete dentist's outfit belonging to one of the passengers. One robber remarked with a laugh "that after they got through their present business they might want to start one of their companions in the tooth-pulling business in Omaha." They said they were sorry more gold was not being shipped out of the Black Hills by stagecoach lately and suspected other methods of transport of treasure were being employed. But they assured their listeners that "they were determined to levy a tribute on the dust going out of the Hills, and that there was no force that could be organized that could capture them. They appeared perfectly cool and went about their work as leisurely as if they were engaged in a perfectly legitimate transaction."[10]

On the Cheyenne route masked robbers dressed in blue blouses and common overalls held up the southbound stage on the night of July 17. T. A. Kent, a prominent businessman of Cheyenne, was a passenger in the coach and described the experience on his arrival home. He said that the passengers, with "ominous muzzles of double-barreled shotguns protruding through the windows" of the coach, were ordered out, lined up, and compelled to remove their boots, coats, and pants. The robbers, "as cool and self possessed as a man holding four aces," went through the clothing diligently but found little of value. They then rummaged through the baggage and opened the treasure box but found no gold. Kent said he had a finely mounted revolver, which he attempted to hide under some straw on the coach floor, but one of the bandits found it and exclaimed, "Ain't that a daisy." The total haul consisted of three revolvers, three rifles, two watches, some bedding and clothing from the baggage, and about $40 in cash. "You don't mean to say, gentlemen, that that's all the wealth you have about you?" grumbled the gang leader. "How is it that you can travel on stages with your linen dusters and only six or eight dollars in your pockets?"[11]

The bandits were bitterly disappointed in the meager proceeds of their night's labors, but another gang that stopped the same coach twelve miles farther down the road must have been even more aggravated when they found the pigeons aboard had already been plucked.[12]

The stage from Deadwood on the Fort Pierre road was stopped by road agents on July 23 near Pine's Springs. This band apparently was much more flush than the ones working the southern routes, for after ordering the passengers out they announced that if any of them had more than $300 they only wanted the overage; they would not rob anyone with less. They got nothing, for no passenger carried that much money. The road agents then threw the baggage off by the side of the road and ordered the driver to go on. When the stage arrived at Pine's Springs a wagon was sent back for the baggage. Only a shirt belonging to a Mr. Holcomb of Yankton had been taken.[13]

It cannot be determined at this late date how many of these July 1877 robberies, if any, involved "Lame Johnny." But he was identified by Superintendent Ed Cook as one of Dunc Blackburn's reconstructed Hat Creek gang that botched the holdup of the Sidney stage near Buffalo Gap on August 23, garnering only $12 for their trouble, while missing $1,000 more.

The other limping bandit named by Cook as a participant in this robbery was a man remembered only as "Lame Bradley." It was said Bradley carried a grudge against Ed Cook and when he spotted him among the passengers deliberately shot a piece off the superintendent's ear. He would have fired again but was restrained by Blackburn, who also made the gang return a fine gold watch taken from Cook.[14]

Although he seems to have been notorious for self-promotion, proclaiming himself "King of the Road,"[15] little is known about the man known as "Lame Bradley,"[16] except that he was often confused with "Lame Johnny."[17] He has been described as a "large, forty-year-old, grizzled and heavily bearded Irishman" who a month before that botched August robbery had been a member of a gang headquartered in Crook City and had outdrawn and killed another gang member named Powell.[18] After a short stint with the Hat Creek gang Bradley is said to have deserted the Black Hills and gone to Dodge, where he spent money freely before moving on to the Texas panhandle. There he was killed by "a youth of nineteen, whom he tried to rob."[19]

Another rather obscure criminal who has been mentioned as a member of "Lame Johnny's" stage robbery gang was James Fowler, alias James Lawton, but best remembered in the Black Hills as "Fly Speck Billy." One old-timer who freighted between Sidney and the Black Hills during that eventful period even elevated "Fly Speck Billy" to the level of Dunc Blackburn, naming those two as the "worst road agents" preying on the stages.[20] Respected historical writer Mari Sandoz described "Fly Speck Billy" as "a slight, almost beardless youth" who got his nickname from a generous "splatter of very dark freckles across his nose." She said that after being jailed in Ogallala for horse theft he came to the Black Hills and "joined Lame Johnny or Dunc Blackburn."[21] The career of "Fly Speck Billy," like many of his ilk, came to an abrupt end. After he shot and killed Abe Barnes, a freighter at Custer City, on February 6, 1881, a mob took him from the sheriff and hanged him.[22]

On October 2, 1877, the Blackburn bunch stopped the northbound coach from Sidney near the site of the August robbery. Again they met with poor pickings, taking a total of only $7 from the two passengers, one of whom was Superintendent Ed Cook, he of the disfigured ear. Cook said he recognized all the bandits, including "Lame Johnny."[23]

For more than a year and a half following that robbery no road agent with a noticeable limp was reported working the Deadwood route as "Lame Johnny" returned to the more lucrative profession of horse stealing. But then in June 1879, at about four in the afternoon, he and two cohorts, Frank Harris and Tom Moore, stopped the stage at Dry Creek, six miles from Buffalo Gap. In a confession made in a courtroom a year later Harris said:

> I stood on the off side of the coach; I stopped the coach; Tom Moore went through the passengers; Lame Johnny stood . . . opposite me and made the passengers throw up their hands. . . . We got two silver watches. . . . After the passengers got out,

Moore went through the coach and found the gold watch. . . . [That] was most all that we got; there was some small change, not more than $10 or $15. . . . Then Moore ordered [the driver] to pitch off the mail sacks, which he did; the passengers were then ordered back into the coach, and the driver ordered to move on. The coach left and we cut the mail sacks open and found a bunch of stamps and several registered letters, but no money in any of them. . . . [Later] Johnnie burned the stamps.[24]

Their stage robbery attempts proving almost totally unproductive, Donahue and Harris once again concentrated on horse stealing. They began making horse-stealing raids on the Pine Ridge Indian Reservation, reportedly killing a guard in the process.[25] This drew the attention of Valentine McGillycuddy, agent at the reservation, who called on the federal government for assistance in capturing the horse thief. Assigned to the task was William Henry Harrison Llewellyn, newly appointed special agent of the Department of Justice.

Llewellyn seems to have fallen rather precipitously and unexpectedly into this important and demanding position. Born on September 9, 1851, at Monroe, Wisconsin, he had attended Tabor College in Iowa before heading for the goldfields of Montana at the age of fifteen. He prospected in the mountains and worked with a surveying party on the plains. By the time he reached his mid-twenties he was claiming a vast knowledge of the western wilderness and firsthand knowledge of many of its colorful characters, including David Charles ("Doc") Middleton, the leader of a notorious horse-stealing outlaw gang operating in Nebraska.[26] Settling at Omaha in 1877, Llewellyn made his first tentative entry into police activity, taking work as a tax collector and deputy jailer for the city.

During this period the activities of Middleton and his minions had aroused great alarm among stock growers of the region and reservation Indians, both groups having suffered heavy losses in their horse herds due to the work of the gang. Someone, evidently having heard Llewellyn's claim of intimate knowledge of the country and the outlaw chief, suggested to powerful political figures that he be enlisted to hunt Middleton down. The idea reached the higher echelons of the federal government in Washington, D.C., and on May 27, 1879, Charles Devens, attorney general of the United States, wrote Llewellyn, offering him the position of special agent with the responsibility

William Henry Harrison Llewellyn, special agent of the Department of Justice, stood trial with Boone May for the killing of outlaw "Curly" Grimes. Courtesy Museum of New Mexico Collections.

to find and arrest not only Middleton and his gang members but any others who "subsist in unlawful traffic in whiskey, and by stealing horses and other stock from the Indians and honest white men [are] in violation especially of the Intercourse Acts of Congress."[27]

Llewellyn took the job and within two months had run Middleton to ground and captured him.[28] Of great assistance to him in that successful campaign was Detective James L. ("Whispering") Smith, an employee of the powerful Union Pacific Railroad, a company with a strong financial interest in reducing outlawry in the region. Unlike Llewellyn, "Whispering" Smith was a veteran outlaw-chaser with wide experience in law enforcement. When he showed up at the Pine

Ridge Agency, Julia McGillycuddy, wife of the Indian agent, was impressed by his appearance, demeanor, and fearsome reputation. "His voice was gentle," she noted (an attribute that no doubt led to his "Whispering" moniker); "he never indulged in liquor; he was not a quarrelsome man; yet he had no regard for human life and was known as a killer."[29]

Born in Maryland about 1838, James Louis Smith reportedly served in the Union army during the Civil War and attained the rank of captain. After the war he was a detective on the police force and warden of the workhouse at New Orleans. By 1876 he had relocated in Omaha, Nebraska, where the Union Pacific Railroad hired him as a detective and he first became acquainted with William Henry Harrison Llewellyn and other special agents employed by the railroad, Nathaniel K. Boswell, William C. Lykins, and Millard F. Leech, who would also play important roles in the war waged against the Deadwood stagecoach robbers.[30]

In July 1879 "Whispering" Smith, then at Sidney, Nebraska, received word that two suspects believed to be "Lame Johnny" and Frank Harris were being held at Fort Robinson by military authorities. Smith hurried to the post, identified the two as the wanted men, and made arrangements for their transfer to Rapid City to stand trial. Deeming their transport together too dangerous, he decided to escort them individually, taking Donahue first and then returning for Harris.

John B. Furay, Post Office Department inspector who was investigating Deadwood stagecoach robberies at the time, had a way with words in his reports to his superiors. "Lame Johnny," he said, "had a keen sense of danger and so in quitting Fort Robinson, he took time by the forelock and bade his companions a long and, as he predicted, a 'last' farewell. He evidently felt a sort of premonition, as it were, that something would interfere with his longevity."[31]

On July 1, 1879, Smith took Donahue, heavily shackled, to the Red Cloud stage station, three miles north of Fort Robinson, to meet the next northbound stage, which turned out to be a treasure coach returning to Deadwood after delivering its bullion box to Sidney. At the reins of this stage was Ed Cook, the division superintendent who had once been robbed by "Lame Johnny," and had first identified him as a road agent. Remarks passing between Cook and the prisoner went unrecorded, unfortunately, but would have been most interesting. Shotgun messenger Jesse Brown, his wife, and two young daughters were seated in the coach, and another shotgun messenger, Boone May, accompanied the stage on horseback as an outrider.[32] After seating Donahue inside with Brown, Smith climbed up on the front boot beside the driver, and the journey began.

At about eleven o'clock that night the coach reached a point near a small creek several miles north of the Buffalo Gap stage station. The site was quite close to the spot where "Lame Johnny" as a member of Dunc Blackburn's gang had robbed the stage back in 1877. Suddenly a band of eight masked men appeared out of the darkness and, with leveled rifles, brought the coach to a halt. From their demeanor it quickly became apparent to Cook and the messengers that they did not intend to rob the stage passengers, but to remove one of them, the shackled captive. It soon became equally obvious that their intention was lynching and not rescue. The presence of Smith, Brown, and May, all fearless fighting men of proven stature, and Ed Cook, whose courage had also been tested often, did not seem to daunt them at all. As Mrs. Brown and her two small daughters watched in terror, the attackers dragged Donahue, kicking and struggling, from the coach and carried him off into the brush. The officers made no effort to stop them. In a few moments Cook put a whip to his horses, and the coach moved on without "Lame Johnny."[33]

Accounts of the actual lynching appeared in several papers, with details that could only have come from eyewitnesses, either the guards, who denied seeing the hanging, or members of the lynch mob. The *Black Hills Daily Times* said that "the doomed robber resisted the vigilantes with all his strength and begged the officer, who had him in charge, for his revolver. He knew well his fate and wanted to sell his life as dearly as possible."[34] According to the *Sidney Telegraph* the vigilantes demanded that "Lame Johnny" confess to his crimes and name his accomplices. "He replied that he had nothing to confess and never would betray a partner, whereupon they told him his hour had come, as they intended to hang him. He replied: 'Hang and be damned; you can't do it any too soon.'"[35]

The next day Pete Oslund's bull train reached the site and found the body of Cornelius Donahue, alias "Lame Johnny," dangling from an elm tree about 100 yards from the road. Oslund cut the corpse down and buried it under the tree. The nearby rivulet came to be called Lame Johnny Creek.[36]

There was a cursory investigation of the lynching. A party of men even went out to the gravesite and dug up the body to ascertain if Donahue had died from a gunshot wound or hanging.[37] The inaction of the officers to protect the prisoner created an air of suspicion about their possible complicity in the affair, but no charges were filed. Black Hills folks seemed to care little about the details of how a notorious horse thief and road agent departed this life. There was general agreement that the passing of "Lame Johnny" Donahue was good riddance.[38]

Examples of the callousness with which "Lame Johnny's" demise was viewed can be found in the reports of Inspector Furay of the Post Office Department. "There were," he said, "two fellows named Frank Harris and 'Lame Johnny' . . . who had been leading away some halters with horses in them. And the boys followed them also and one of them, Lame Johnny, got so badly strangled with a rope while the stage stopped to rest, as he was being conveyed to jail, that he only lived a few minutes."[39]

In another report Furay recounted how "Lame Johnny," arrested in Nebraska and taken by officers to Dakota for trial, died near Buffalo Gap "by strangulation." In a display of sarcasm he said, "the following tenderly expressed thoughts rudely etched upon a wooden slab" at the gravesite "shows the sacredness and care observed by the living over the spot where he lies:

Pilgrim, Pause! You're standing on
The moldering clay of "Limping John."
Tread lightly, stranger, on his sod
For if it moved, you're robbed, by G——d.[40]

Jim "Whispering" Smith went back to Fort Robinson a few days later and, without incident, brought Frank Harris to Rapid City to face a federal indictment for stealing Indian ponies and a territorial charge of grand larceny. Convicted, Harris made an effort for clemency before sentence was imposed by offering the court a signed affidavit in which he confessed to the January 1879 stagecoach robbery and named "Lame Johnny" and Tom Moore as his confederates.

Shotgun messenger Daniel Boone May was hated and feared by the road agents for his diligence in combating them. Author's collection.

He was outraged when the judge, after taking due note of the confession, still gave him five years in the penitentiary for horse theft.[41]

Federal agent William Henry Harrison Llewellyn and Boone May teamed up to bring down another desperado at this time.

Leon Grimes, or "Curly" as he was widely known, went by a number of names, including William Curley, Lew Curley, and Lee Curley. A horse thief by profession — he had been an associate of "Doc" Middleton, generally recognized as the premier purloiner of horseflesh on the plains — Grimes was a former stage driver who had bragged to his friends that he was going to the Black Hills to "make a raise" by robbing stagecoaches. So dangerous that even his outlaw confederates held him in awe, Grimes was an expert at "fanning" his handgun and was reputed to have had committed several murders. Witnesses to his feats with a revolver claimed that when he took his time and aimed he could drill an oyster can every shot at 100 yards. But Grimes was so ornery that "Doc" Middleton banned him from his gang of thieves and cutthroats.[42]

On July 5, 1879, Grimes and two other Middleton gang members, Joe Johnson and Jack Nolan, robbed the Bone Creek, Nebraska, post office, near the Deadwood-to-Sidney route, which got the attention of Llewellyn and Furay. While in Deadwood in late January 1880 Furay got a tip that Grimes was driving a team with a freight outfit near the town and passed the information to Llewellyn. Enlisting the help of Boone May as a special deputy, Llewellyn went to Fort Meade, arriving there on Sunday evening, February 1, and remained overnight. The next day he and May located the bull train on Elk Creek, some thirty-five or forty miles from Deadwood, and arrested Grimes without incident. They cuffed their prisoner, placed him on a borrowed horse, and started out on the return journey to Deadwood.[43]

It was bitterly cold, with the temperature hovering several degrees below zero, and a heavy snow began to fall. Grimes complained that his hands would freeze unless the handcuffs were taken off and swore he would not attempt to escape if they were removed. The officers freed his hands, and the three of them rode on into an increasingly severe blizzard.

After stopping to eat and warm up a bit at Bull Dog Ranch, they were within two miles of Fort Meade shortly before midnight when Grimes, in a desperate bid for freedom, suddenly dug spurs into his pony and headed for a nearby copse of woods. Llewellyn and May shouted at him to halt, but he kept on. They opened fire. Grimes was dead when they reached him, riddled with buckshot and pistol bullets. Leaving him where he lay, they went on to Fort Meade and reported the incident. When the storm subsided a party rode out from the fort, found the frozen body, and buried it on the spot. Meanwhile Llewellyn and May went on into Deadwood, where they asked the coroner to hold an inquest, but he declined.[44]

Some in Deadwood questioned the officers' account of how "Curly" Grimes met his end. Because of recent events, a cloud of suspicion that

Llewellyn and May were too quick on the trigger when dealing with suspects hovered over the heads of both men. Llewellyn had been accused by some of attempting to assassinate "Doc" Middleton rather than capturing him, and others believed May was complicit in the lynching of "Lame Johnny."

An examination of the saddle and bridle Grimes had been using when shot indicated he had been "lying along the side of his horse holding by its mane and one heel wedged into the saddle. The shot riddled him, and the saddle shows marks of the terrible fire that rained on him and his horse. The cantle of the saddle is perforated by a dozen shots from the heavy mail guard's guns, the holes being as large as the end of a lead pencil."[45]

There were even a few around Deadwood who voiced a suspicion that it was not "Curly" Grimes who was killed, but an innocent freighter named Joe Bowers.

Amid much argument, an inquest into the death was finally held on February 11, and a coroner's jury found that the killing was unjustified. Murder charges were brought against Llewellyn and May, and at a hearing a judge set bail for each of the two at $10,000. There was no lack of sureties; men who represented over half a million dollars in assets signed the bonds.[46]

The ruling of the coroner's jury infuriated Editor Glafcke of the *Cheyenne Daily Leader*, who wrote that the folks in the neighboring territory were "a little too fast in the matter of condemning Boone May and Detective Llewellyn for the killing of Curley, the reputed road agent. The people want to see every bandit in the country fixed, but as soon as one is planted in any particular locality the people . . . generally succeed in creating sympathy for the dead robber."[47]

A comment by an Omaha newspaper editor less involved in the ongoing outlaw-lawman battle taking place in Wyoming and Dakota was perhaps more dispassionate:

> Boone May, the intrepid messenger of the Black Hills Stage line, passed through the city yesterday, en route for St. Joe. May and Llewellyn will stand the racket raised by the coroner's jury on Deadwood, which found that the killing of "Curley," the outlaw, who attempted to escape from their custody, was unjustifiable. Parties [who are] best informed hardly regard the charge as worth considering for a moment, but the fact that it

comes in a legal form entitles it to at least the attention of being disproved. May states that he will return on Thursday and meet Llewellyn, and the two will proceed to Deadwood and deliver themselves up. There is little doubt in the public mind but that they shot a desperate character, and will be readily justified in the examination. May himself declares that he was personally acquainted with "Curley" and knows that Joe Bowers, the inoffensive freighter, was not the man they killed.[48]

The trial of Llewellyn and May took place in Deadwood on August 23, 1880. Commented the *Black Hills Daily Times*: "This is a remarkable case. Two men who acknowledge that they shot this man Curley [have asked] to be indicted that they may have a chance to vindicate themselves for ridding the world of a monster. This is something that does not often occur. They do not deny the killing and never did, but from the first courted an investigation [and] plead justification."[49]

The jury delivered a "not guilty" verdict without ever leaving the jury box, and a resounding cheer went up from those in the packed courtroom.[50]

— 6 —

THE TOM PRICE GANG

Lynch law as a rule is not to be upheld, but there appears to be no other way to rid the country of the thieving outlaws and murderers that infest it. . . . All law-abiding citizens trust that the good work will go on until the country is well rid of these outlaws, who have become the terror of those subjected to their operations, and who have set the law at defiance and almost invariably escaped its officers.
— Edward A. Slack of the *Cheyenne Daily Sun,*
September 24, 25, 1878

In addition to assaults on the Deadwood stagecoaches by desperadoes and hardcore criminals — members of robber bands led by Joel Collins, Dunc Blackburn, "Lame Johnny," "Persimmon Bill" Chambers, and "Big Nose George" Parrott — ambitious young misfits and amateur outlaws followed the example set by these professionals and entered the highway holdup business during the years 1877 and 1878.

In late July 1877 a trio of aspiring young brigands from Deadwood, Prescott Webb, C. P. ("Perry") Wisdom, and G. W. Conner, schemed to hold up a southbound stage at Robbers' Roost. Unfortunately for the would-be bandits, one of them was loose-mouthed in a Deadwood saloon, and soon rumors of their plans reached the ears of the intrepid messenger Boone May. Enlisting the aid of Mike Goldman and Jim Lebby, two sporting men said to be plucky and proficient with guns, May laid plans of his own, a trap for the road agents. He and the gamblers, heavily armed, were to ride in the coach with two other male passengers and surprise the highwaymen when they stopped the stage. It did not concern May that two other male adults were making the trip, but a problem developed when, just before the stage left Deadwood, a woman and a small child boarded the coach. Anticipating a possible gunfight with the bandits, May objected vehemently to risking the lives of the woman and child by permitting them to go along, but the woman insisted and the journey began. With these innocents in the possible line of fire, Goldman and Lebby lost much of their enthusiasm for a gun battle with bandits.

As the stagecoach approached Robbers' Roost that night, one of the passengers, a man named Schofield, noted, "the moon was shining so brightly that ordinary print could be read."[1] As expected, the robbers appeared and ordered the driver to pull up. Boone May tried to jump down from the coach and fight it out, but was restrained by the others. In disgust, he threw his expensive 45-caliber Sharp's rifle from the window and, fuming, submitted to a search by the robbers.[2] They found little of value except the weapons of May, Goldman, and Lebby. Later, when the coach arrived in Cheyenne, Schofield told a newspaper reporter that in anticipation of a robbery the passengers had resolved to bring no valuables with them. He himself was relieved of $15 and his tobacco. Said Schofield:

> One man did the robbing while the other two stood vigilant guard, looking more like walking arsenals than human beings. After being searched, one of the passengers asked for a chew of tobacco. The captain of the band said, "Certainly, boys, you all can have a chew if you like," and a plug was handed to one of the end men in the row. He took a chew and passed it along the line, each one partaking thereof. A flask of whisky belonging to one of the passengers was found and drank by the thirsty robbers. . . . The scene assumed more of a ludicrous than tragical appearance.[3]

Perhaps more "tragical" was an open debate among the robbers as to whether to kill Boone May, the avowed enemy of all road agents, but they finally decided against the execution of the noted messenger. It was a decision they would come to regret.

The three highwaymen returned to Deadwood in high spirits, gloating over their humiliation of Boone May. But their revelry was short-lived.

Only a month later May and Goldman were walking down the main street in Deadwood when they spotted Prescott Webb, one of the robbers. Webb saw and recognized them at the same time. He pulled two revolvers and began shooting, hitting May in the left arm. Undaunted, May returned the fire, emptying his six-shooter and a backup derringer at Webb, who, dodging and weaving, avoided the shots and reached a horse tied in front of the post office. Leaping into the saddle, he wheeled the animal and spurred for the hills. The roar of gunfire had brought Sheriff Seth Bullock and Deputies John Cochran and A. M. Willard to the scene, and they opened up on the fleeing Webb. Struck by the barrage, Webb's horse went down. Boone May, badly wounded but still in the fight, grabbed a rifle from a bystander and pumped a round into Webb's right shoulder. The officers quickly collared the embattled suspect.[4]

Taken to the offices of Dr. L. F. Babcock for treatment of his wound, Webb warned the physician to take care in his handling. "I come from a good family," he said, "even if I do look rough."[5] Described as 120 pounds in weight, about twenty-two years old, "smooth-faced, very youthful in appearance and regarded handsome," he was said to be "a full-blooded southerner, which is betrayed by his accent." Still defiant, he said if they would "turn him loose with a good six-shooter" he would "whip the crowd."[6]

Later that day Sheriff Bullock and his deputies arrested Wisdom and Conner, Webb's companions. They resisted but were quickly overpowered. The three men turned out to be, like the original members of Joel Collins's Texas gang, drovers who had come up the cattle trail and earned their living whacking bulls for freight outfits and hunting wild game to supply Deadwood's restaurants before trying their hands at stagecoach robbery.[7]

The arrests triggered a spate of telegrams between Dakota and Wyoming territories. On August 28 Bullock fired off a telegram to Sheriff Jeff Carr at Cheyenne: "Three supposed coach robbers are in jail here. Get a requisition and come and get them. Have telegraphed Voorhees their names." The same day stage company agent W. F. Bartlett wired Luke Voorhees: "Deputy Sheriff Boon [*sic*] May says that he can convict the three robbers in jail here. Sheriff Seth Bullock wants Sheriff Carr to come and get them. Their names are W. P. Webb, Perry Wisdom and George Conners [*sic*]. Have it attended to immediately."[8] The next day J. W. Murray, a special deputy appointed by Sheriff Carr, advised his boss by wire that Bullock had agreed to turn over the prisoners to Murray's custody as soon as Dakota governor John L. Pennington received a telegram from Wyoming governor John Thayer advising him that a requisition was on the way. The territorial executives complied, and on August 30 Deputy Sheriff Murray telegraphed Carr: "W. M. Ward, Jesse Brown and myself leave for Cheyenne with Webb, Wisdom and Conner, the road agents, on Saturday morning next [September 1] at 3 o'clock. We will be met at the Stockade by a strong escort and conducted through the dangerous localities. Deputy Sheriff Boon [sic] May, who was shot by Webb, is still suffering severely from his wounds and will not be able to travel for several days."[9]

The bullet that struck May, according to Special Deputy Ward in an interview several days later, entered the left arm "just below the elbow, and touching the bone slightly, the result of which was to split the ball in halves, one piece of the lead passing clear through and out of the arm and the other piece remaining until removed by a surgeon."[10]

On their arrival in Cheyenne with their prisoners Special Deputies Murray and Ward and Jesse Brown, a deputy of Sheriff Bullock who had assisted in the transport, were met by a crowd of some 150 men and boys who followed them to the jail. At a preliminary hearing in Cheyenne the prisoners were bound over for trial in the district court and committed to jail in default of $1,000 bond each.[11]

The *Sun* reporter who interviewed Ward described Prescott Webb as the youngest of the three at about twenty-five years of age, sallow of complexion, five feet eight inches in height, and weighing perhaps 155 pounds.[12] The slug that Boone May had implanted in his shoulder still remained there, giving him some pain. George W. Conner and Perry Wisdom were older, about thirty-two, and larger, both standing about five feet ten inches in height and weighing 160 to 175 pounds. Conner had short sandy hair and whiskers and was a little cross-eyed. Wisdom was dark haired with a sandy mustache and no beard. None of the three, the reporter said, were "desperate looking men, but would pass in a crowd without exciting comment."[13]

Locked up in the county jail, the three neophyte highwaymen had a chance to discuss the finer points of banditry with more experienced knights of the road, Dunc Blackburn and Jim Wall, who were also awaiting trial. Interestingly, when Blackburn attacked Sheriff Carr and made his last desperate bid for freedom, none of the three joined him in the escape attempt.

A defense team of Cheyenne lawyers led by J. W. Kingman got the court's approval to try the three defendants separately. The first case called, that of Perry Wisdom, began on December 18, 1877, before Judge J. W. Fisher. Judge C. F. Miller, conducting the prosecution, called as his first and primary witness Boone May, who had recovered from his gunshot wound. May described the robbery and said he was "quite confident" Wisdom, Webb, and Conner had committed the crime. He also told of the gunfight and arrest of Webb in Deadwood and estimated that fifty shots had been fired in that exchange. Under a strong and lengthy cross-examination he did not change his testimony. Mike Goldman followed May to the stand and corroborated his story in every detail. Judge Miller then rested the case for the prosecution. The defense introduced two witnesses who placed Wisdom far from the scene at the time of the robbery. The defendant was called and denied having any part in the robbery or knowledge of it. He was followed to the stand by the other defendants, Webb and Conner, who testified to the same effect.[14] Closing statements by the defense and prosecution attorneys and Judge Fisher's charge to the jury came the next day. The *Cheyenne Daily Sun* commented that "Judge Fisher's charge amply demonstrates the fact that, while the people in general may entertain, perhaps unconsciously to themselves, a sentiment bordering on prejudice against all those charged with road agency, the same feeling and sentiment does not find its way to the bench of the First Judicial District of Wyoming Territory."[15] The jury failed to agree on a verdict, eight voting for acquittal and four holding out for conviction.[16]

Judge Miller then dismissed the territorial indictments against the three defendants, and they were released on $700 bonds to appear at the next term of U.S. court to answer to federal charges.[17] When court convened in March 1878 attorneys for the federal government, admitting an inability to produce prosecution witnesses, requested dismissal of all charges. The resolution of these cases, as Editor Slack of the *Daily Sun* noted, was highly unusual:

Wisdom, Webb and Conner [were] discharged from further custody and thus after having been in the clutches of the law since the 27th day of August last, when they were arrested in Deadwood; with nine indictments hanging over the three at one time; having stood trial after trial in the Territorial and United States courts, on the charge of robbing the Deadwood coaches, these three men find themselves at last out of the woods and at liberty, they being the only parties ever tried in the district court here on the charge of "road agency," who have not gone "over the hill" to the penitentiary for a term of years.[18]

"In time," according to one Deadwood historian, "all three crooks turned over a new leaf and became exemplary citizens — Webb was a county official, G. W. Conners [sic] a trusted employee of Gilmer and Salisbury and C. P. Wisdom worked for a freighting outfit."[19]

On November 1, 1877, a couple months after the arrest of Webb and company and before the passage of the Posse Comitatus Act, U.S. cavalrymen from Fort Laramie under the command of Second Lieutenant George F. Chase captured a pair of suspected stagecoach robbers, described in a news dispatch as "two small, vicious looking creatures,"[20] and a week later turned them over to civilian authorities at Cheyenne.

One of the suspects, twenty-one-year-old George F. Duncan, alias Duncan Ryan, alias Fonce "Lorenzo" Raines, or Reins, was recognized immediately by several Cheyenne residents, for he had grown up in that town. Sheriff Jeff Carr recalled spanking the boy for petty thievery and setting fires.[21] From the age of seventeen he had been in trouble with the law. On February 10, 1874, a court had sentenced him to a year in prison for horse stealing. Shortly after his release in 1875 for that offense, he was arrested again on a charge of burglary. Convicted, he went back behind bars for another year and six months. Released June 12, 1877, he soon turned to the currently popular felony of stage robbery.[22]

Charged as Duncan's accessory in road agency was John F. Babcock. At thirty-four, Babcock was thirteen years older than his companion. A native of New York State and a Union veteran, he went west after the Civil War and worked on railroad bridges as a carpenter and joiner. In the summer of 1877 he had been employed by Wyoming pioneer and diarist John Hunton.[23] It was his claim that he was

George F. Duncan, alias Fonce Raines, juvenile delinquent turned road agent, still displays an air of arrogance in this prison photo. Courtesy Elnora L. Frye, *Atlas of Wyoming Outlaws at the Territorial Penitentiary.*

forced into outlawry by young Duncan. He said that he had been walking along the road north of Fort Laramie when he was overtaken by Duncan, who was riding a horse and leading another. Duncan pulled a pistol and robbed him of his own revolver and $20.25 in cash. Unloading Babcock's weapon, Duncan returned it to him, saying, "You can't harm me now. I've use for you; we'll go and rob the stage coach."[24] Or so went Babcock's story.

On the night of October 3, 1877, Duncan and Babcock stopped the stage near Eagle's Nest, only about twelve miles south of Fort Laramie. Up on the boot were the driver, O. R. Manchester, and an extra, H. E. ("Gene") Barnett. Five passengers were in the coach when it left

John F. Babcock protested that George Duncan forced him into out-lawry, but he still went to prison. Courtesy Elnora L. Frye, *Atlas of Wyoming Outlaws at the Territorial Penitentiary.*

Deadwood: Mrs. Ella King, A. C. Schryver, S. M. Wheaton, William Smith, and W. J. Scott. At Fort Laramie another unidentified man joined them. They had been sleeping soundly when they were roused rudely by the shouted command, "Stop that coach!" As Scott related the story:

> Two men rushed up from a little ravine, one with a gun in his hand and the other with a revolver in each hand, all the weapons being leveled at us. One of the robbers, who was the spokesman and superintended the affair, was a medium sized man and, I should judge, about 25 or 30 years old. His face was blackened, and he possessed a peculiar indescribable voice — one which I would be able to recognize were I to hear it again. The other

man had a silk handkerchief tied over the lower portion of his face, leaving him the full use of his eyes and ears.

The robbers ordered the passengers out of the coach, and the men were lined up and searched. Scott continued: "From S. M. Wheaton they took $40; Wm. Smith, $1, Schriver, $50 and a revolver, and from myself $3 and a revolver. Smith saved a $10 bill by sticking it down the back of his neck. The other passenger, whose name I have forgotten, lost about $140."

After going through the valises of the passengers the robber who appeared to be "chief" approached Mrs. King and asked her if she had any money. "She was," said Scott, "somewhat embarrassed, to say the least, and hesitatingly responded that she had a little. 'Let us have it,' said he. She made no response by word or gesture, and he told her he guessed it would be necessary to search her. Mrs. King, during the progress of the robbery of the other passengers, had managed to secrete $140 in her hair. In the search it dropped out and became the prey of the villain. He previously took her gold finger ring, but returned it as soon as he found the money."

The road agents then tackled the treasure box and used a carbine to smash it open. When one told his companion to be careful not to damage the carbine, the reply was, "Damn the carbine. I want the sugar." But no "sugar" was found in the box, only papers and letters.

Scott said the "chief," with great bravado, told him to relay a message to Luke Voorhees. They hoped hereafter he would send out the cavalry to guard the stage, as they could handle a number of soldiers and would be able to capture some horses, something they needed badly.[25]

When news of the robbery reached Cheyenne, Editor Glafcke of the *Leader* railed: "Is there no God in Israel? Is there no law in Wyoming?" The people of the territory were not being protected by men in power from this "dark incubus," he declared, and called again for the liberal use of hemp:

> Every one of the villains now operating on the Stage lines is known to the civil and military authorities. Every one of them should have stretched hemp long ago, but no aid is extended the Stage company in its efforts to ferret out and punish them, and

it appears the people are paying for protection from the lawless-ness and are not being protected. If robbers and Indians are to run this country, why not disband our troops and abolish our civil offices. These are harsh words, but we have heard the same old stories of bold and successful robberies day after day for months and the villains still ride the Plains and rob whomever they meet.[26]

Following the stage robbery of October 3 Duncan and Babcock went on a crime spree, stopping and robbing freighters on the road. On October 31 at a point only three miles from Fort Laramie they held up another down coach from Deadwood, robbing all seven passengers, including the U.S. marshal for Wyoming, William S. Sweezy. The next morning they robbed a four-wagon freight outfit, taking all the blankets. Discovering a Chinese with the group, they stripped him of all his possessions and, driven by sheer racial hatred, beat him soundly with the teamster's whip.[27]

Perhaps responding to Glafcke's tirade and embarrassment that the robberies were being committed within the shadow of Fort Laramie, the officers in charge of that post dispatched a detail of cavalrymen under Lieutenant George F. Chase to hunt down the brigands and bring them to justice. Assisting Chase was William Reed, an experienced scout and thief-catcher. Not far from the fort they met another party of freighters who had just been victimized by the brigands. They provided Chase and Reed descriptions of the men and the direction they had headed. Later that day, after a hard ride of eighty-six miles, the military unit caught up with Duncan and Babcock near Rawhide Buttes and fired several shots over their heads before the bandits surrendered.[28]

On November 8 Lieutenant Chase and a unit of troopers rode into Cheyenne with an ambulance containing their prisoners. A crowd assembled, and Duncan, "with chains on his feet and a broad-brimmed hat on, presenting something of a dare-devil appearance," savored every minute of the interest he engendered and played to the hilt the part of "young Dick Turpin of the border land."[29] Among his other exploits he bragged falsely that he had put a bullet into Scott Davis during the September 26 stage robbery attempt.[30] Babcock, on the other hand, claimed innocence, insisting he had been forced into outlawry by his companion, whose true name, he said, was Fonce Reins.

ASSAULT ON THE DEADWOOD STAGE

At their trial in mid-November for the robbery of the freighters Babcock's attorney, a man named Langworthy, attempted to prove his client had been bullied into criminal acts by calling Duncan to the stand. Although cautioned by his own counsel and the court that he need not testify to anything that might incriminate himself, the young firebrand, once on the stand, could not resist the opportunity to brag of his exploits. Said Editor Slack of the *Daily Sun*:

> His natural disposition to tell big yarns and to convey the impression that he is a desperado of high degree led him to recount a long list of daring robberies, hair-breadth escapes, and Turpinian adventures, to the great damage of himself as far as his chances are concerned in the trials yet to take place. After all his admissions made yesterday, the whole legal fraternity of the country could not save him from his impending doom. A greater part, however, of his statements and admissions are probably nothing but mere bosh.[31]

On November 23, 1877, a jury convicted Duncan and Babcock of grand larceny and highway robbery for the October 3 affair.[32] When asked by the court if they had anything to say before sentence was pronounced, Babcock silently shook his head. Duncan, on the other hand, ranted at length how he had been forced into criminal acts because everybody was prejudiced against him. He seemed resigned to his fate, however, and when Judge Fisher interrupted his tirade to remark that he was probably beyond all hope of redemption, Duncan mechanically nodded assent. Judge Fisher sentenced Duncan to fourteen years for robbery, two years for grand larceny, and one year and a fine of $99 for "federal highway robbery." (The federal charge was later dismissed.)[33]

The unfortunate John F. Babcock, who may have been dragged against his will into the road agent business by the wicked Duncan, received a sentence of ten years in prison and a fine of $99 for grand larceny and federal highway robbery.

When Duncan entered the territorial prison at Laramie a physical examination revealed he had "marks of buckshot on both hips," remembrances, evidently, of earlier escapades. He acquired another scar on June 18, 1878, when in an unsuccessful escape attempt from the prison he was shot in the thigh by a guard.[34]

Prison photo of road agent gang leader Tom Price. Courtesy Elnora L. Frye, *Atlas of Wyoming Outlaws at the Territorial Penitentiary.*

Another bunch of amateur road agents from Deadwood led by a disgruntled miner named Tom Price became active on the Deadwood routes in 1878.

A native of Virginia, thirty-year-old Price came to the Black Hills in 1876 and eked out a precarious living as a gambler, teamster, speculator, and miner until, tempted by dreams of riches to be obtained by robbery of the Deadwood stages, he recruited a bunch of other similarly disenchanted types and took to road agency.[35]

Joining him were a number of young men in their twenties: John H. Brown, a freighter; Charles Ross, alias James Patrick, a farmer from Illinois; Albert Spears, a bridge builder from Indiana; Thomas Jefferson ("Duck") Goodale, son of a wealthy Iowa hotel owner; William ("Billy") Mansfield, a carpenter; and Archie McLaughlin, who sometimes used the alias "Cummings."[36] Others who dropped into and out of the Price gang included Charles Henry Borris, an immigrant farmer from Prussia, at thirty-five years of age one of the gang's elders; George Howard, whose alias was "Tony Pastor," a name borrowed from a nationally popular entertainer of the day; Andy Gouch, called "Red Cloud" because he had spent some time at that Indian agency; Charles Carey, a taxidermist; Dave Black; Lew Hagers; Frank McBride; and, according to one Black Hills historian, "Big Nose George" Parrott for at least one job.[37]

On July 2, 1878, the Tom Price gang stopped the Deadwood coach at Whoop Up Canyon, on the Cheyenne road, some sixty-five miles south of Deadwood. On the boot handling the ribbons of his six-horse team was John Flaherty, and passengers E. S. Smith and J. S. Smith of New York, A. Liberman and H. Liberman of Chicago, Mrs. M. V. Boughton of Cheyenne, and Daniel Finn, formerly a Union Pacific freight conductor, occupied the coach. As the bandits came to learn, Dan Finn would prove to be a remarkably uncooperative robbery victim.

Two outlaws stepped out in front of the coach and with leveled weapons ordered Flaherty to rein in, while six other gang members crouched in the roadside shrubbery. Following the standard road agent procedure, the outlaws ordered the passengers from the coach, lined them up, and began a search for valuables. Mrs. Boughton was not molested, but from the Smiths and Libermans they obtained an undisclosed amount of money and two gold watches. When they advanced on Daniel Finn, however, they met a surprise. With a sudden movement that gentleman jerked a revolver from his pocket and put a bullet into one of the highwaymen. The robber fell to the ground, and Finn cocked his pistol to shoot again. But before he could pull the trigger a bullet from another road agent slammed into his face. It struck him just left of his nose, passed through his mouth, destroying two teeth, and came out in front of his right ear. It was an extremely painful but not life-threatening wound.

Disconcerted by this unexpected resistance, the robbers then retreated with their stricken comrade, firing as they fled. E. S. Smith was hit in the leg below the knee and A. Liberman in the thigh. After everyone scrambled back into the carriage Flaherty drove on to the next station, where the passengers' wounds were treated, and then the coach continued on to Cheyenne.[38]

The story of the holdup and shooting went out from Cheyenne on the Associated Press wires and was reprinted in newspapers across the land, although some readers had to wait as long as a week to read about the dramatic event.[39] The editor of a Worcester, Massachusetts, paper found amusement in the goings-on in the wilds of far-off Wyoming. "The stage was robbed," he wrote,

> with remarkable system and punctuality by an association of gentlemen who are among the ornaments of society in that agreeable town where the route ends. . . . As the stage approached a place known as "Whoop-Up" two "road agents" appeared, signaled the driver to stop, and politely asked the passengers to alight. Having arranged the eight passengers in a line, the robbers proceeded to levy the usual tribute, but when Mr. Finn's turn came, instead of giving them his watch and pocketbook, as they expected, he gave them the contents of his pistol, which doubtless seemed to him at that moment the most valuable thing he had about him. This irregularity deranged the whole proceedings. The robbers, greatly offended by so gross a departure from the customs of the road, went away at once, firing two or three shots as tokens of their displeasure, one of which grazed Mr. Finn's head, inflicting a slight wound, and others unfortunately hit in the legs two other passengers, who had not deserved such treatment, since they had punctiliously observed the proprieties of the occasion by surrendering on demand what property they had with them. Mr. Finn's conduct seems commendable at this distance, but in the Deadwood region, where the etiquette of such affairs is better understood, and is rigidly enforced by public opinion, it is not universally approved. The road agents' association have adopted strong resolutions of censure, taking the ground that his behavior is not only adapted to break up a profitable business, but it also tends to disturb the pleasant relations that have hitherto been maintained between themselves and their traveling friends, whom they have robbed up to this time with the utmost consideration and personal courtesy. They fear that they will be obliged hereafter to adopt methods much harsher than those that have proved so satisfactory until now.[40]

The robber shot by Finn was John H. Brown, the young freighter turned road agent.[41] He would later confess to his part in the robbery. "Gentlemen," said he,

I never robbed but one coach so help me God, and never killed anybody. Charlie Ross . . . and me stopped the coach on the second of last July, four miles from Whoop Up. Charlie hollered to the driver to halt; he was on one side of the road and I on the other; the coach stopped. I told the man on the box to get down; he did. And I told him to go round to the other side, where Ross was standing them up in line. Then Ross went through them while I stood guard. The first thing I knew the man Finn shot me. I thought I was badly hurt. I shot at him twice, and Ross shot six times, at least he told me he emptied his pistol. We got $32 and two watches. Ross kept them both. I had one but gave it back. I got $18. . . . Our horses were about fifty yards from the coach. After the robbery we rode to Deadwood.[42]

Brown was badly wounded, and the horseback ride to Deadwood must have been a terrible ordeal. Ross took him to a small cabin on the edge of town where other gang members were hiding out. Brown received no professional medical attention, as the gang feared exposure if a doctor was called. When he did not recover after a number of days, but seemed to be sinking, a remarkable woman was called on for help.

Although not as well remembered as "Calamity Jane," a flamboyant frontier female going under the mellifluous name Lurline Monte Verde played a significant role in the history of Black Hills banditry. For romance and adventure this woman's life story rivals that of any of her colorful male contemporaries. From a prominent and well-to-do family of Missouri, her name was Belle Siddons at birth, but she would adopt others during her temerarious career. Arrested as a Confederate spy by Union officers during the Civil War, she was released after several months' confinement on a promise to stay out of Missouri until the cessation of hostilities. In Texas she married an army surgeon, who schooled his bride in the rudiments of medicine and the intricacies of gambling. When her husband died she took to the gambling tables as a profession and, under the name "Madame Vestal," became a prominent figure in the western sporting world. She arrived in Deadwood in spectacular fashion in 1876, riding in an omnibus drawn by four matched horses and outfitted as a rolling boudoir with carpeted floor, four-poster bed, and curtains on the windows. A correspondent for a

New York paper said she "stood upon a board and was borne through the town on the shoulders of four strapping miners."[43]

Taking a new name in the new town, she became Lurline Monte Verde and opened a combination restaurant, saloon, and gambling house. Men of Deadwood flocked in to risk their money at the gambling table presided over by the brunette beauty. She had a "husband," or "solid man," as male consorts of sporting women were called in those days, with whom she lived, but, according to legend, a dashing young fellow named Archie McLaughlin, the apprentice road agent, caught her eye and her interest.[44]

McLaughlin, during the hours spent with the alluring Lurline, had learned of her earlier marriage to a medical doctor and the knowledge of healing she had obtained from him, and so when his pal John Brown lay near death from Daniel Finn's bullet in the Deadwood cabin, he called on her for help. She went to the outlaws' cabin, ministered to Brown, and probably saved his life.

Months later, following the demise of the Price gang, she told her story to a reporter for the *Cheyenne Daily Sun*. She had not told anyone about her involvement with the outlaws before, she said, having taken an oath to keep silent, but with the death of several of the gang members and the arrest and confession of others, she now felt free to talk. Although denying she was in any way connected with "their business," she admitted familiarity with the gang members. Her Deadwood establishment became a place of resort for them, and in the course of their conversations she necessarily learned a great deal about their doings, including what she called "that Finn shooting affair."

About the middle of July she was approached by "a particular friend" she identified as Billy Mansfield, but was in all probability Archie McLaughlin, who said her help was urgently needed to care for a very sick friend. "After some argument on my part," she said,

I accompanied him down the main street of Deadwood to a small house near the bridge, where I met McLaughlin and another member of the gang, and in the presence of these men I was made to take a solemn oath of secrecy. I was afraid to refuse for a person's life was not worth much in that region.

I was conducted from the deserted shanty near the bridge to another not far distant, where the pretended sick man lay.

There, in a dark corner, upon a pallet or bunk made of pine poles, lay a man whom I at once recognized as Johnny H. Brown. . . . The men told me he was not wounded, just sick, but I declined to believe it, and insisted upon knowing the "truth" before I would prescribe. Brown was in a high fever and delirious. Blood and pus were thrown from his mouth during each convulsion. He was raving and would not permit anyone to approach him, saying that the gang wished to poison him or kill him to prevent him "giving them away." Finding that "taffy" and nonsense would not do, the men told me the truth — that Johnny Brown had been engaged in the robbery of the coach on the 3rd [*sic* 2nd] of July, and had got shot. He had lain there ten days without medical attention, fearing that a regular physician would expose the gang if he were introduced.

I obtained control over the suspicious sufferer by means of chloroform, which I administered from the wounded man's head, while I held his pulse in my right hand. When I knew the excitement was reduced sufficiently, I told him what I wanted to do to save his life. He had a bullet in his side which I wanted to cut out. I asked him if he could stand the pain, or whether I should give him chloroform. He said, "No, I can trust you as you are not interested in my death." I turned him over and found where the bullet had lodged between two of his ribs after passing through his side and liver. I cut out the bullet and inserted a wire loop I had prepared, and in less time that it has taken to tell you, I flipped the bullet out. Johnny, the brave boy, made but one groan during the entire operation. I was then permitted to go home, with the promise to return the following night.[45]

She said she saw Brown every night until he was out of danger. The gang members, she said, made a practice of hiding out in the woods during the day and coming in to the Deadwood cabin at night. Once she was startled to discover Charley Ross and Charley Borris hiding under Brown's bed. Suspicious of her intentions, they were listening for any indication of treachery on her part. Had they found any, she was sure they would have killed her.[46]

Charley Ross, who was an inmate of the Cheyenne jail when Monte Verde's account appeared in the *Sun*, demanded an interview with a reporter for the paper to refute the story. He denied knowing the

Charles Ross went to prison claiming he was "not half as bad" as charged. Courtesy Elnora L. Frye, *Atlas of Wyoming Outlaws at the Territorial Penitentiary*.

woman at all and certainly was not hiding under the bed, as she charged, while she was attending to Brown. Ross, twenty-two years old, said he had left his home in Illinois three years earlier and gone to Denver, and then to Deadwood in November 1876. He said Monte Verde's story was cooked up by friends of "that infernal scoundrel Burris [*sic*] . . . , to ruin me, to get me out of the way and save themselves. . . . I am not half as bad as they would make me out to be."[47]

But back in July 1878 both Ross and "that infernal scoundrel Burris" were still part of the Price gang that returned to the outlaw trail and embarked on another stagecoach foray.

About two o'clock in the morning of July 25, 1878, the southbound stagecoach from Deadwood was stopped near Lance Creek some twenty-eight miles from Hat Creek by six masked men armed with Winchester rifles. Only one passenger was on board, the Reverend

J. W. Picket of Colorado Springs, Colorado, and he was seated on the box beside the driver. The clergyman later told of his experience to a reporter for the *Greeley Tribune*. He said for hours the driver had regaled him with stories of previous holdups, but after passing Robbers' Roost, the two thought they were through the danger zone. And then suddenly the road agents appeared out of the darkness.

The minister said he called out in his clear, Sunday sermon voice: "Men, you make a lean job this time, only two of us, one the driver and the other a preacher." The robbers ordered them down off the box and asked how much money they had. Both answered they had only a few dollars, and they were bothered no more. The driver informed the bandits that the treasure boxes were empty and showed them the waybills as proof, but, disbelieving, the road agents hacked open one box with a hatchet and hefted and shook the other to confirm this advice. In a desperate effort to find something of value, they turned at last to the mailbags. Cutting the straps of the pouches, they emptied the contents on the ground and opened the registered letters in search of money. Finally, disgruntled by their failure, they permitted driver and preacher to proceed on their way.[48]

Unwittingly, with this robbery the neophyte highwaymen opened the door for federal involvement in the stagecoach robbery problem on the Deadwood stagecoach route, a door that only a month earlier seemingly had been closed.

On June 16, 1878, the U.S. Congress passed the Posse Comitatus Act, which prohibited uniformed forces of the U.S. government from assisting state, territorial, county, or municipal law enforcement officers in the pursuit or apprehension of law violators. The act was passed as part of an effort to mollify the grievances of white citizens of the former Confederacy who were outraged by what they believed to be oppressive military occupation of their states during the Reconstruction period following the Civil War. But it worked an extreme hardship on western lawmen, hard-pressed to run down felons in the vast expanses of their jurisdictions without the help of the military stationed in the many forts scattered throughout the region.[49] For the operators of the Cheyenne and Black Hills Stage Company and law officers of Wyoming and Dakota it was a severe blow, for it meant they could no longer call upon U.S. Army units to aid in the search for road agents.

But the ransacking of the U.S. mail the night of July 25, 1878, prompted Editor Slack of the *Cheyenne Daily Sun* to repeat the cry for a federal government crackdown on road agency that his counterpart, Herman Glafcke of the *Leader*, had raised a year earlier. In an editorial headed "The Death Knell of Road Agents," he opined: "Last season the depredations of the road agents along the route between Fort Laramie and Deadwood were mainly confined to the robbing of passengers and plundering of the treasure-box. They in no instance attempted to interfere with the mails. Whether this fact was due to fear of 'Uncle Sam' . . . we know not." But the looting of the mails at Lightning Creek changed all that, he said, and he reminded his readers that "the United States government is possessed of abundant means and considerable vitality, and when once aroused will leave no stone unturned to crush out all obstacles which lie in the path of its legitimate authority." Even the Indians knew that and, fearing federal government retaliation, never interfered with the U.S. mail, he said.

> But these thieving road agents appear to be far less discreet than the Indian. They have now made war direct on the government, and there can be but one result from this in our judgment. The United States authorities will now take hold of the matter of suppressing lawlessness and road agency, and if it takes one half of the troops now in the Department of the Platte to do it, we predict that the route between this city and Deadwood, as well as all others that are molested, will be protected by the strong arm of United States authority. Not only this, but scouts, spies, detectives and cavalry will be put on the track of the marauders and they will be hunted down, cost what it may, and when they are found the chances will be good for such summary punishment as will put a quietus on their operations.[50]

The ransacking of the U.S. mail by the robbers did indeed get the attention of the federal authorities. Soon arriving on the scene at Deadwood to investigate was Inspector John B. Furay of the Post Office Department. A resident of Omaha, Nebraska, Furay at the age of thirty-three was a Far West veteran. Enlisting as a private in the Eleventh Ohio Volunteer Cavalry at the outbreak of the Civil War, he had risen to the rank of first lieutenant and served with the unit on the Oregon Trail. Just before coming to the Black Hills he had traveled throughout the West inspecting the work of postmasters. Traveling by conveyances ranging from railroad to mule back, he had covered forty thousand miles in less than a year.[51] Furay would play an important part in bringing about the ultimate defeat of the robbers of the Deadwood stage.

Since the robbery of July 25 had yielded little of value, the Tom Price gang struck again a few nights later, attacking in the same locality the northbound coach, carrying three passengers, one a woman. Again the driver was John Flaherty. Although this was a return trip for the bullion-carrying stage and the treasure box was empty, messenger Eugene S. Smith, riding several hundred yards ahead of the coach, resisted the road agents forcefully. Single-handedly he beat off all six of the outlaws in a gunfight, firing off seventeen rounds from his rifle and four from his pistol while the outlaws unloaded fifty shots at him.[52] The only known casualty on either side was Smith's horse, which was killed in the first volley. Witnesses were "profuse in their commendation of Smith's bravery and coolness."[53]

These two unproductive assaults cooled any ambitions the Tom Price outfit may have had for additional stagecoach robberies, and they began looking for easier targets. Early in September they learned, probably by loose-mouthed saloon talk, that S. M. Booth, a Custer City merchant, was about to drive his wagon and team to Cheyenne and would be carrying a great deal of money. They kept Booth under surveillance, and when he set out in company with a friend and neighbor, D. K. Snively, driving another team, three of them closed in. On the afternoon of September 11 they waylaid the travelers in Red Canyon and stripped Booth of almost every valuable possession he had with him, including $1,200 in cash, his fine team of horses, his provisions, his packed clothing, his watch, and even his shirt studs, cuff links, collar button, and the boots he was wearing. He was left to walk barefoot back to Custer City. Snively was also robbed of his valuables, but the bandits let him keep his wagon and team. He was allowed to continue on southward, but was forced to depend upon "the tender mercies of incoming freighters for provisions to subsist him to Cheyenne."[54]

On the way back to their hideout the jubilant road agents came on two telegraph line repairmen, resetting a pole, and added to their day's haul by stealing the money, supplies, watches, and firearms of the pair, but showed their generosity by allowing the men to keep their horses.[55]

Meanwhile another upstart road agent outfit, led by an amiable, charismatic character named William Wallace Johnson,[56] who, at six feet four inches in height, was widely known as "Lengthy." Johnson had taken advantage of the Tom Price gang's hiatus from stage robbery to take up operations on the Deadwood-Cheyenne trail.

On the night of September 10 Johnson and two accomplices stopped the northbound stage between Lightning Creek and the Cheyenne River and robbed the two passengers, a man and a woman, but garnered very little. From the woman they got $1.25, and the man coughed up $5.00 and an ulster overcoat that had taken the fancy of the bandit captain.[57]

They were plundering the mailbags when the coach from Deadwood arrived. They threw down on that driver and ordered the passengers, three men and a woman, out of the coach. Messenger Eugene Smith, the hero of the earlier robbery attempt by the Price gang, remained inside and prepared to do battle, but one of the bandits grabbed a passenger, and using him as a shield, demanded Smith's surrender. Under the circumstances the messenger had little choice and complied. He was stripped of his shotgun, two pistols, $15 in cash, his overcoat, and a watch and chain valued at $150. The driver contributed $6 to the outlaw haul, and one of the passengers gave up $10. The bandit leader, eyeing the man's boots, asked what size they were, which brought on a ludicrous tableau at the scene of a stagecoach holdup. The man sat down and held "his foot aloft, while the captain placed his against it," but when a difference of several sizes became apparent, the passenger was allowed to keep his footwear. The outlaws pulled several valuable rings from the fingers of the woman, including her wedding ring, the return of which she pleaded in vain. A "ruffian gruffly informed her that a wedding-ring was as good for him as her." The road agents ransacked the mail, broke open the treasure boxes, and removed whatever they contained, before mounting their horses and galloping off. After their departure some of the passengers "congratulated themselves that a more thorough search was not made, as one had ten dollars under the lining of his hat, another a substantial roll concealed in his coat-sleeve, and the lady one hundred and ninety dollars within her stocking, under her foot."[58]

The two cohorts of the road agent gang, wearing masks, were not positively identified, but the leader, unmasked and easily recognizable by his unusual height, was "Lengthy" Johnson.[59] About a week later Johnson was arrested at Fort Robinson, Nebraska, and taken under strong guard to Sidney. There Deputy U.S. Marshal F. O. Horn took him in charge and brought him to Cheyenne. Remarked Editor Glafcke of the *Leader*: "Lengthy loafed about this city several months last spring and summer, and is not a stranger to our police force."[60] Described as "the terror of the Spanish Valley in the Black Hills, a hard citizen, a sleek horse gobbler,"[61] Johnson was close to forty years of age, slim, with about 175 pounds distributed over more than six feet in height, and "inclined to be stoop-shouldered." He had brown hair and a full but short beard. Evidently fairly well educated, he displayed an extensive vocabulary as he denied emphatically that he had any connection with the road agents.[62]

Johnson had a $100 bill in his possession when arrested. He first said it had been given to him by Ed Cook, superintendent of the northern division of the stage company, for "work performed." When officers scoffed at this, he changed his story, saying it was part of the proceeds from the sale of a ranch he had owned. Officers found little credibility in that explanation also, and believed the bill had come out of one of the treasure boxes rifled on September 9.[63]

When Deputy Marshal Horn arrived in Cheyenne with Johnson he also brought with him news that the bodies of two suspected outlaws had been found hanging from pine trees at the foot of Lookout Mountain, a few miles east of Spearfish, Dakota Territory. "The news is almost too good to be true," said Slack of the *Sun.* "Lynch law as a rule is not to be upheld, but there appears to be no other way to rid the country of the thieving outlaws and murderers that infest it."[64] He added in the next day's edition: "All law-abiding citizens trust that the good work will go on until the country is well rid of these outlaws, who have become the terror of those subjected to their operations, and who have set the law at defiance and almost invariably escaped its officers."[65]

Lawyers in Cheyenne soon "habeas corpused" Johnson out of jail on $5,000 bond. Newspaper reporters who interviewed the suspected road agent found him affable, garrulous, well educated, and "quite witty." He said he was originally from Rochester, New York, and had been in the region of the Rocky Mountains for thirteen years. He claimed to be innocent of the charges against him but admitted to being well acquainted with all the desperadoes infesting the surrounding country. It was "a degree of familiarity," remarked the reporter, "which is, to say the least, suspicious." Nevertheless Johnson felt confident that he would be cleared of all charges.[66]

He was in fact released in October for lack of evidence. Many in Cheyenne believed the dismissal of charges in his case resulted from a deal he had cut with the authorities in which he had provided information about outlaws with whom he was familiar in exchange for his freedom. They pointed to the recent elimination by vigilantes of the two suspected outlaws near Spearfish. Their bodies had been identified as belonging to George W. Keating and Orbean ("Beans") Davis, who were believed to be the accomplices of "Lengthy" Johnson in the stage robbery. In any event, either to escape the wrath of his outlaw pals or further harassment by the law, "Lengthy" Johnson disappeared, and his tall frame ceased to cast a long shadow on the Black Hills trail.

On September 26, 1878, the Tom Price gang emerged again to attack a stagecoach on that trail, resulting in the most memorable battle between road agents and shotgun messengers of the entire period.

— 7 —

THE HEAD OF FRANK TOWLE

The fact that these men dug up a corpse, cut off its head, and brought it several hundred miles to obtain a reward was a bad sample of civiliza-tion, but to leave the head to be gnawed and eaten by vagrant dogs is inhuman and shocking.
— Edward A. Slack of the *Cheyenne Daily Sun*, May 2, 1879

Following the departure of Joel Collins and most of the members of his gang from the Black Hills, Frank Towle became associated with two of the older, well-established outlaw bands of the region, the gangs of "Persimmon Bill" Chambers and "Big Nose George" Parrott.

An acquaintance described William F. Chambers, better known as "Persimmon Bill," as "about 31 or 32 years of age. About five feet eight or ten inches high; rather well built; would weigh perhaps 140 pounds; had short, thick arms and a short bull shaped neck. His hair was dark brown, and was cut short; eyes bright blue; small, well-shaped nose; thin lips, shaded by a small blonde mustache. His chin was covered by a short brown beard. . . . The only features indicating his ferocious disposition [were] his very heavy, protruding eyebrows and his thick, heavy, lower jaws."[1]

This observer said he had an opportunity to witness a demonstra-tion of "Persimmon Bill's" skill with weapons:

Picking out a cottonwood tree as a mark, which stood about forty yards away, he took two navy revolvers in his hands, and holding them at arms' length, fired every cartridge at the tree *without cocking the pistols.* He merely pulled the hammers of the pistols back and let them go, never stopping to pull a trigger. The twelve shots sent out of his two holster pistols seemed like one continuous discharge from a mitrailleuse.[2] He fired from his other two revolvers shot after shot, each after whirling around on his heel and without apparently taking aim; but he seldom, if ever, missed his mark. He was equally skillful with his two rifles, one of which he carried swung upon the left side of his saddle, the other hanging by his right hip.[3]

Chambers arrived in Cheyenne in 1867 before the coming of the railroad. Although believed by some to be a native of Tennessee,[4] he said that he was born in Murphysville, Cherokee County, North Carolina, in 1845. He claimed that during the Civil War he served in both Confederate and Union military units. He first joined the rebel forces, was captured, and switched sides, becoming a "galvanized Yankee" as former Confederates were known. When he killed a Union soldier in a dispute over a woman he fled and rejoined the Confederate forces. Captured again, he spent the rest of the great conflict confined in the Union prisoner of war camp at Johnson Island in Lake Erie. After his release he went west and ended up in Wyoming, where he caroused with a tough crowd, drank rotgut whiskey to excess, and first got crossways with the law. Vigilantes hanged some of his cronies, but he gained his release on a promise to leave town. He went to Sioux City, Iowa, where he continued to raise hell. On a drunken spree in 1870 he shot his own horse and wounded a deputy sheriff who attempted to corral him. He was arrested, but escaped and, with a $1,000 reward on his head, fled the state and returned to Wyoming.[5]

For at least two years he stayed out of trouble, working cattle for early-day Wyoming ranchers. One of those cattleman was Malcolm Campbell, who later served as a deputy of Sheriff Nathaniel K. Boswell at Laramie, and later still, was the first sheriff of Converse County, Wyoming. Campbell remembered "Persimmon Bill" as the best herder he ever had "before he went bad."[6]

As many outlaws before him, Chambers yielded to the temptation of stealing Indian horses, an activity that many Indian-hating whites of the time did not consider a crime, but this soon led to his killing of a U.S. Army sergeant named Sullivan, which set him on the owl-hoot trail with no turning back.

An early employer of "Persimmon Bill" Chambers, Malcolm Campbell was a deputy under Sheriff Nathaniel K. Boswell and later was elected sheriff of Converse County, Wyoming. Courtesy American Heritage Center, University of Wyoming.

The story of that killing was told by Malcolm Campbell, who was at Fort Fetterman when some Arapahoe Indians rode in and complained to the officer in charge that Chambers had driven off some of their ponies. The officer sent Sergeant Sullivan, together with two of the Indians, after the stolen horses with the admonition, according to Campbell, "If you find the thief, bring him back dead or alive." With the help of the Indians, Sullivan located the horses without difficulty, but as they were driving the animals past a ranch on their way back to the fort, "Persimmon Bill" suddenly rode out of a thicket and, addressing the sergeant, roared, "Turn them horses loose or I will kill you." Sullivan "made a move as if to start on toward the Fort. Bill thereupon drew a gun from his hip and shot the soldier off his horse." While the Indians and some cowboys from the ranch "looked on too stunned to move," Bill dismounted and went through the pockets of the dead man. Finding more than $400 dollars in cash, he waved it in the air, shouting, "I've got his money, too." The Indians wheeled their horses and galloped off. "Bill mounted and rode away un-harmed. For several days, the soldiers of the Fort searched for him diligently, but without success."[7]

"Persimmon Bill" told the story differently. Making no mention of stolen horses, he said he passed Sergeant Sullivan on the road, rode on a little ways, and then remembered seeing Sullivan with a wad of money at Owens's ranch a few days earlier. "So I just turned 'round and plugged him in the back. The sergeant fell from the horse he was riding, which galloped on toward the fort." Laughing as he related this cold-blooded murder, he said he took from his victim's body about $300 in cash, a gold watch, and his needle gun and ammunition. "I am death on soldiers and government property," he admitted.[8]

This murder occurred on March 3, 1876, and following its descrip-tion in a telegraphic dispatch from Cheyenne, made news around the country, permanently sealing the fate of "Persimmon Bill" Cham-bers. Ever afterward he would be denounced in the press as "a rene-gade and horse thief, a bad man and a coward [who] shot Sullivan in the back without giving him a chance to defend himself."[9] The fed-eral government offered a reward of $1,000 for his capture "dead or alive."[10] His notoriety reached such heights that when he simply stopped overnight at a remote camp it made news in papers as far away as San Francisco: "Persimmon Bill, the outlaw, made his ap-pearance in a camp five miles south of Hat Creek five days ago. He had supper and breakfast and stayed over night in the camp. The last heard of him was at Rawhide Buttes, very drunk, and with consider-able money."[11]

He was believed guilty of committing another brutal murder later that month. H. E. ("Stuttering") Brown, division superintendent of the Cheyenne and Black Hills Stage Company, concerned about the loss of his fine stage horses from stations on the Deadwood route, was convinced that Chambers and his followers were responsible for the thefts. When a particularly fine team disappeared from Hager's ranch on the Cheyenne River, Brown went to the ranch to investigate and found Bill calmly sitting there, "toasting his feet at the fire." Brown exploded at such effrontery and chased the suspected thief out of the place at gunpoint, threatening to kill him if he did not quit the road. Shortly afterward, on April 19, 1876, unseen assailants shot the stage line official from ambush and killed him. Luke Voorhees and others were convinced "Persimmon Bill" and his gang were the murderers.[12]

Chambers dropped out of sight for a while, but in March 1877, when road agents stopped the first Deadwood coach and killed Johnny Slaughter, his name was often mentioned as a prime suspect. However, some habitués of the Cheyenne and Deadwood saloons, who claimed to have knowledge of the movements of the outlaw gangs, were willing to bet "Persimmon Bill" was not even in the Black Hills at that time.[13] The attempted robbery and murder of Slaughter was the work of the Texas gang led by Joel Collins, of course, and the only connection to "Persimmon Bill" was the participation of Frank Towle, who later left Collins to join up with Chambers's band.

Actually there is no real proof that "Persimmon Bill" ever led a road agent attack on a Deadwood coach, although Luke Voorhees and John Furay were convinced that he did. When the Deadwood stage was robbed on the morning of July 25, 1878, and the mail ransacked, Furay was called in to investigate.

Inspector Furay of the Post Office Department was a strong believer in the use of underworld informants in investigative work and the practice of "using a crook to catch a crook," as he made clear in one of his reports. The few honest inhabitants in that sparsely settled country, he said, "will give no information, knowing full well that their lives will pay the forfeit if it becomes known. The only way to get evidence is to buy up certain members of the 'confidence gang' at Custer, Lead City, Central, and Deadwood, have them go out and join the outlaws, be captured with them and then turn state's evidence."[14]

Based on information obtained from his underworld contacts, Furay reported that he was convinced that the six men who committed the crime were "Persimmon Bill," Frank Towle, Jack Campbell, Tom Reed, Jackson Bishop, and a Third Cavalry deserter, name unknown. He later added that possibly Jack Watkins had also taken part.[15] But Furay was new to the Black Hills, and his informants, aware of his lack of knowledge of road agent history there, may have led him astray. Jackson Bishop was a Colorado murderer and outlaw, as Furay himself acknowledged, and was not active in the Black Hills. Jack Watkins of the Hat Creek gang had disappeared from the country when the gang broke up and had not been seen for months. Frank Towle, Tom Reed, and "Jack Campbell," one of the aliases of Charley Ross, were known road agents, but Furay's report is the only known record tying them to "Persimmon Bill." In his report of the July 25 robbery Furay had to admit that "there is not a particle of legal proof of the [guilt of those named] as they were closely masked, and the passengers and driver could not, as they say, possibly identify them."[16]

So with no worthwhile case against "Persimmon Bill," Furay and other lawmen made no real effort to find him. A search might have been useless, however, as Chambers had already disappeared from the Black Hills region, never to return. He was not, as one historical writer has written, killed by messenger Boone May.[17] His followers drifted off to other gangs.

And those gangs had proliferated, as Furay emphasized in one of his reports to his superior, Chief Special Agent D. B. Parker of the Post Office Department in Washington, D.C. The country for 150 miles, said Furay, "is infested with various gangs of the most desperate outlaws to be found anywhere perhaps on this continent. They have various places where they receive food and information, which places are well known, but the buffalo are in the country in which they are staying and they profess to be 'hunters' and when they rob the stages and mails, they know they can not be identified sufficiently to make a conviction."[18]

Frank Towle, Tom Reed, and Charley Ross, alias Jack ("Sandy") Campbell, now joined another of the outlaw bands infesting the region, this one led by a notorious brigand called "Big Nose George" Parrott.

"Big Nose George," whose real name was George Francis Warden,[19] said he was born on April 13, 1843, at Dayton, Ohio, but this has never been verified.[20] At another time he said was born in Indiana and raised in Ottumwa, Iowa.[21] But then lying was one of this character's minor sins. A newspaper reporter in 1880 described him as "a man about 35 years old, five feet ten inches tall, rather spare built and

"Big Nose George" Parrott, like some others of his ilk, closed out his career dangling from the end of a rope. Courtesy Robert G. McCubbin Collection.

[weighing] about 160 pounds, dark complexion, black hair and beard, sharp rather piercing eyes and a very prominent nose," but added that he was "really not as bad a looking fellow as one would expect," presumably because of the dreadful reputation he had acquired and his unflattering nickname.[22]

Allied with Parrott, Towle, Reed, and Campbell in Black Hills road agency were "Dutch Charley," a man of many aliases, including

Charles Randall, Burris, Baylis, and Bates;[23] Joe Minuse; John Irwin; Cully McDonald; and a man calling himself "Sim Wan." The last named was thought by some to be none other than Frank James, the legendary bank and train robber and brother of the notorious Jesse James.[24] While no specific Deadwood stage holdups can be attributed to this gang, editors Porter Warner and W. P. Newhard of the *Black Hills Daily Times* asserted at the time that Parrott and his followers concentrated on coaches traveling over the Deadwood-to-Sidney route rather than the Cheyenne run.[25] Others speculated that was because Parrott had once freighted between Cheyenne and Deadwood and the chances that he would be recognized were greater there.[26]

The Parrott gang first gained wide attention, however, when on August 14, 1878, they attempted to derail and rob the westbound pay car of a Union Pacific train east of the coal-mining town of Carbon, Wyoming. Section foreman John Brown thwarted the plan when he discovered the loosened rail and stopped the train. When news of the derailment attempt got out, posses scoured the area for the bandits. Two intrepid Carbon County deputy sheriffs, E. R. ("Tip") Vincent from the town of Carbon, and E. R. ("Bob") Widdowfield from Rawlins, tracked the outlaws to a camp in the Elk Mountains, but were ambushed and shot down.

"Big Nose George" later described the killing in detail to a newspaper reporter. When the gang members spotted the two approaching riders, he said,

it was decided to hide our horses in the brush and conceal ourselves and let the men pass should they not be officers, and to kill them should they be such. . . .

They rode up the trail to our camp fire, when the large man [Widdowfield] got off his horse and stuck his hand into the fire, remarking, "It is as hot as hell; they have been here and we will catch them before long." . . . Frank Tolle [*sic*], one of our party, then said, "Let's fire," and loud enough for all to hear. Part of us shooting at the man on the ground and part of us at the man on the horse. I fired at the man on the horse. After our volley the horses and rider run about fifty yards, when the latter fell off his horse, and attempted to get up, holding his gun in his hands. Some twenty shots were fired at him and the firing ceased when we were certain he was dead. Jack Campbell took Widdowfield's boots and Dutch Charlie the best saddle. After taking what valuables they had, we got scared and did not know what to do with the bodies but finally concluded to carry them down in the brush and cover them up which we did.[27]

When nothing was heard from the two sheriff's deputies for several days, search parties went out and found the bodies of Widdowfield and Vincent, partially covered with dirt, where the gang had left them. Widdowfield had been shot four times and Vincent three. Tracks indicated that seven outlaws had been in the party that killed the two officers.[28] The young men had been well liked, and their brutal murders aroused more rage against the road agents throughout Wyoming. The Carbon County commissioners offered a reward of $1,000 for each of the killers.[29]

According to information uncovered by operatives of the Rocky Mountain Detective Association, the Parrott gang, knowing that when the bodies were discovered the hunt for them would be intensified, fled north after the murder of the two officers. They rendezvoused for a time on the Dry Cheyenne River, and then broke up into smaller groups. One, a mysterious man who some believed to be the famous bandit Frank James, headed for Montana. "Dutch Charley" and Joe Minuse stayed together. John Irwin took over leadership of another band. Others, including Frank Towle and Tom Reed, returned to the Deadwood trails and resumed the assault on the stagecoaches.

About eleven o'clock on the night of September 13, 1878, six men stopped the coach from Cheyenne at Old Woman's Fork. Although the outlaws brandished rifles, this holdup, according to reports, seems to have been a rather quiet, genial affair as armed robberies on the Deadwood trail went:

> The spokesman asked the driver, "How many passengers have you?" receiving the answer, "Two, a lady and a gentleman." "Get out and hold up your hands." The command was obeyed by the gentleman, but the lady was allowed to retain her seat. The gentleman was approached and asked, "How much money have you?" He replied, "Thirty dollars." The highwayman said he would take one half of it, but by advice of his comrades compromised with ten dollars, giving that back when

he ascertained that his victim was a laboring man, with the words, "We don't want to molest the passengers, but must have the treasure." They next asked for eatables, and the driver produced a box of fruit in reply, which was broken open and a good portion devoured, the ruffians offering the passengers a share.

The mail-sacks were handed down, and one cut open and one found unlocked. Their contents were poured out upon the ground, sorted over and returned to the pouches. The gentleman's trunk was taken off the rack, but not broken open.[30]

The driver was then allowed to proceed. Several miles farther on he met the southbound stage, advised the occupants of the holdup, and warned them to be on the alert. The stage from Deadwood also carried two passengers and mail, but since it was also conveying gold in its treasure boxes, it was guarded by two shotgun messengers, John Zimmerman and Boone May.

The messengers were following the stagecoach on horseback. When they learned of the possible robbery attempt in the vicinity of Old Woman's Fork they dropped back some 200 yards in hopes of catching the road agents unawares.

The robbers stopped the coach as anticipated and were going through the mail sacks when the messengers, now on foot, stealthily crept up on them. Zimmerman was armed with a rifle, May with a shotgun. In the dark the messengers got within fifteen feet before being discovered, and a gun battle erupted. One of the highwaymen was killed before the others ran off, two of them limping from wounds.[31]

When the shooting began, the driver whipped up his team, and the coach careened down the road. May and Zimmerman, realizing they could not chase the bandits in the dark, returned to their horses and followed the stage, leaving the dead robber and the scattered mail pouches in the road.

In the morning a party from the next stagecoach station returned to the scene to pick up the rifled mail sacks. The body of the slain robber had disappeared, but a pool of blood remained in the road where he had fallen. Boone May said he was sure he had killed the man, adding that he recognized another of the band as Tom Reed.[32] The identity of the supposed dead road agent and what became of his body remained a mystery for several months.

Sheriff Nathaniel K. Boswell of Albany County, Wyoming, led a great roundup of road agents. Courtesy American Heritage Center, University of Wyoming.

And then in late December the newly elected sheriff of Albany County, Wyoming, Nathaniel K. Boswell, was advised that a bunch of tough-looking characters, suspected road agents, were hanging out and planning deviltry in the vicinity of Rock Creek, some fifty miles west of Laramie.

At forty-two years of age, Boswell, an imposing figure of a man— tall, with a steely gaze and a fierce bushy beard—was a veteran lawman. Born in New Hampshire in 1836, he came west at the age of twenty-three and labored as a miner and lumberjack in Colorado before settling in Laramie, Wyoming Territory, where in 1869 he was appointed the first sheriff of the new county of Albany. As Laramie city marshal in August 1876 he arrested and jailed Jack McCall, the slayer of "Wild Bill" Hickok in Deadwood. He became the principal agent of the Rocky Mountain Detective Association in the region and held a commission as a deputy U.S. marshal. Voters elected him county sheriff again in November 1878, and, although he would not officially assume office until the following January, he acted on the report of suspected road agents at Rock Creek.[33]

Frank Howard, one of the gang, had grown tired of the perilous outlaw life and contacted C. D. Thayer, son of John M. Thayer, the former Wyoming governor, who kept a hotel and store in Rock Creek. Howard told Thayer who was in the gang, where they were camped, and their plans for their next operation, a train robbery and a raid on the Thayer hotel. When Boswell received this information from Thayer, he gathered together an impressive roster of fourteen possemen,[34] and made arrangements with officials of the Union Pacific Railroad for a special car to take his posse to Rock Creek. The railroad company was cooperative, and offered a reward of $150 for each member of the gang captured.

At three o'clock on the bitterly cold morning of December 23 Boswell led his posse out from Rock Creek to the point where Howard said the outlaws were encamped. There he found evidence of their stay, but they had moved on. Nearby was the cabin of a man named Oscar Osterman,[35] whom the officers suspected of being in cahoots with the gang. They rousted Osterman out of bed, and under threat of lynching got him to disclose the gang's new location. Boswell found the camp without difficulty and deployed his men around it. Surprising the sleeping outlaws, they made their arrests without firing a shot. Taken in the haul were Joe Minuse, Charles ("Kid") Condon, Henry ("Hank") Harrington, and Frederick C. Robie, alias Frank Ruby. A saddle and a pistol recognized as the property of Bob Widdowfield and "Tip" Vincent were found in the camp, providing strong evidence that those arrested were part of the gang who murdered the Carbon County deputies the previous August.[36] In addition, Joe Minuse had in his possession an overcoat that Boone May had worn the night of the September 13 holdups and shootout, an indication that he was a member of that band.[37]

ASSAULT ON THE DEADWOOD STAGE

After Boswell returned to Rock Creek with his prisoners he also took into custody Frank Howard, the admitted road agent who had blown the whistle on his comrades. On suspicion of gang activity he later jailed John Vassar,[38] Tom Reed, and Albert C. Douglas, a twenty-two-year-old employee of the Rock Creek–Fort Fetterman Stage Line who was thought to be in league with the bandits. (A Laramie correspondent of the *Cheyenne Daily Sun* called Douglas "the undoubted leader of a gang of five robbers."[39]) A few days after Boswell had lodged his prisoners in the Laramie calaboose, officers in Cheyenne arrested a drunken gun-wielder for firing his pistol in the McDaniels Theater, and the hell-raiser turned out to be John Irwin, another wanted member of the gang. Irwin joined Boswell's catch in the Laramie lockup.[40]

J. H. Hayford of the *Laramie Daily Sentinel* heaped praise on Sheriff Boswell and his men:

> Even this early in the winter, the harvest of road agents has exceeded our most sanguine expectations. Sheriff N. K. Boswell went at this good work some weeks before the commencement of his official term and with a most able and efficient corps of deputies and detectives, has already done much to rid this country of those outlaws. If the good work goes on for a few months longer, robbery and murder will not be so fashionable here next year as it has been the past summer and people can ride . . . into the north country with reasonable safety.[41]

Meanwhile, Sheriff Boswell was working on Joe Minuse, who seemed to be bossing the outlaws he had captured, seeking a confession of particular crimes, including the attempted train derailment near Carbon, the murders of the Carbon County deputy sheriffs, and the attempted stagecoach robberies of September 13, as well as information regarding the possible whereabouts of other gang members. Together with Union Pacific authorities, he employed a technique modern-day ACLU lawyers would declare abhorrent but tough frontier lawmen found quite effective. He threw a rope over a rafter, put a noosed end around the neck of the prisoner, and pulled him up off the floor until he indicated an inclination to talk. By means of the imminent threat of death by strangulation technique, Boswell was able to confirm from Minuse that the gang led by "Big Nose George"

Joe Minuse, photographed in prison. Officers
used a rope to persuade him to disclose
information about his outlaw associates.
Courtesy Elnora L. Frye, *Atlas of Wyoming
Outlaws at the Territorial Penitentiary.*

Parrott and "Dutch Charley" was responsible for these crimes.[42]
When pressed for details as to where these two ringleaders were
currently located, Minuse said Parrott was nowhere in the vicinity,
having gone off to Montana. He did give Boswell a lead to "Dutch
Charley," however, and on December 31 officers identified in one
Cheyenne Daily Sun report only as "two detectives from Laramie City,
assisted by Sheriff [John W.] Dykins"[43] collared the notorious outlaw
at Green River City, and he soon joined the others in the Laramie jail.

Boswell learned from Minuse for the first time the identity of the
outlaw slain in the gun battle with shotgun messengers Boone May
and John Zimmerman of September 13. The accurate fire of the two
messengers had brought to an abrupt end the road agent career of
Frank Towle, veteran of the Texas gang, the "Persimmon Bill" gang,
and the "Big Nose George" gang. Minuse said other gang members
had dragged the body from the scene and buried it nearby in a shallow
grave. Boswell passed this information on to Boone May, who rode
out to the scene of the robbery, found the grave site, dug up Towle's
body, cut off the head, and brought it back 178 miles to Cheyenne in
the hope of collecting the reward offered for road agents, dead or
alive.[44] He presented the head to the Laramie County commissioners
as proof that he had killed Towle. Weeks dragged on with no response
from the commissioners, but finally they denied May's petition on the
ground that there was no proof that he, in fact, had been Towle's
killer. May, still in possession of Frank Towle's gradually deterio-
rating head, then filed an affidavit with the authorities of Carbon
County, hoping to cash in there:

Sheriff John W. Dykins of Sweetwater County, Wyoming, collared the notorious outlaw "Dutch Charley." Courtesy Ann Gorzalka, *Wyoming's Territorial Sheriffs.*

Territory of Wyoming, County of Albany. Boon [sic] May being first duly sworn on oath, say: That on the night of 13th September A.D., 1878 he shot and killed Frank Toll [sic], one of the murders [sic] of Widdowfield and Vincent on the Old Woman's Fork on the Black Hills Stage road running from Cheyenne to Deadwood; that affiant has the head of Frank Toll in his possession sufficient to identify him and that affiant is prepared to prove that the man killed by him as above stated is the identical Frank Toll and the murderer of Widdowfield at Elk mountain in said Carbon County.

(Signed) Boone May.

Subscribed and sworn to before me this 29th day of January A.D. 1879.[45]

Boone May was no more successful with Carbon County than he had been with Laramie. Finally, in disgust, he buried the head of Frank Towle on the outskirts of Cheyenne. A few months later the head turned up, "pulled hither and thither by dogs and swine," as Editor Edward A. Slack of the *Cheyenne Daily Sun* reported. "It was lying there yesterday, exposed to the sun, its ghastly jaws grinning hideously at passers-by." The fact that May had "dug up a corpse, cut off its head, and brought it several hundred miles to obtain a reward," Slack believed, "was a bad sample of civilization, but to leave the head to be gnawed and eaten by vagrant dogs is inhuman and shocking."[46]

Frank Towle was dead, his head separated from his body by almost 200 miles, and he was soon joined wherever outlaws went when they left this life by "Dutch Charley." During the hempen ordeal administered to Joe Minuse by Sheriff Boswell, the outlaw said that "Dutch Charley" had bragged to him about shooting down Bob Widdowfield and "Tip" Vincent, and that was enough for Carbon County authorities to demand custody for a murder trial. On January 5, 1879, Albany County Deputy Sheriff Ed Kerns placed "Dutch Charley" in the baggage car of a Union Pacific train at Laramie for transfer to Rawlins. At 9:25 that evening, as the train pulled in to the station at Carbon, hometown of the slain deputies, a party of masked men broke open the door of the baggage car, overpowered Deputy Kerns, and took "Dutch Charley" out and hanged him.

Editor Slack of the *Cheyenne Daily Sun* greeted the news with a gleeful headline: " 'DUTCH CHARLEY' TAKES HIS LAST DANCE IN A HEMP NECK-

TIE, WITH A TELEGRAPH POLE FOR A PARTNER."[47] In another edition he wrote facetiously that "German Charles . . . was met by a select company of about one hundred and fifty anxious friends, who led him to a telegraph pole and called before the curtain, where his feet got tangled up in the footlights and his trachea got mixed up with the curtain cord in such a way that the weight of his overshoes broke his neck."[48]

J. H. Hayford, editor of the *Laramie Daily Sentinel*, was more restrained in his comments regarding the lynching of "Dutch Charley," saying only that "the general sense of the people is that he deserved his fate and everybody breathes freer that there is one less murderer among us."[49] But in another editorial aside a week later, while praising Boswell for his great outlaw haul, he seemed more amenable to summary execution by vigilantes: "The only fault we have to find with the proceedings so far is that every one of the desperadoes is not shot or hung as soon as he is caught. They don't deserve any more pity or sympathy than they awarded to their victims and the laws they have outraged and defied, should not extend to them the protection of the courts or the courtesy of a trial."[50]

Some said "Dutch Charley" was game to the end, refusing to name any additional participants in the Widdowfield and Vincent murders.[51] Others reported that he "begged piteously for his life, falling upon his knees in the snow, begging for mercy and talking in a wild and incoherent manner."[52] In one account he went to his death in a cowardly fashion, confessing to the Elk Mountain murders and was about to name his accomplices when none other than "Frank Howard, one of his pals in crime now turned state's witness, kicked the barrel from under him . . . , fearful that Dutch would tell the part played by himself and Big Nose George." The authors added that "kids growing up in Carbon, old men tell you today, played a game called 'Stretch yer legs before we stretch yer neck like Pa done to Dutch Charlie.'"[53] Another story has it that Elizabeth Widdowfield, sister-in-law of the murdered deputy, was the one who kicked the barrel from under "Dutch Charley."[54] The next day Carbon residents cut the cold, stiff body of "Dutch Charley" down and threw it, "his newly acquired necktie still around his neck," on a coal car to continue his ride to Rawlins.[55]

The cases of the other gang members were quickly disposed of, for the law moved swiftly in those days.

Frank Howard, whose original recital to C. D. Thayer had led to the capture of the gang, was not prosecuted. The *Cheyenne Daily Sun* reported in January 1879 that Howard, "a desperado without even the honor which is said to be current among thieves," had been shot and killed by a man named John R. Smith,[56] but other accounts say he survived and later became a highly regarded detective for the Union Pacific Railroad.[57]

On January 3, 1879, federal officers placed a hold on Henry ("Hank") Harrington, charged with larceny of the U.S. mails. Bail was set at $100 on February 18 as he awaited trial scheduled for March 22. The bonds were given, and he was released. He agreed to turn state's evidence and testify against his former gang members, and shortly afterward, on his way to Fort McKinney to identify road agent suspects, was reportedly murdered.[58]

The U.S. marshals on January 9 also put in a claim for Tom Reed to face a federal charge of larceny of the U.S. mails. Tried on February 20, he was acquitted and released from custody. Reed, who by most accounts had been a major force within the Parrott gang, got off scot-free and disappeared from the pages of history.[59]

The U.S. marshal on January 15, 1879, placed a hold on John Vassar, charging him with highway robbery in northern Wyoming. Tried on February 27, he won an acquittal and was also released.[60]

A few weeks before they were due for trial John Irwin and "Kid" Condon, together with two other jail inmates, attempted to tunnel out of confinement. Somehow, with the aid of "a common shoe-knife" that had been smuggled in, they broke through the cut-stone ground floor, dug down five feet, and excavated a passage almost thirty feet long before their operation was discovered. Sheriff Boswell allowed them to continue their tedious project, but posted a twenty-four-hour guard at the point where they would emerge. When the first escapee "pushed his head to the surface [he] was rather embarrassed to discover Deputy Sheriff Butler waiting to receive him."[61]

On February 20 in federal court John Irwin and Charles ("Kid") Condon were tried and convicted of "robbing the United States mails by force of arms" and sentenced to life terms. Albert C. Douglas, charged with being an accessory after the fact in the robbery of the mails, was convicted, but was sentenced to only fifteen days in jail and a fine of one dollar and costs.[62]

Frederick C. Robie, alias Frank Ruby, stood trial on March 20 in federal court, charged with robbing the mails. He was convicted but received a much lighter sentence than his comrades Irwin and Condon, only two years in the prison at Laramie. He was released on February 20, 1881, after serving one year and eleven months.[63]

The trial of Joe Minuse, charged with complicity in the murder of sheriff's deputies Widdowfield and Vincent, originally scheduled for April 17, 1879, was held over until September 11, when a jury acquitted him. As the editor of the *Laramie Daily Sentinel* remarked, "The popular verdict is 'guilty' for him, but not proven."[64] He was released but rearrested immediately by Green River, Wyoming, officers on a charge of horse theft in their jurisdiction. Convicted of that crime, he served two years in prison before walking out a free man on Christmas Eve, 1881.[65]

So by the first months of 1879 the criminal gang of "Big Nose George" had been pretty well broken up, but Parrott, the leader, remained on the loose. Parrott and one remaining gang member, Jack Campbell, operated in the vicinity of Miles City, Montana, throughout most of 1879 and 1880, stealing horses and robbing whatever victims they thought were easy touches. They avoided the Deadwood stage lines, evidently fearful of the company's shotgun messengers, Boone May and his compadres, whose reputation for swift and deadly response to attacks by road agents had grown apace since May and Zimmerman had dispatched Frank Towle. Sheriff Tom Irvine of Custer County, Montana, once arrested "Big Nose George" on suspicion, but when a deputy U.S. marshal who knew Parrott by sight did not appear in time to make positive identification, Irvine was forced to release his prisoner.[66]

Parrott continued his depredations in Montana, and rewards totaling $2,000 for his arrest and $1,000 for the arrest of Jack Campbell were eventually posted by that territory. On July 19, 1880, "Big Nose George" and Campbell, who was going by the name of Carey, showed up again in Miles City, and two of Sheriff Irvine's deputies, Lem Wilson and Fred Schmalsle, set out to collar them. They first approached Parrott at John Chinnick's cabin, where he was staying. The wanted man was sitting in the doorway enjoying the evening breezes when Schmalsle, as one newspaper reported, "told him to throw up, placing a pistol to his left ear." Parrott did not vomit, but raised his hands "with an exclamation of surprise." The officers then proceeded to a saloon where they found Carey. "When ordered to throw up, [Carey] made a motion for his pistol, but changed his mind as he saw the hammer of Schmalsle's self-cocker slowly rise."[67]

Sheriff Irvine locked his prisoners up and wired Carbon County, Wyoming, that he had the men in custody who had for two years been wanted for the murders of Widdowfield and Vincent. Governor John W. Hoyt issued a requisition for Parrott the week of July 24, and Carbon County Sheriff Isaac M. Lawry dispatched his best deputy, James G. ("Jim") Rankin, to go after "Big Nose George." Joining him on the long, arduous journey was the county's prosecuting attorney, a man named Smith. They went "by train to Ogden, Utah, and taking the Utah Northern Railroad to Butte City; thence by buckboard of mail stage to Bozeman; by horseback east through the Yellowstone River country, 150 miles to Miles City."[68] (Evidently not believing he had enough evidence against Campbell to prosecute him for the Elk Mountain murders, Prosecuting Attorney Smith had not secured a requisition for him, and Campbell was released.)

Then, with their well-shackled prisoner, Rankin and Smith worked their way back the many miles to Rawlins, Wyoming. The return trip was "by livery conveyance 175 east to the terminus of the Northern Pacific at Medora, Dakota Territory, thence on to Sioux City, picking up the Union Pacific train and on to Wyoming, taking a total of 12 days travel."[69] Their arrival at Omaha was noted and reported on the national wire services. An August 6 dispatch from Chicago predicted that when "Big Nose George" got back to Wyoming, friends of Widdowfield and Vincent at Carbon would "treat him to a lynching as they did Dutch Charley." It added that the arrest of the notorious gang leader would "probably break up the contemplated organization of a band of outlaws on the northern frontier, who, it is thought, were preparing to raid the Union Pacific and other roads and to rob the stage coaches."[70]

In anticipation of an escape attempt by Parrott or the threat of possible action by a lynch mob, Deputy Sheriff Rankin shackled his prisoner to the seat of the car. Short stops at Cheyenne and Laramie passed without incident, but when the train pulled into the depot at Carbon on August 13 a band of masked and armed men was waiting. They overpowered Rankin and Smith and, using a sledgehammer, broke the iron bands binding "Big Nose George" to his seat. They dragged him from the train, put a noose around his neck, and subjected him to the same treatment Sheriff Boswell had given Joe Minuse back in 1878, strangling him until he confessed to the murders of Widdowfield and Vincent. But they did not go all the way and string him up as they had his pal "Dutch Charley" the year earlier; they chose to let the law deal with "Big Nose George" and returned him to the care of Jim Rankin, who continued on with his prisoner to Rawlins.[71]

On September 13 "Big Nose George" Parrott was arraigned for murder. He first pleaded guilty to the arraignment and then four days later changed his plea to not guilty. A special grand jury handed down an indictment for first-degree murder. The foreman of that grand jury was Isaac Carson Miller, who would succeed Isaac Lawry as sheriff of Carbon County that fall and would be in charge during the last chapter of the outlaw's violent career.

The trial of what one newspaper called the last of "one of the worst band of road-agents and robbers that ever infested Wyoming"[72] began in November. At the outset Parrott's lawyers filed for a change of venue, charging the presiding judge, Jacob B. Blair, with prejudice. The venue change was not granted, but William W. Peck, associate justice of the Wyoming Supreme Court, was called in to hear the case. The jury was sworn in on November 16, and testimony began the next day. Parrott, meanwhile, had again changed his plea to guilty, and his attorneys filed a motion for arrest of judgment and sentence. Justice Peck took the matter under advisement, delaying further action for several weeks. On December 15 he denied the motion and on the 17th sentenced the defendant to hang on April 2, 1881.[73] According to an Associated Press report, "when sentence of death was passed on him, he wept like a child and broke down completely."[74]

"Big Nose George" was returned to a cell in the Rawlins calaboose to await his execution.[75] His jailer was Robert Rankin, brother of the deputy sheriff who had brought him from Montana. (There were three Rankin brothers, all involved in law enforcement. James, the deputy sheriff in 1880, would be elected Carbon County sheriff in 1884. Robert would tend the jail. Joseph, an early day scout, would be appointed U.S. marshal for Wyoming and serve from 1890 to 1894.[76])

Having publicly repented his murderous career, "Big Nose George" seemed to have accepted his date with the hangman, but at about 7:30

on the night of March 22, 1881, less than two weeks before that lethal meeting, he made a desperate attempt at escape. Newly elected sheriff Isaac Miller was out of town, and Robert Rankin had full charge of the jail. With the help of a case knife he had somehow acquired, Parrott sawed through the rivets on his homemade leg shackles, extricated himself from them, and attacked Rankin, striking him over the head with the heavy irons. Although stunned and bleeding from the blow, the jailer fought back. His wife, Rosa, in an adjoining room, heard the fracas and realizing an escape attempt was under way, locked the door, grabbed a pistol, and fired a shot, alerting others, who came running. They subdued and double-manacled the prisoner.[77]

This was the last straw for Carbon County citizens who had for two and a half years sought retribution for the murders of their friends Bob Widdowfield and "Tip" Vincent. At ten o'clock that night an armed mob, determined to end the career of the man most responsible for those slayings, moved on the jail. They

took the criminal to a telegraph pole, placed him on a barrel, put a rope around his neck, and threw the other end over the cross arm of the pole. The barrel was then kicked from under the victim, but the attempt at hanging was a failure. The mob then got a ladder which they compelled him to climb and jump off. This also failed to break his neck. His arms were then unloosed and he was compelled to climb up the pole, meanwhile begging the crowd to shoot him. His last words were, "Boys, I'll jump and break my neck." He jumped and strangled to death. The inquest will be held to-day.[78]

The coroner's jury at the inquest, of course, found that the infamous desperado and road agent came to his demise by hanging at the hands of persons unknown. The Rawlins jail registry for March 22, 1881, contains the notation that the prisoner Parrott "went to jine the angels" that day.[79]

A comment in a Canadian newspaper reporting on the passing of "Big Nose George" some years later is no doubt greatly hyperbolized: "They say his nose was so big that the coffin lid would not nail down; so they had to squeeze it down by sitting on it."[80]

— 8 —

THE BATTLE AT CANYON SPRINGS

I turned and backed my way across the road, shooting at anything and everything that looked like a robber.

— Scott ("Quick Shot") Davis

Over the years 1877 and 1878 as road agent gangs mounted a criminal offensive against the passengers and treasure carried by its coaches, the Cheyenne and Black Hills Stage Company made every effort to safeguard the persons and property committed to its care.

Transport of the Black Hills gold was a lucrative part of business for the stagecoach company, which charged one dollar for every hundred in bullion entrusted to its care.[1] To protect the treasure shipments, Luke Voorhees ordered construction of a special iron box, lined with chill steel. Designed and built by the Master Safe and Lock Company of Cincinnati, Ohio, and called a "salamander safe," possibly because of its length and green color, the box or safe was sixteen by thirty inches in outward size, with walls at top, bottom, ends, and sides three inches thick, leaving a space ten by twenty-four inches for valuables. The manufacturing company gave assurance that the Yale combination lock was of the most modern design and could not be opened by brigands within six days.[2] As a conveyance for the "salamander safe" and its treasure the owners of the stage company contracted with coach manufacturer A. D. Butler of Cheyenne to build two specially designed coaches with interiors lined with steel plates, five-sixteenths of an inch thick, capable of withstanding the impact of the heaviest charged rifle bullet. Two portholes were made in the doors from which messengers within could direct fire at road agents. The steel-walled "salamander safe" was to be bolted to the floor of this heavy coach, the first model of which was delivered in May 1878 and came to be called the "Iron Clad" or the "Monitor." A second coach, called the "Johnny Slaughter" to memorialize the popular driver murdered by road agents, was received in September.[3] Guarding the treasure coaches were the elite corps of messengers headed by Captain Scott Davis.[4]

On the morning of September 26, 1878, employees of the Gilmer stage company in Deadwood prepared a shipment of gold and other valuables for transport to Cheyenne. They placed within the "salamander safe" about $27,000 in valuables, $9,500 in gold bullion, $14,500 in gold dust, and some $3,000 in currency and jewelry, and bolted the box to the floor of the armored "Monitor" coach.[5]

Holding the reins of the six-horse team as the "Monitor" rolled out of Deadwood at seven o'clock that morning was H. E. ("Big Gene") Barnett, an experienced driver who had been on the boot when George Duncan and John Babcock robbed the stage near Eagle's Nest on the night of October 3, 1877, almost a year earlier. Beside Barnett sat Gale Hill, one of the messengers. Inside with his back to the horses was messenger Eugene Smith and across from him sat the messenger captain, Scott Davis. Although company policy forbade the taking of passengers when transporting treasure, an exception had been made for this trip. Hugh O. Campbell, an employee of the Black Hills Telegraph Company, described as "a tall, fine-looking man,"[6] had been given permission to ride in the coach as far as Jenney Stockade, fifty-seven miles south of Deadwood, where he was to assume a new position as telegraph operator. William Ward, northern division superintendent for the stage company, under instructions from Luke Voorhees to accompany the coach as far as Hat Creek, rode along on horseback. For reasons never explained, Ward disobeyed orders and left the stage at the Pleasant Valley dinner stop and returned to Deadwood, thereby missing out on the excitement to follow.

According to Deadwood pioneer and historian John S. McClintock, a plan was afoot to rob this treasure coach, and what followed he called "the most heartless, as well as the bloodiest stage robbery ever perpetrated in the Black Hills." At least six men were implicated in the plot, he said. Four of them, Charles Carey, "Duck" Goodale, Frank McBride, and Andy Gouch, called "Red Cloud" since he came from that agency, were well known to McClintock, who believed "Big Nose George" Parrott and Al Spears were also in the gang.[7] In preparation for the robbery, all of gang members, with the exception of "Red Cloud," went by spring wagon to the vicinity of Canyon Springs station, about forty-five miles down the Cheyenne trail, to await word from their confederate, who remained in Deadwood to watch the coach.

When Gene Barnett wheeled the "Monitor" and its valuable cargo out on the morning of September 26 and turned his lead horses south toward Cheyenne, "Red Cloud" Gouch stole a prize racehorse owned by a prosperous Deadwood prostitute named Blanche White and rode ahead to notify the gang of its coming.[8]

Canyon Springs station, situated in rough, heavily timbered country on Beaver Creek, was one of the smaller stops on the Deadwood-to-Cheyenne stage route. Designed only as a relay post for the changing of teams, it had no accommodations for meals or lodgings, only a corral for the stage horses, a barn, and a rude shack that served as living quarters for William Miner, the stock-tender.

Miner later described what happened that day: "Shortly before the arrival of the coach a man on horseback rode up and asked for a drink of water. Upon dismounting, he at once ordered me to throw up my hands, which I did. He then pushed me in the grain room of the stable. By this time the band of five (I thought there were six of them) all got in and proceeded to make arrangements for the capture of the coach. They removed the dirt from between the logs near the door of the stable, where the stage always stops, and upon its arrival opened fire from their positions on the inside."[9]

When the stage rolled in and Gene Barnett reined his team to a halt by the barn where the stock-tender would normally be waiting to assist in the change of horses, he found no one. Gale Hill called out to Miner but received no answer. Jumping down to the ground, Hill used a chock to block the wheels of the coach to keep it from rolling during the team change. As he walked toward the barn to look for Miner, shots rang out.

A bullet struck him in the left arm. Seeing that the fire was coming from the stable, he jerked out his pistol and returned the fire. Then

Shotgun messenger Galen E. Hill was severely wounded in the shootout at Canyon Springs station. Author's collection.

another ball from a large bore rifle struck him in the back, passed "entirely through his body, entering rather close to the backbone, piercing his left lung and tearing a big hole out through his breast."[10] With blood gushing from his wounds and his mouth, Hill staggered toward the stable, but kept firing through a dense haze of black powder gunsmoke.[11]

As he related the story later, Hill was only a few feet from the stable when suddenly a man he instantly recognized as Charley Carey emerged from the cloud of smoke, thrust the muzzle of his gun almost in the messenger's face, and fired. Carey was so close Hill "could feel the hot air on the side of his neck as it came from the gun barrel," but in his haste he had missed. Hill returned the fire, but, half-blinded by the smoke and weak from his wounds, he also missed.

"Carey then fell back into the stable and Hill made a dash for the corner of the building. . . . A rattling fusillade was still going on and [Hill] saw a man up in front who was down on one knee and pumping a Winchester for all he was worth." Although he was losing blood and strength rapidly, Hill took deliberate aim and dropped this outlaw before passing out.[12]

Meanwhile messengers Smith and Davis were carrying on the fight, shooting through the door ports. The bandits returned the fire, and a bullet grazed Smith's head, stunning him. He slumped over with blood running down his face, and Davis thought he had been killed. "I fired a good many shots from the coach into the barn door and the port holes from which the robbers were firing," Davis related,

> but from my position in the coach was unsuccessful in hitting the attacking foe. I told Campbell that I was going to get out of the coach and go across the road to where there was a large pine tree from which I could get better aim. . . . Campbell said he was going to the tree with me. We both climbed from the coach but Campbell had no gun with him to defend himself. I turned and backed my way across the road, shooting at anything and everything that looked like a robber. When we were about half way across the road, Campbell swerved to the left while I was shooting at the port holes, hoping that I might hit a hidden robber. Suddenly Mr. Campbell went down on his knees in the middle of the road. The holdup men then fired another volley, killing him instantly.[13]
>
> Before I reached the tree, one of the robbers appeared at the head of the horses. I had been urging the stage driver to make a run for it and leave the coach. The instant I saw the robber at the horse's head, I turned quickly and fired. The shot wounded him badly. He threw up his hands, fell over backwards, crawled around behind the horses and made his getaway to the back of the barn.[14]

Although severely wounded, Gale Hill managed to crawl around to the rear of the barn, pull himself up to the rear window opening, and "with his arm resting on the sill," continue firing. He put a bullet in another robber, later identified as Frank McBride, before fainting from loss of blood.[15]

During all this shooting, Gene Barnett had remained on the boot of the coach. Now one of the bandits ran up, ordered him down, and then, using him as a shield, advanced on Davis's position behind the tree. "Surrender!" he yelled.

"If you come an inch farther I'll kill you," was Davis's response.

"For God's sake, Scott, don't shoot," shouted a terrified Barnett.

Scott Davis knew that both of his fellow messengers had been hit in the first volley from the stable. Believing Eugene Smith was dead in the coach and hearing no more shots from Gale Hill's position in the barn, he had to assume Hill had been killed also. Left alone to carry on the fight and unable to fire at the advancing robber for fear of hitting Barnett, he was faced with the choice: surrender or flee. He chose flight. Backing off through the brush and trees, he made his escape.[16]

When it was clear that Davis had gone and Hill had lost consciousness and was no longer a threat, the road agents emerged from the stable and disarmed Smith, who was just recovering his senses. Leaving the body of Campbell lying in the road, Hill apparently breathing his last, and stock-tender Miner tied up in the grain room, they placed blindfolds around Barnett and Smith, shoved them into the coach, and drove it some distance away. In a copse of woods they tied their captives to the wheels and began an attack on the treasure box. After about two hours work with sledgehammer and chisel they managed to break open the safe and remove the contents. Gathering up their wounded comrades, they loaded their loot on packhorses, promised their tied-up captives they would send someone from Cold Springs ranch to release them, and rode off in a southwesterly direction.[17]

It was after nightfall, about ten o'clock, before Barnett, after a struggle, managed to free himself, and untied Smith, whose hands, with the circulation cut off, had swollen to almost twice their normal size.[18] The two men returned to the station to find Miner, the stock-tender, gone. He had also worked loose and started on foot for Cold Springs ranch, two miles away.[19] There he obtained a saddle horse and rode to Deadwood to report the robbery and get medical help for the badly wounded Gale Hill. Fearing that he might encounter some of the bandits along the way, he avoided the road and kept to the timber and brush, making his ride of more than forty miles an arduous one.[20]

ASSAULT ON THE DEADWOOD STAGE

Scott Davis, meanwhile, after scurrying away through the underbrush, had legged it seven miles to the Ben Eager ranch, where he got a mount and rode hard for Beaver station, where he expected to find Boone May, Billy Sample, and Jesse Brown, the messengers waiting to escort the treasure coach on south.[21] But on the way he met his fellow messengers who, with several others, including a Post Office inspector named Adams and W. H. Taylor, who left an account of the affair, had started out to investigate when the stage did not arrive at Beaver on time. The party then went to Canyon Springs station, which, as Taylor said, "resembled a shambles" with the riddled body of Hugh Campbell stretched out in a pool of blood and Gale Hill appearing "so near death that nothing much could be done for him. . . . At every expiration the air could be heard coming out of his back as well as the wound in his breast."[22]

Although Hill had lost so much blood it seemed he was done for,[23] his fellow messengers helped him as best they could while they awaited Miner's return from Deadwood with medical assistance. When the stock-tender got back after his grueling round-trip by horseback, he was accompanied by Dr. L. F. Babcock, the stage company physician; B. P. Smith, an undertaker; and "a hurry party of citizens."[24] The doctor removed Hill to the nearby ranch of Charles L. Snow and turned him over to the care of a Mrs. Frazier, who nursed him until he was well enough to be taken to the hospital in Deadwood. Despite the loss of a great deal of blood, Gale Hill survived, although he was troubled by his wound for the rest of his life. Two years after the shootout a jagged bullet fragment worked its way out of his arm.[25]

Undertaker Smith attended to the removal of Hugh Campbell's remains to Deadwood, where an examination of the body revealed that in addition to the fatal wound in the head he had received three bullets in the legs and one through the body.[26] Fellow Masons conducted the young man's funeral and buried his body in Mount Moriah Cemetery.

Among the "hurry party" of Deadwood folks rushing to the scene of the robbery was Seth Bullock. When news of the holdup reached Deadwood, Jack Gilmer, who happened to be in the town at the time, went to Bullock and urged him to organize a posse to pursue the road agents. Bullock was reluctant, saying he no longer held any law enforcement position and was busy with his large hardware store, but

Gilmer's formidable powers of persuasion, together with his assurance that the stagecoach company would provide full assistance, including permission to appropriate any horses stabled at his stage line stations that he might need, and the posting of large rewards for capture of the bandits, finally won him over. Together with Mike Whalen, a former deputy sheriff, Bullock mounted up and rode to the scene of the robbery and shooting in less than six hours.[27]

Bullock and Whalen joined a group gathered at Canyon Springs that included stage line superintendent W. M. Ward, Judge John H. Burns, Post Office Inspector Adams, W. H. Taylor, June Dix, Hank Beeman, driver "Big Gene" Barnett, stock-tender Bill Miner, and shotgun messengers Scott Davis, Eugene Smith, Boone May, Billy Sample, and Jesse Brown. As Bullock later related it, in an attempt to disclose every detail of the holdup to provide leads for the pursuit, "an impromptu court was organized in a stable near the springs under the hill, where the Deadwood party put the driver and the stock tender and one or two others who had been in the vicinity for some time through a severe cross examination."[28]

One of those "others" was a young man who wandered onto the scene while the inquiry was in progress and turned out to have more information about the robbers than the interrogators could have imagined. He was former-freighter-turned-highwayman John H. Brown, who, still not fully recovered from the wound he had received at the hands of passenger Daniel Finn in the botched stagecoach robbery the previous July, was recuperating in a shack near Canyon Springs. Apparently drawn by unbridled curiosity, he walked into the meeting and was immediately recognized by Gene Barnett and the messengers as one of the Tom Price gang.

The self-appointed chairman of the kangaroo court, not identified by Bullock in his account, but probably William Ward, senior representative of the stagecoach company, subjected Brown to an intense grilling and directed others to administer what Bullock coyly called "the Montana argument," the threat of immediate hanging as a noose was tightened around the neck. Brown broke down under this treatment and confessed to having taken part in the earlier holdup in which he had been shot, but denied involvement in the robbery and gunfight at Canyon Springs. Members of that gang had pressured him to join them in the holdup, he said, but he begged off, claiming he was still incapacitated by the bullet fired by Daniel Finn, a memento that still remained in his body, despite the nursing of Lurline Monte Verde in Deadwood. He did know the road agents who had pulled the job at Canyon Springs, however, and named them for his interrogators. He said they had divided up the loot and separated into different groups before heading out in a southerly direction.[29]

This information was dispatched to officers in Deadwood, Cheyenne, and Sidney, and the hunt for the road agents who had attacked the stage at Canyon Springs began.[30]

— 9 —

ROAD AGENT ROUNDUP

The hunt for the robbers who robbed the treasure coach and murdered poor Campbell is being vigorously pushed and the large reward offered by the stage company for the capture of the bandits is having its effect. New parties are being organized nearly every day to go out on the trail, and the search will be kept up until they are run down or out of the country.

— *Cheyenne Daily Leader*, October 19, 1878

The robbery of the seemingly impregnable treasure coach and the murder of an innocent passenger caused an uproar in the Black Hills and at all points on the roads leading to the diggings.[1] Editor Edward A. Slack of the *Cheyenne Daily Sun* certainly expressed the views of many when he editorialized: "It would seem as if the stage company had been plundered past all endurance, and if there is such a thing as a county government, a territorial government, and a United States government, the line should be protected. Governments are supposed to exist for other purposes besides the collection of taxes, that it would seem that is about all the use that is being made in this locality."[2]

The theme was echoed by Herman Glafcke of the *Cheyenne Daily Leader*: "When robbery is supplemented by the murder of an innocent passenger, the offense at once rises to the highest point, and an outraged community grows justly indignant. When life is no longer secure in traveling between two large cities it is high time to inquire into the state of our civilization and learn where and why it fails in its first duty — protection."

Glafcke went on to reveal how, even prior to the sensational affair at Canyon Springs, he, as postmaster at Cheyenne, together with Wyoming governor John W. Hoyt and U.S. Marshal Gustave Schnitger, had opened correspondence with Washington authorities, urging greater federal assistance in the protection of the U.S. mails and the war on road agents. In response, the Post Office Department had appropriated $2,000 for this purpose. Schnitger appointed Charles Adams, a post office special agent working for Inspector John Furay, as a deputy U.S. marshal assigned to the mission. Adams in turn deputized Scott Davis, Boone May, and eight other worthies to help him in the battle. These fighting men were each to be paid $5 a day from this special fund. Additionally, they would receive a bounty of $400 for every road agent taken, dead or alive, the cost of which would be shared equally by the U.S. government and Laramie County. In an independent action, Laramie County commissioners had engaged another force of five man hunters under the leadership of Ed Ordway to go after the bandits with the same remuneration inducements.[3]

It was originally intended that these developments be kept secret from the general public, but Glafcke, apparently believing it was more important that the citizenry, shocked by the Canyon Springs robbery and murder, be made aware of the important steps being taken to combat road agents, ran the story in a column alongside news of the holdup.

The editor of the *Laramie Daily Sentinel*, who missed no opportunity to take shots at his competitor, under the headline "The Secret's Out," commented:

> The *Cheyenne Leader*, having seen fit to expose the operations of the government and the United States Marshal of this Territory looking to the capture of road agents, which those gentlemen had hoped to keep from the public prints for obvious reasons, we may now state the Northern part of Laramie County is at present being scoured by armed parties, working for good pay and a handsome reward for each robber taken; the expenses being borne jointly by the government and Laramie County. Upon the whole, however, as the *Leader's* circulation is but a small affair, this breach of journalistic courtesy will probably do no great harm.[4]

The Cheyenne and Black Hills Stage Company contributed to the campaign by posting a notice offering a substantial reward for recovery of monies stolen by the Canyon Springs robbers and the apprehension of the culprits:

$2,500 Reward.

Will be paid for the return of the money and valuables and the capture (upon conviction) of the five men who robbed our coach on the 26th day of September 1878, at Canyon Springs (Whisky Gap), Wyo. Ter., of twenty-seven thousand dollars, consisting mostly of gold bullion. Pro rate of the above will be paid for the capture of either of the robbers and proportionate part of the property.

Luke Voorhees, Supt. Cheyenne and Black Hills Stage Co.
Cheyenne, Wyo. Sept. 28, 1878.[5]

Two days later citizens of Cheyenne had an opportunity to see a real live road agent when John H. Brown, heavily shackled, arrived on a stagecoach in the custody of J. L. Jelm, an agent of the Post Office Department working under the leadership of Inspector Furay. After the impromptu court of inquiry at Canyon Springs had elicited Brown's confession and gotten all the information it could from him about the treasure coach robbery, Scott Davis, Boone May, and W. H. Taylor had taken the prisoner, described as about thirty years of age with a mustache but no whiskers and wearing "a sort of hangdog expression which would almost convict him,"[6] to Fort Laramie and turned him over to the post office authorities.[7]

Davis, May, and Taylor, acting on information provided by Brown, then went to a location near Jenney Stockade and collared another highwayman, Charles Henry Borris. When Post Office Agent Jelm arrived in Cheyenne with Brown on September 30, he told reporters that Borris would be along on another stage if his guard was "not compelled to kill him on account of an effort to escape."[8]

A week later May and Taylor came in on the stage with Borris. Taylor said they had arrested their quarry at a road agent rendezvous, the cabin of the notorious "Mother Ogden," a woman he described as "tall, masculine and fierce." Threatened by his captors with summary hanging, Borris had confessed to participation in the Canyon Springs holdup as well as two other stagecoach robberies.[9]

ASSAULT ON THE DEADWOOD STAGE

Wyoming Territorial Penitentiary, where many of the road agents were incarcerated. Courtesy Wyoming State Museum.

Other passengers in the coach with the prisoner and his guards described "a ghastly looking spectacle" they had witnessed near Jenney Stockade. The bodies of two men, presumably suspected road agents, with blackened faces, sunken cheeks and eyes, and tongue protruding, were hanging from a tree. From their appearance it was believed they had been dead for some time. This was duly reported in the press, but nothing more appeared in the papers, and the identity of these lynching victims was never disclosed. It was evident, however, that an aggressive offensive against the road agents had begun.[10]

That first week of October Brown and Borris appeared before U.S. Commissioner Joseph W. Fisher to answer a charge of obstruction of the U.S. mails. Fisher remanded them to the Wyoming Territorial Penitentiary at Laramie to await the next term of federal court, scheduled for May 1879.[11]

In November indictments for road agency were brought against both men by Wyoming authorities. Although they had admitted complicity in the Whoop Up stagecoach robbery and entered guilty pleas, trial dates for the robbery charges were not set, pending disposition of the lesser federal charges. This was obviously a ploy to keep the two locked up and available for further interrogation by officers seeking additional information about other gang members. For the next seven months Brown and Borris occupied cells in the Laramie penitentiary.

Meanwhile, spurred on by a sense of outrage at the audacity of the Canyon Springs road agents and with an eye, no doubt, to the reward money offered by the stage company, law officers and civilians alike were engaged in an extensive outlaw hunt.

In the days immediately after the robbery posses were organized in the Black Hills and struck out in every direction in search of the brigands.

As soon as Scott Davis got back to Deadwood he formed a party and rode into the Inyan Kara country, but failing to find a lead, headed southwest toward Rawhide Buttes.[12]

At Rapid City stage line superintendent Ed Cook and Pennington County Sheriff Frank Moulton led a party that included Deputy Sheriff Bill Steele, Bob Burleigh, Howard Worth, Dr. D. M. Flick, Ellis T. ("Doc") Peirce, Dr. N. C. Whitfield, and C. B. Stocking, "a noted trailer and gunman,"[13] said to be equally adept "with six shooter and knife."[14]

Several different parties were formed from the large group of men congregated at Canyon Springs. Stage line superintendent William Ward, heading up one that included Seth Bullock, Judge John Burns, June Dix, and Hank Beeman, struck south toward Robbers' Roost.[15] For the next week this posse rode hard, covering some 700 miles at a rate of 100 miles a day. It was a terrible physical strain on the men, but the mounts they were riding suffered even more. The horses of Burns and Dix fell dead. Burns secured a mule to replace his dead mount, and Dix appropriated "a buckskin broncho from a boy on his way to school,"[16] and they rode on.

At one point Superintendent Ward left Bullock's party to see if he could secure fresh mounts as promised by Gilmer, but ended up carrying out his own investigation. Following up on some leads, he engaged Uriah Gillett, "a veteran frontiersman, a crack shot, and experienced trailer, and, of course, a brave man," to assist him in the search. At Newton's Fork Ward hit pay dirt. There they learned that a man known only as "Frenchy" had sold a team and "dead-axle" wagon to two men, identified by Ward from Frenchy's description as Charles Carey and Frank McBride.[17]

Assault on the Deadwood Stage

Carey, twenty-seven years old, was said to be a former scout for Custer. Six feet tall, with light complexion, brown hair, and a sandy beard, he had noticeable pockmarks on either side of his nose. He was known to wear a Winchester cartridge belt over a new ulster overcoat and ride a gray, unshod pony. Frank McBride, twenty-four, was a small man, weighing about 145 pounds, with very sharp eyes, small features and feet, and light brown hair, mustache, and goatee. He rode a dark sorrel barefoot pony, bald faced, and blind in one eye. McBride was suffering from the gunshot wound, presumably the bullet Gale Hill had put in him during the Canyon Springs fight.[18]

Boone May, his brother Bill, and detective Noah Siever were with a party searching the Rapid Creek country. Hearing of Ward's discovery, they hurried to the spot. Frenchy told them he had been paid $250 in cash for two horses and the wagon, which Carey needed to carry his badly wounded crony, McBride. The May party set out on the trail of the wagon and were soon joined by the Rapid City posse led by Ed Cook and Sheriff Moulton. The combined posse followed the trail to Wasta Spring Road House, some eighteen miles east of Rapid City, where link up was made with Seth Bullock and his riders.

Along the trail this large body of man hunters picked up bits of information from locals. A miner disclosed that three outlaws, two of them badly wounded, had appeared at his camp the morning following the robbery. One, believed to be McBride, was shot in the groin. The other, described as "a tall young man with a smooth face," was suffering from seven buckshot wounds in the breast and stomach. This fellow died the following evening and was buried nearby.[19]

A hunter named Frost, who said he was a former hunting partner of Charles Carey and therefore knew him well, verified this story, saying Carey and two wounded men, one of whom was McBride, had stopped at his cabin and remained several hours. Unaware that his onetime partner had turned to outlawry, Frost had been amazed at the large amount of gold Carey had in his possession.[20]

The miner's story that one of the outlaws had died of his wounds received some verification from a man named Jim Sherman, who said two men stopped at his place at Newton City. One came in to purchase supplies while the other lay in the wagon, "very sick," according to his partner. "They made a very short stay and then departed . . . as fast as their team could go."[21]

The large, combined posse doggedly followed the trail to a point a few miles from Mitchell Creek, where, according to Dr. Whitfield, "it being very dark, nothing could be distinguished ten feet from the road. As the cavalcade crossed a little sag, a horse to the left of us was heard to neigh."[22]

Scouts investigated and determined that the wanted men were in the brush where the horse had been heard. An argument then ensued among the posse leaders as to their next move. Bullock and some others wanted to surround the camp and shoot the horses. By setting the outlaws afoot, they contended, they could be assured of recovering the treasure. But Cook rejected this argument and insisted they wait until morning. It was important that these bandits should not be killed in a gunfight, he argued. They must be taken alive so that information could be obtained from them with regard to the other gang members. The robbers, he said, were unaware of the posse's presence and would not decamp before daylight, when they could be easily captured.[23]

Cook's plan was adopted, and the possemen, as a disgruntled Bullock said, "shivered until daylight."[24] With the rising sun the posse made what Dr. Whitfield called "a grand charge." They found the wagon, "but the birds had flown and the nest was cold." All the officers had for their trouble, recalled the doctor sadly, was "one old coat, some bacon, flour, two belts with cartridges, a gun case, pistol scabbard, one axe, some shelled corn, a heavy double harness and some other articles."[25] Since the wagon had been abandoned, it was surmised that it was no longer needed as McBride had died somewhere along the route and been buried.[26]

Seth Bullock and those who had wanted to attack when the fugitives were first discovered were understandably irate. "A hotter party was never gathered on the prairie and serious trouble in the crowd was only averted by the persuasive tongue of John H. Burns."[27]

Finally the posse moved on, but Dr. Whitfield, who was riding a Mexican pony that could not maintain the pace, turned back. Out of curiosity he revisited the site of the last encampment of the outlaws and found a pair of old overalls that the other possemen had ignored. Kicking at the garment, he was amazed and elated to find that it contained a gold brick. He kept this find in his possession until learning that the stage company was offering a reward of 10 percent of the value for recovery of any of the treasure stolen at Canyon Springs. Whitfield then turned the brick over to Major John R. Brennan, the founder of Rapid City, who weighed it, determined its value at $9,500, and paid Whitfield his reward money of $950 in cash.[28]

The possemen, meanwhile, weary and disgruntled after blowing their opportunity to capture some of the robbers, split up shortly after that misadventure. Many of them returned to their homes. The stage company officials, Ward and Cook, however, continued on all the way to Pierre, where they learned that a suspicious-looking individual had recently crossed the Missouri River there. They sent out his description to points along the river, and the man was quickly apprehended at Fort Thompson. He turned out to be Andy ("Red Cloud") Gouch, the gang member who stole the prostitute's valuable horse and raced to Canyon Springs to announce the approach of the treasure coach. Gouch, reported the *Black Hills Daily Times*, "was the advance guard of those who were in the wagon, keeping in advance of them most of the time, riding into all camps they saw on the route. He was seen by a great many persons, and all describe him as being just ahead of the wagon, and as one of the party."[29] "Red Cloud" cooperated with his captors, leading agents of the stage company to a cache of stolen gold buried near Pine's Springs, and was rewarded by not being prosecuted for his part in the robbery.[30]

Meanwhile, in Deadwood, other members of the Tom Price road agent gang and stage company officials were engaged in a game of cat and mouse. As recounted in the *Black Hills Pioneer* of Deadwood: "For some time past parties in this city have been in communication with the robbers, who made overtures to them to dispose of $31,000 worth of bullion, for which they were to secure one-third, or about $10,000. The parties here entered into the agreement, and a meeting was appointed in [Wes] Travis' stable on Main Street."

On Sunday, October 13, the story continued, Archie McLaughlin, a member of the Price gang, showed up at the stable. He did not have the bullion but did have $300 in currency, which he wanted to exchange for gold dust. Travis pulled a gun and demanded that McLaughlin identify his partner in this scheme. McLaughlin named Billy Mansfield and disclosed his location. Travis and some unnamed assistants then nabbed Mansfield, took the two suspects by wagon to City Creek, put nooses around their necks, and under threat of lynching extracted confessions of stagecoach robbery from them. They took the statements down in writing and then turned McLaughlin and Mansfield over to the custody of Sheriff Manning.[31]

Jesse Brown remembered it differently. Mentioning nothing about an offer proposed by the bandits, he said shotgun messenger Bill May spotted McLaughlin, a suspected road agent, when he entered the Travis stable, arrested him, and immediately took him to the sheriff's office. There he met Brown and told him of the arrest. McLaughlin had indicated his buddy Mansfield was also in town, so Brown and Bill May went out and located the other suspect in a house on Sherman Street. "We got to the door before he saw us," Brown related. "He was standing at a table drinking a glass of milk. He set the glass down quickly and reached for his gun, but he was covered before he got it. He threw up his hands as commanded and we put him in a separate cell from Archie. In the afternoon we went up to the jail and had an interview with each one separately. They both told the same story in regard to their companions, [Jack] Smith[32] and Tom Price, and where their camp was."[33]

As reported in the *Pioneer*, on the morning of October 17 "Travis and the two Mays [Bill and Jim] and a few determined men started for the neighborhood of Ten-Mile ranch, where the old camp of the robbers was, accompanied by Archie McLaughlin, who had been persuaded to show them where the gold was cached." They found the camp of the robbers, but it was deserted. The outlaw hunters were standing around, debating what to do next, when they heard a sound from the dense underbrush nearby.

Immediately all seized their weapons and saw within 30 feet two of the robbers who had come unexpectedly upon them. They were ordered to throw up their hands, instead of which they threw up their rifles and opened fire, which was returned by Travis and party. A fierce fight was then commenced and kept up without abatement for some minutes, until Tom Price, one of the robbers, fell mortally wounded by a shot in the stomach.[34] His partner was also silenced. During the melee the prisoner [McLaughlin] escaped and commenced to run away, whereupon one of the party started after him, capturing him after a short race. The wounded man [Price] was taken to Ten-Mile station and his wounds dressed and left there under guard. . . .

Later advices received are that Tom Price has died. . . . Thus one by one are the perpetrators of the robbery and murder brought to justice. The treasure will most probably be all secured.[35]

As Jesse Brown related the story, the search party consisted of Bill and Jim May, Wes Travis, and himself, with Archie McLaughlin along as a guide. When they approached a heavily wooded valley McLaughlin indicated it was the place where the gang had hidden out. The others went down to investigate while Brown remained on the hill to guard McLaughlin. When the shooting started, Brown said, "I made Archie sit down on the ground and place his arms around a tree, and I handcuffed his hands on the opposite side of the tree. Then I ran down to where the battle was going on." By the time he got there the shooting had ended. The others told him one man was lying in the thicket, badly wounded, and another, believed to be Jack Smith,[36] had disappeared. "We surrounded the brush patch as well as we could, watching in every direction, but saw no Smith. Then we went into the brush and searched back and forth but never got a glimpse of him, neither then nor since."[37] Brown said nothing about his prisoner escaping briefly and having to be run down.

Tom Price, shot up by the May posse, did not die from the effects of his gunshot wound as reported by the *Black Hills Pioneer*. Dr. L. F. Babcock, the same physician who had worked to save the life of messenger Gale Hill, ministered to Price in Deadwood. For twenty-one days "everything he ate passed through the hole in him," according to Jesse Brown,[38] but Price did recover.

The *Black Hills Times* reported Price talked freely of his capture, saying "the May-Travis party escaped death by the merest scratch, by the skin of their teeth." He said "the robbers never approached their camp, excepting upon that fatal occasion without first making a thorough reconnoiter. But upon that evening they thoughtlessly entered it and got their medicine. Price says he was struck in the shoulder at the first shot, which felled him to the ground and he blames his captors for continuing to fire upon him when he was down and had surrendered." His partner, whom he did not identify, stayed with him when he went down, firing his rifle over Price's body. "God, he made his Winchester sing!" Price was amazed that his captors were not hit, for, he said, his partner was "a dead sure shot and always cool."[39]

In February 1879 Price was fit enough to travel, and Boone May took him to Cheyenne to stand trial. May, described by the *Daily Sun* as "one of the bravest and most intrepid thief catchers and stage messengers in this region," said in an interview after his arrival that Price claimed innocence and "flattered himself that no proof could be brought against him." Asserting that he had been "shot down for the purpose of robbery and for nothing else," Price said that $630 in cash he had on his person when captured had disappeared. May called his prisoner "a shrewd rascal," adding that he believed the robber gang was still numerous, and would give further trouble. "There will have to be much new hemp before the country is rid of these pests," he predicted.[40]

At the May term of court Tom Price was convicted of highway robbery and sentenced to five years in prison. He was transferred to the Nebraska State Prison on May 27, 1879, and released February 27, 1883, after serving three years and nine months.[41]

Canyon Springs robbery suspects Archie McLaughlin and Billy Mansfield, in custody at Deadwood, were destined to share a different fate. On October 18, 1878, the two men who, under extreme duress, had admitted taking part in the stage robberies at Whoop Up Canyon and Canyon Springs, were taken from the jail at Deadwood by Jesse Brown and Jim May and conveyed to Cheyenne to stand trial. The guards, fearing enraged citizens somewhere on the direct route to Cheyenne might attempt to lynch the prisoners, chose to take their charges by stagecoach to Sidney and from there to Cheyenne by rail. Later events would prove their caution was well-founded.

On their arrival in Cheyenne on October 21, McLaughlin and Mansfield were lodged in the county jail.[42] There they remained until November 3, when officials decided, since the next term of court would not be held for several months, the two should be returned to Deadwood, where they could be tried more expeditiously. The same two guards, Jim May and Jesse Brown, took them in charge and put them on a northbound stage.

"We started back on the coach, stopped at Fort Laramie for supper, and started out again at about eight o'clock," recalled Brown.

I rode inside with the prisoners. Jim May was out with the driver. We had just entered the timber approaching the Platte river about a mile from the Fort, when that ominous cry was heard, "Halt!" The driver pulled up his team quickly but had scarcely stopped when I struck the ground. I jumped right into the arms of a big fellow who caught my gun and yanked it from me. I looked ahead and there was May standing disarmed and I was ordered to stand alongside of May. Then one of these men went to the coach door and ordered McLaughlin and Mansfield to come out, and when they did so one man took them and left the road. The other fellow told May and myself to follow up. . . . They only went a little ways when they halted and one of them picked up a rope. It commenced to dawn on me that there was going to be some dastardly work done, and it was done quickly. The rope was placed around Mansfield's neck first, and he was drawn up. Archie was next. . . . The rope went up and he was hoisted between heaven and earth and left there.[43]

That was Brown's recital of the lynching. Other accounts differed considerably in detail. Five masked men, reported one chronicler, placed McLaughlin and Mansfield on top of the coach with nooses around their necks and drove the coach under a large cottonwood tree to which they tied the ends of the ropes. Mansfield was said to have "shed tears and begged for mercy," but the "avengers of the law" ignored his pleas. McLaughlin, "made of harder stuff . . . , defied his captors and refused the opportunity to confess the whereabouts of the hidden spoils of the recent stage robberies. He said he had eight thousand dollars stashed away where it could be reached by friends, but declined to answer all questions put to him. He died cursing his lynchers" as they drove the coach off, leaving their victims dangling.[44]

Early the next morning F. L. Greene, deputy coroner at Fort Laramie, arrived at the scene and arranged for the bodies to have a decent burial. A jury was impaneled at the fort, but found that the lynchings had been performed by persons unknown, and the identities of the five masked men were never disclosed.[45]

Two other members of the gang that had pulled off the Canyon Springs robbery and murder and so incensed the citizenry were "Duck" Goodale and Al Spears, who fled together. It was their misfortune to become the particular targets of Millard F. Leech, the intrepid bounty hunter of Ogallala, Nebraska, who had recently been commissioned a deputy U.S. marshal to enhance his arrest powers.

While harboring deep suspicions regarding these two characters for some time, Leech investigated the background of Goodale and found that he was the son of a prominent resident and hotel proprietor of Atlantic, Iowa. Playing a hunch that young Goodale after the Canyon Springs holdup would head back home with his share of the loot, Leech, in collaboration with Luke Voorhees, sent an undercover detective, described in the press as "a secret agent in the employ of the Cheyenne stage line,"[46] to Atlantic with instructions to lay low and watch for the appearance of the wanted fugitive. On October 10 Goodale turned up. Telling his family he had struck it rich in the Black Hills, he turned over to his father for safekeeping a lady's gold watch and two silver watches, as well as gold bar stamped "NO. 12 DEADWOOD MINING CO. OUNCES 248.87," valued at $4,482 in its crude state. Almond Goodale, the father, seemingly accepted his son's story and placed the valuables in the vault of the Cass County Bank of Atlantic.[47]

Luke Voorhees, alerted by the detective that Goodale had indeed returned to his home base, obtained an arrest warrant and a requisition from the Wyoming governor and sent William Ward to Atlantic after Goodale. In addition to the valuable items tucked away in the bank vault, the fugitive when arrested had in his possession 986 grains of gold dust, a seven-set diamond ring, two plain gold rings, one shotgun, and two revolvers, one of which was ivory-handled.[48] When questioned by Ward about how he acquired these items, Goodale spun an unbelievable tale, saying he and several others had happened on the camp of a band of robbers who fled, leaving their stolen goods, which he and his friends had divided up.[49]

Ward and Iowa officers escorted Goodale to Des Moines, Iowa, for a preliminary hearing, and then when Iowa governor John H. Gear granted the Wyoming requisition, they returned with their prisoner to Atlantic and gave him an opportunity to meet with his parents and other relatives before being taken back to Cheyenne to face trial. On October 23 Ward, Goodale, and A. S. Churchill, an attorney Almond Goodale had engaged to represent his son, boarded a westbound train. At a stop in Council Bluffs Ward had a railroad blacksmith rivet shackles to the legs of his prisoner, but allowed him free use of his hands.

Just west of Central City, Nebraska, shortly after seven o'clock that evening, Goodale asked permission to visit the water closet, which Ward granted. As Churchill later related the story to a reporter, "Ward got up and walked with Goodale to the closet. Goodale went into the closet and Ward stepped out of the car onto the platform. Presently Ward came into the car and looked into the closet, and seeing that Goodale was not there, at once hollered with great force, 'Churchill, Duck's gone!' "[50]

Ward arrived back in Cheyenne on October 24 to face an infuriated Voorhees and explain how he had let the road agent get away. He had gone to the platform between the cars, Ward said, and watched the windows, although he thought any escape attempt by the heavily shackled prisoner through a window was highly unlikely. After waiting a couple of minutes he returned to the car and opened the water closet door to discover that Goodale had raised the sash and leaped from the train during the few minutes the window had not been under observation. Ward said he immediately notified the conductor, who stopped the train before it had run more than half a mile, and had the engineer back it up to the point where it was believed Goodale had leaped off.

In the hours following the escape he had employed fifteen men to scour the country, Ward said. He sent others to warn farmers to keep a watch over their horses, as Goodale would undoubtedly be looking for one. Goodale's trail, found about two miles from the track, indicated he was still shackled and traveling northward. The search was continued all night and the following day without success.

Before going on to Cheyenne, Ward said he had posters describing Goodale and offering a reward for his capture printed and distributed throughout the area. He believed everything was being done to recapture Goodale, and thought it "scarcely possible" the man could long elude his pursuers.[51]

From the start Ward's story was received with skepticism. It was "passing strange," opined the editor of the *Central City Courier*, that "a man weighing 165 pounds, heavily shackled, could throw himself from a car window, the train going at a rate of twenty-two miles an hour, and escape in an open country thoroughly searched over by a body of mounted men," and suggested that Goodale was not even on the train when it passed through Central City.[52]

Even before he saw a report that Goodale's shackles had been found in the water closet,[53] Luke Voorhees strongly suspected that the escape was not a result of Ward's negligence, but of outright complicity on the part of Goodale's guard, probably in collaboration with attorney Churchill. According to one newspaper report, Voorhees had concluded that Goodale simply walked off the train at Central City, or, as an alternative theory, climbed out of the water closet window to the roof of the car and rode it to another station. A rumor circulated that Ward had been paid $3,000 for allowing his prisoner to escape. Although he never publicly accused Ward of complicity in the escape, Voorhees did say his subordinate's actions were "a case of gross carelessness, if nothing else." Within a week of Ward's return to Cheyenne, Voorhees fired him.[54]

As W. H. Taylor noted, "The remarks and comments made on the subject [of Goodale's escape] by Voorhees, [Gale] Hill and some of those most interested were edifying but difficult to sort out for printing. They were not poetry by any means, and were too lurid even for blank verse."[55]

On October 28 Voorhees arrived in Atlantic to pick up the stolen property that Goodale's father had turned over to the county. Voorhees announced that the stage company was offering a reward of $700 for the recapture of Goodale and that Laramie County, Wyoming, had added another $200 to that figure.[56] Goodale was described in the company circulars as "about 27 years old, 5 feet, 11 inches in height, 180 pounds, dark hair, and when he escaped wore a thin beard of two weeks' growth."[57]

The rewards were never claimed; Thomas Jefferson ("Duck") Goodale was never captured.

One of the particular quarries of Millard Leech had slipped away, but within a week of Goodale's escape, the indefatigable detective collared another.

On his way back to Wyoming from Atlantic, after recovering Goodale's stolen goods, Voorhees stopped at Ogallala, Nebraska, Leech's home, to discuss the progress of the road agent roundup campaign. Leech told him that he had continued to track Al Spears, who escaped with Goodale after the Canyon Springs robbery. According to infor-

Mug shot of road agent Albert Spears, who was hunted down and arrested by the intrepid bounty hunter Millard F. Leech. Courtesy Elnora L. Frye, *Atlas of Wyoming Outlaws at the Territorial Penitentiary.*

mation Leech had uncovered, the two outlaws had separated at North Platte, Nebraska. Goodale had gone on to Atlantic, while Spears remained in Nebraska. Voorhees encouraged Leech to stay on the case and catch Spears with stolen goods if possible.

Within days Spears showed up in Ogallala and made the mistake of trying to unload about $500 in jewelry and $800 in gold dust in Leech's hometown. The detective quickly learned of the attempt, but before he could corner him, Spears moved on to Grand Island, Nebraska, with his stolen goods. Leech dogged his trail and caught him there in the act of disposing of the stolen valuables. "Spears made a motion to draw his gun, but Leech, who was sharply watching his movements, quickly covered him with a murderous looking revolver."[58] Spears, described in the Wyoming papers as "the brains of the outlaw gang, cunning, cool, desperate and temperate," was quoted as saying Leech had been very lucky, "for he would have shot him had not Leach [*sic*] got the drop on him."[59]

Leech brought his prisoner to Cheyenne without incident and lodged him in the county jail on November 1. There was little doubt of his guilt. Some female holdup victims who happened to be in the stage company offices that day readily identified jewelry he had tried to sell as property stolen from them. Also, the gun Spears was packing when arrested was one taken from Gale Hill after the Canyon Springs battle.[60] Spears, saying "he was tired of running around a fugitive from justice, and he did not now care whether he lived or died," confessed to taking part in the Canyon Springs robbery. He told Voorhees he had buried his share of the gold taken from the treasure coach near the barn of J. D. Firman, two miles from Wood River Station, Nebraska. Voorhees went there and found gold worth $4,000 buried three feet deep.[61]

District court was meeting that month, and officials wasted no time in bringing Spears to trial. On November 28 he pleaded guilty to murder in the second degree in the death of Hugh Campbell and was sentenced to life in prison. Described in the penitentiary records as twenty-six years of age, blue-eyed, with red hair and beard, he had two false teeth in his upper jaw.[62]

By 1878 the facilities of the territorial penitentiary at Laramie had become overloaded, and the Wyoming authorities contracted with Nebraska to incarcerate certain convicts in the Nebraska State Prison at Lincoln, and Spears was sent there to serve his life term.[63]

Commented Editor Slack of the *Cheyenne Daily Sun*: "Some of the road agents now serving a sentence in the Nebraska State Penitentiary have written to Attorney W. P. Carroll of this city requesting him to come down and *habeas corpus* them out of prison. What they need is someone to go there and cold *corpus* them. Their present punishment is altogether too light for the crimes they have committed."[64]

An Omaha, Nebraska, newspaper in December of that year reported that Gale Hill, still not recovered from the wounds he received in the battle at Canyon Springs station, had gone to Edgerton, Missouri, to spend a few weeks in recuperation, adding: "It is expected that on his return he will pay a visit to Lincoln to have a talk with Al Spears, who was recently condemned to imprisonment for life for complicity in the attack and robbery in which Hill was wounded. It is not improbable that Spears may be induced to give some information as to his confederates in the bloody affair."[65]

Whether Hill did indeed stop at the Nebraska penitentiary for a chat with Spears, the outlaw who ended up with Hill's gun and may well have been the one who shot him, is not known, nor is it known if Spears was ever "induced" to divulge information about his erstwhile cohorts to Gale Hill or anyone.

That someone was leaking that information was evident, however. Before the year ended Laramie County Sheriff Thomas Jefferson Carr, acting on a tip, went all the way to Eureka, Nevada, where on December 21 he located and arrested Charley Ross, alias James Patrick, alias Jack Campbell,[66] a principal in both the "Persimmon Bill" and Tom Price gangs.[67]

Sheriff Carr brought Ross back to Cheyenne, where he was held in the Laramie County jail, together with fellow road agents Tom Price, still recovering from the gunshot wounds he received when captured, and John H. Brown, who had been brought from the prison at Laramie to Cheyenne to testify in a trial. On April 11, 1879, Ross, Brown, and Charles Clark, a Fifth Cavalry trooper accused of murdering a fellow soldier, attempted a daring escape from the jail. As reported in the *Daily Sun*:

> The prisoners were confined in a large, spacious, well-lighted room upon the ground floor. In the center of this is an iron cage, and within this cage a large, wrought-iron box, divided off into cells, which open out into the cage. Between the doors of the cells and the bars of the cage there is a corridor, or walk, and during certain hours of the day the prisoners are allowed to come out of their cells and exercise by walking up and down this corridor....
>
> The prisoners had taken from a pair of fine boots two pieces of strap steel about four inches in length. These they had bound together with wire. With a small pen-knife blade they had by patient, hard work, cut teeth in the bands of steel and improvised a saw. With a piece of ash wood, cut from a broom-stick, a key was made which exactly fitted the lock upon the cell door. The impression of this key was obtained in a piece of soap, pressed upon the key in the hand of a prisoner who was some-

times permitted to lock up the prisoners in the evening. This wooden key was a perfect counterpart of the iron key. A rope nearly an inch in thickness was made by twisting together a lot of rags saved from the bandages of the wounded road agent, Price. . . . With the wooden key the robbers unlocked the cell door, with the saw they cut through the inch and a half bars of the outside cage, thus furnishing themselves with a crow-bar, and also cutting off their shackles.[68]

Certain unusual scurrying sounds made by the prisoners in their preparations aroused the suspicions of recently elected Sheriff George W. Draper. He and a deputy, John Martin, searched the cells and discovered the hidden tools. "The escape of Ross, Brown and Clark would have turned loose upon the community three of the worst desperadoes on the frontier," said the *Sun*. "Charley Ross and Johnny Brown are the remains of the once notorious gang of Deadwood coach robbers. . . . Several of the above named gang have been lynched, and had these two escaped, they would most likely have been hunted down and shared the same fate of McLaughlin, Mansfield or Dutch Charley."[69]

Tried and convicted of assault with intent to kill for his part in the Whoop Up robbery, Charley Ross received a twelve-year sentence, and was sent to the Nebraska State Prison.[70]

If John H. Brown and Charles Henry Borris were imprisoned without bail and without trial for seven months in an effort to extract information from them to aid in the road agent apprehension, as seems likely, the stratagem may have been successful. Any help these two may have given the authorities is not known, but the lawmen's record of success in rounding up road agents during this period is impressive.

In the days immediately following the robbery Frank McBride and the "tall, smooth-faced man," never identified, died of gunshot wounds while trying to escape, and Tom Price, badly shot up, later was convicted and sent to prison. Two suspected road agents, also unidentified, were hanged near Jenney Stockade. And in the ensuing months Archie McLaughlin, Billy Mansfield, and "Dutch Charley" were captured and lynched; Henry ("Hank") Harrington was killed soon after avoiding prosecution by turning state's evidence; Albert Spears, Charley Ross, John Irwin, and Charles Condon were con-

Sheriff Thomas Jefferson Carr of Laramie County, Wyoming, brought Charley Ross all the way back to Wyoming from Eureka, Nevada. Courtesy American Heritage Center, University of Wyoming.

victed and sentenced to long prison terms; "Reddy" McKimie, arrested and tried in Ohio, also received a lengthy prison sentence for crimes committed there; Fred Robie, Joe Minuse, and Albert Douglas were convicted and given shorter sentences; and Thomas Jefferson ("Duck") Goodale was taken into custody, escaped, but was never seen in that country again. Charles Carey, Jack Smith (Dave Black), and Tom Reed avoided capture but also disappeared from the Black Hills.

It is significant that when Brown and Borris finally stood trial in May 1879, all federal and territorial charges against Brown were dropped, and he was released. Robbery charges against Borris were also dropped, but for some reason the federal attorneys pressed the obstruction of the U.S. mails charge, and he was fined $100 and costs. After payment he, too, was released.[71] Both men wasted little time in seeking other climes.

Of particular relief to Luke Voorhees and the owners of the Cheyenne and Black Hills Stage Company was the recovery during the course of the campaign of about three-fifths of their property stolen at Canyon Springs.[72]

The robbery of the treasure coach and shootout at the Canyon Springs stage station on September 26, 1878, was one of the most dramatic events in the history of the Black Hills gold rush, and it became legendary in Wyoming, the Dakotas, and Nebraska. As late as 1914, thirty-six years after the incident, frontier veterans, led by Jim Dahlman, one-time sidekick of Scott Davis and the current mayor of Omaha, performed reenactments of the dramatic holdup and shooting in Nebraska.[73]

— 10 —

DEBACLE AT SIDNEY

*These gentry of the road know no mercy, nor can they be dissuaded
from their course, it seems, by any other than the heroic treatment —
cold lead pills.*
— Edward A. Slack in the *Cheyenne Daily Sun*, March 26, 1879

Following the great roundup of road agents in the closing months
of 1878 law officers, managers of the stage lines, and travelers to
and from the Black Hills looked forward to the coming of spring
in 1879 with high hopes that the plague of highway robberies had
passed. In a January 1879 editorial Edward A. Slack of the *Cheyenne
Daily Sun* praised the efforts of the U.S. government in the campaign
directed against the outlaws. "The pursuit of the mail robbers in
Albany county is being pushed by the United States authorities with
energy and success, and will soon rid the county of 'road agents' and
robbers," he wrote. "The United States marshal has now got nine
prisoners in the penitentiary charged with mail robbery and there are
five in the county jails of Carbon and Albany counties, against whom
charges will be preferred by the United States. It is the determination
of the U.S. Marshal and his deputies to hunt down or drive from this
region all the road agents and mail robbers now infesting the mail
routes of Wyoming. From present indications, it is safe to predict the
success of the Marshal in his efforts."[1]

But only a few weeks later Slack was having second thoughts. "The
idea which had gained ground that all the road agents were either

dead or captured appears to have been erroneous," he observed in his edition of February 12.

Slack's competitor at the *Leader*, Herman Glafcke, on March 1 quoted a letter from a Yankton, Dakota, reader, declaring that road agents had diverted their attention to the Fort Pierre route to the Black Hills, prompting Glafcke to comment, "Wyoming is at last free from the curse of Indians and road agents. Let us hope she will hereafter remain so."

In an interview for the *Sun* two weeks later James L. ("Whispering") Smith, now employed as a detective for the Union Pacific Railroad, stated that his investigations had shown that there was

> a regular cordon of robbers' roosts extending from Green River on the west to Elk Creek valley in Nebraska on the east. The gangs of train robbers, horse thieves, stage stoppers and highwaymen who infested the roads in western Nebraska and northern Wyoming of late have an organized system or line of communication more than 500 miles in length, by which they transmit news, give alarms, transfer stolen property, and elude pursuit and capture. This line extends to Fort Keogh, takes in the Fort McKinney road, Fort Fetterman and the Black Hills country. They have haunts which pass for ranches but are nothing more or less than dens for thieves. These are located at intervals throughout the country convenient for refuge. Their system is so perfect that it is almost impossible to break it up. It is dangerous to interfere with it with small bodies of men. . . . With the advent of pleasant spring weather lively times are anticipated.[2]

Perhaps motivated in part by this warning, Editor Slack composed a lengthy piece calling attention to what he called "the greatest evil with which this territory has to contend — highway robbery."

"These gentry of the road," he said, "know no mercy, nor can they be dissuaded from their course, it seems, by any other than the heroic treatment — cold lead pills. . . . Road agency must be suppressed and that immediately. Already have a few robberies occurred, which fact proves that even the extended and thorough search for road agents made last fall and winter failed to drive or scare away those who escaped capture or death. It [is] reasonably certain that these white savages will be as numerous . . . as they were last summer. . . . They must be suppressed."[3]

Meanwhile the officials of the Cheyenne and Black Hills Stage Company had been embarrassed by the fiasco of the Canyon Springs robbery. Within hours the bandits had successfully broken open the "salamander safe," which the manufacturer had claimed could not be cracked in six days. Luke Voorhees now demanded from the Cincinnati firm a better, virtually impregnable safe to protect the Black Hills treasure shipped over his stage line. What was needed, he said, was a strongbox that could not be breached in twelve hours without the use of gunpowder. The company agreed to build such a safe, pay the freight fees to Cheyenne, and accept no payment unless the product met all requirements. When the new box arrived, Voorhees hired a large, muscular blacksmith named Richardson to test it out. It took the blacksmith, using chisels and a sledgehammer, less than an hour and a half to break it open. Voorhees ordered another, stronger version, and when it was delivered Richardson cracked it in three hours and forty minutes. "This," said the *Daily Sun*, "virtually settles the question as to whether a safe can be made for use in a stage coach or wagon which can successfully resist the strength and perseverance of skillful blacksmiths to break it open. The safe that has just been smashed was one of the best and finest ever made. The safe manufacturers did their very best to make a success of their effort, but failed. The best and safest way to keep robbers away from the Black Hills treasure chest is a good and sufficient guard."[4]

Voorhees agreed, and in the following months abandoned the idea of protecting gold shipments by means of an impregnable strongbox and relied entirely for that protection on the coterie of tough, straight-shooting fighting men he had employed as shotgun messengers.

And the policy worked. Throughout the year 1879 stages carrying treasure from Deadwood went through to the safety of the railroad without interference from those scattered road agents still roaming the expanses of Dakota and Wyoming. And it followed that when the road agents lost their interest in tackling the treasure-laden coaches, assaults on stages carrying passengers also diminished dramatically. In a book published in 1880 a commentator on stagecoach travel to and from Deadwood would write that highway robbery "became unprofitable business for the road agents, and it soon became also accompanied with too great risk to pay them to follow it. The messengers became more bold, and several of the highwaymen were killed, others were captured by the sheriff and posse, so that finally the business was broken up and no further molestation occurred. . . . At present there is as much safety and security to person and property in the Black Hills as in any country on the frontier."[5]

Quietly, without publicity, the Cheyenne and Black Hills Stage Company in 1879 began routing its fortnightly shipments of gold from the mines to the Union Pacific Railroad station at Sidney, Nebraska, rather than Cheyenne. This change soon became generally known, and a news dispatch in September of that year headed "HOW BULLION IS CARRIED IN THE BLACK HILLS" appeared in papers across the country, relating the story of the Canyon Springs robbery (with some errors of fact) and describing the measures the stage company had taken to protect the treasure.

> All the bullion produced in the hills is also carried to Sidney by stage-coach, but no passengers are taken at the same time. A coach is prepared for the purpose by lining it with sheet iron to make it bullet-proof. The box containing the bullion is placed on the floor of the coach, and the whole is given in charge of six messengers, who are the bravest and most daring men to be found in the West. Four of these men, armed with carbines, which are never out of their hands, and with a whole arsenal of navy revolvers within reach, sit in the coach and keep guard over the treasure, while the fifth rides in front and the sixth behind the coach on horseback. No coach with a full complement of messengers has ever been attacked, but about a year ago, when only about twenty-five thousand dollars was being sent out in charge of three messengers, the "road agents" secured the stock keeper of one of the stations, and, firing into the stage as it came up, killed two of the messengers and wounded the other. The wounded man shot one of the robbers so that he died very soon after, but the robbers got away with the bullion. An alarm was given as soon as possible and the thieves were pursued, and one or two of them caught. All but about six thousand dollars of the bullion was recovered. A hundred men would fare hard if they were to attack the treasure coach with its present outfit and I doubt if they could capture it.[6]

The advantage Sidney held as a transfer point over Cheyenne, of course, was the matter of a savings in distance. Custer City, the southernmost mining camp in the Hills, was about fifty miles closer to the railroad than Cheyenne. This meant to travelers ten or twelve fewer hours of stagecoach hardship, a consideration not to be ignored. And Sidney, lying some 120 miles to the east of Cheyenne, was that much closer for railroad passengers coming or going in that direction.

Sidney was a much smaller community than Cheyenne, having in the late 1870s less than a third of the population of its Wyoming counterpart. Both towns had violent early-day histories, but Cheyenne, having burgeoned to a community of more than a thousand permanent residents, had outgrown to a great extent its notorious past. Sidney, on the other hand, was in many respects still a rough frontier outpost.

Jesse Brown, who had good reason to know, having been to the town many times in his job as stage messenger, observed that Sidney during these years was "one of the roughest, toughest towns along the Union Pacific line," a mecca for sure-thing gamblers, the place where the gold brick con scam was hatched. The little community "supported fifty-three saloons, and numerous dance houses of the knock down, drag out type," he said, and they all contributed to making Sidney "the gayety of the wildest town in America."[7]

An article about the town that appeared in an 1877 edition of the *New York Herald* was reprinted in the *Cheyenne Daily Sun*. While undoubtedly exaggerated, it revealed how many people viewed the town of Sidney. A *Herald* reporter, interviewing a visitor to New York City who had spent several months at Sidney, asked if the town was as rough and lawless as stories in western papers would indicate. The man replied that it was worse.

"I don't know what the papers say of it, but I know it's worse'n any language can tell. It's the orneryest [*sic*] this side of hell. There's no law an' no Sunday. Every man's his own court, an' his revolver is lawyer, judge, an' executioner — especially executioner. An' the gamblin', drinkin' and fightin' goes on all the time, day and night. You wouldn't know when Sunday comes around if you put it down in a book.

"Murders? Oh, yes, there's plenty of them, but they don't call them that. At least three a day on an average some fellow gets the worse of an argument an' is laid out. It's putty dull in town them days when somebody don't get killed. . . .

"There's funerals every day, but most of 'em are quiet like an' don't go much on style."[8]

A writer for the *Omaha Bee* in 1899 commented that early visitors to the wild communities springing up in the West had designated Cheyenne as "the roughest town in the world," but evidently, he said, these observers had never visited Sidney, for had they done so they would certainly "have located their blood curdling tales at the latter place. . . . Crime ran rampant [there] until the vigilantes took the law in their hands and did some regulating."[9]

The town was still in that state of near anarchy on March 9, 1880, when in the late afternoon the steel-walled coach "Iron Clad" rolled into Sidney. Its treasure box was loaded with four large gold bricks valued at $119,040, two smaller bars, and $1,040 in cash.[10] Guarded by five of the best messengers in the employ of the stage line, brothers Scott and Ross Davis, Boone May, Jesse Brown, and Gale Hill, the coach had made the trip from the Black Hills without incident. Now the tired messengers were anxious to turn their burden of responsibility over to the railroad and get some rest before the long journey back. A spring snowfall had resulted in muddy roads, delaying the trip down, and just as the stage and its outriders wheeled up to the express office the eastbound Union Pacific train to which the treasure was to be transferred pulled in.[11]

Messenger Captain Davis thought there was enough time to make the transfer, but Chester K. ("Chet") Allen, the freight agent, disagreed. "You are too late," he said. "You'll have to hold it over until tomorrow."

"Hold nothing," Davis protested. Turning to former Cheyenne County Sheriff Cornelius M. ("Con") McCarty,[12] who stood nearby observing this dispute, Davis pleaded his case, but McCarty declined to intervene, saying it was none of his affair. "Allen was stubborn," said Davis, "so we drove back to the stage office, unloaded the treasure and put three of our men to guard it. Allen said he would receive it next morning at 11:30 and we delivered it and got his receipt."[13]

The train was due to arrive just after noon, but when it failed to show up on time Station Agent Allen suggested they all repair to the nearby hotel for lunch. Davis hesitated. Looking at a baggage cart as it stood in the express office weighted down under its heavy golden burden, he suggested that the bullion be put back in the safe. But Allen assured him that wrestling those heavy bars around again would be unnecessary. He said he would lock up the office, and all of them would be just across the street and could keep an eye on the place. The gold would be perfectly safe.

With a paper in his pocket signed by the station agent proving that Allen had assumed responsibility for the shipment, Davis did not argue the matter further.

They all went to lunch.

After eating, Davis came out of the hotel at 12:40 to see a crowd gathering outside the express office. He heard a man say the express office had been robbed. Hurrying to the building, he found Allen sitting in a chair, his face hidden in his hands. "They got it all," he moaned. Davis saw at a glance how robbers had gotten into the office and departed with the gold through a square hole cut in the wooden floor.[14]

The express office had been constructed on pilings above the ground to put it on a level with the train platform, leaving an open space under the building where coal was stored. Going outside, Davis surveyed the ground around the building. A light snow had fallen, and knowing that a wagon would be required to move the heavy gold bars, he looked for tracks and found nothing. Convinced now that the bullion remained on the premises, he entered the space under the building and discovered how the hole in the floor had been made. At some time previous dozens of holes in the form of a square had been bored almost through the floorboards from below. The weakened square had been supported by a jack to keep it from collapsing. Then, after everyone left the room, the thieves, after only a few minutes work with chisel and hammer, opened the hole. Observing foot tracks leading from the hole in the floor to the coal pile, Davis began tearing into the coal with the help of a couple of his men.

"In a short time we struck something heavier than coal," he said. "It proved to be one of the Homestake gold bricks, then another and kept on until we had the whole shipment except the currency and the two small bricks."[15]

He and his men heaved the gold bars back up through the hole in the floor to the empty express office. Allen and McCarty were gone. The express agent had appeared on the verge of a nervous collapse and probably was in need of a fortifying drink at a nearby saloon. Davis was sitting in a chair guarding the gold when they returned. "The two stared at me as if greatly surprised," Davis continued. "I says, 'There is your gold, Allen, all except two small bars and the currency.'" Knowing that the still-missing items could have been carried off in the deep pockets of a man's bulky winter coat, Davis looked at McCarty with suspicion. He was aware that the former sheriff, owner of the Capitol Saloon and Gambling Hall, the largest establishment of its kind in Sidney, was reputed to be in league with the town's criminal elements, and he saw that the man was wearing a chinchilla coat with big pockets.[16]

At Davis's suggestion Allen locked up the bullion in the express office safe until the shotgun messengers saw it safely aboard an eastbound train. Telegrams describing the robbery were dispatched to offices of the Union Pacific Railroad at Omaha and the Pacific Express Company at Cheyenne. Soon officials descended on Sidney, among whom were General Superintendent Morsman of the Pacific Express; J. T. Clark, general manager of the Union Pacific; John M. Thurston, the railroad's legal representative; Robert Law, superintendent of the line's Mountain Division; Luke Voorhees; and an ace detective of the railroad, James L. ("Whispering") Smith.[17] Those from Cheyenne came by special train, making the 106-mile trip to Sidney in a record-setting two hours.[18]

Smith was an excellent choice to conduct an investigation. He had been a resident of Sidney and was well acquainted with all the residents there, including Chet Allen, "Con" McCarty, and others associated with the former sheriff who came under suspicion. He had also worked with Scott Davis and his crew of shotgun messengers, and before they left to return to Deadwood he talked to them at length, soliciting their opinions and suspicions with regard to the robbery. The messengers and the stagecoach company that employed them had no legal responsibility for the financial loss incurred by the robbery, as that responsibility had passed with the signing of receipt by

Allen, but Davis and his friends had a strong personal interest in seeing the thieves brought to justice.

His investigation led Smith to reach the conclusion that McCarty and Allen were involved in the scheme to steal the gold shipment, along with several shady pals of the former sheriff, Dennis L. Flannigan, alias Douglas Black, a professional gambler who had served time in an Omaha jail for theft; Patrick H. ("Patsy") Walters, another gambler who tended bar and managed McCarty's Capitol Saloon; and Thomas Ryan, a onetime McCarty deputy, now acting as county assessor.[19]

Based on strong circumstantial evidence provided by Smith, John Thurston, the Union Pacific attorney who had secured appointment as a special prosecutor to pursue the case, attempted to bring indictments against McCarty, Walters, Ryan, and Allen, but soon learned that his cause was lost from the outset. McCarty cohort Dennis Flannigan managed to get himself appointed to the grand jury, and the county judge who was to hear the case moonlighted nights as a faro dealer in McCarty's Capitol Saloon. Of course with the deck so stacked against him Thurston failed to get McCarty and his cronies indicted, and only Chester Allen, not a gang member, was held for trial.[20]

"Whispering" Smith was furious. On the night of May 24, 1880, he clashed with Patrick Walters in a Sidney saloon. After a heated verbal exchange both men went for their guns. Getting his Webley .45 in action first, Smith pumped a bullet into his adversary's abdomen and missed with a second shot. He was triggering off a third round when a slug from Walters's pistol struck Smith's Webley and glanced upward through his wrist and arm. Walters fired several more wild shots before collapsing to the floor.[21]

Fearing retaliation by other members of the McCarty gang, Smith fled to the hotel, where Scott and Ross Davis, in town for the Allen hearing, were staying. When Sheriff Robert C. ("Mose") Howard sent deputies to the hotel to arrest Smith, the Davis brothers met them at the doorway of their room and demanded to see a warrant. The deputies admitted they had none, and the messengers refused to let them in. "Ross and I disarmed them," Scott Davis said, "and told them that we would deliver Smith at the jail next morning, which we did."[22] After having his wounded arm treated, Smith surrendered to the authorities on condition that he be allowed to keep a loaded rifle in his cell until the Union Pacific got him out on bail. He also insisted on being guarded by the shotgun messengers rather than any local officers.[23]

Walters recovered from his wound, and Smith, charged with attempted murder, won acquittal on a plea of self-defense. At a trial in October a jury also found Chester Allen not guilty of complicity in the gold bullion robbery.[24]

"Whispering" Smith remained in Sidney, still trying to build a case against the members of the "Con" McCarty gang. Frustrated in his efforts, he confronted Dennis Flannigan on New Year's Eve 1880 and shot him down. Mortally wounded, Flannigan died the next day. As in the Walters shooting, a plea of self-defense won Smith's release in this case.[25]

The gold bars and currency, valued at approximately $13,000, that disappeared from the Sidney express office were never recovered, and no one was ever tried for the theft, but the officials of the Union Pacific Railroad, losing patience with the violence and skullduggery going on in the town, issued a warning to the residents in the spring of 1881: either clean up Sidney or the railroad would move its section headquarters elsewhere. Taking heed, a vigilante group took action. They posted notices about the town ordering the criminal element to move on. Those who did not comply were rounded up on the night of April 1 and thrown in the city's hoosegow. Among those locked up were former sheriff "Con" McCarty; "Patsy" Walters, almost fully recovered from the bullet wound administered by "Whispering" Smith; and a gang hanger-on named John MacDonald. As a newspaper dispatch noted, "The desperadoes are awed." A couple nights later they were awed even further when a mob dragged MacDonald from the jail and hanged him from a telegraph pole. Why this particular individual was singled out for quick execution is uncertain, but the lives of the others were spared, at least temporarily. McCarty, Walters, and the others were taken out, whipped, and run out of town under threat of immediate hanging if they returned.[26]

Apparently McCarty and his cronies never showed up in Sidney again, but Scott Davis ran into Billy Feen, one of the McCarty crowd, several years later in Chicago. Not one to mince words, Davis asked him point-blank how much McCarty realized for the two gold bricks that disappeared. Feen told him that he had been given the bricks by McCarty for disposal. At Denver, Feen and a pal named Dempsey reworked the bars, "sawing and remelting," and then peddled the gold to a fence for $1,100, and divided the money between themselves. McCarty, who, according to Feen, "engineered the job from start to finish," realized nothing from the Sidney express station robbery except the cash, which totaled a little more than $1,000.[27]

The poorly conceived and badly bungled robbery attempt at Sidney was the last real effort by outlaws to steal golden treasure as it was transported out of the Black Hills. It was only fitting that quick and decisive action by Scott Davis and the stage company's shotgun messengers foiled the plan.

Over the decade of the 1880s, until the arrival of railroads connecting the Black Hills to the outside world, the shotgun messengers continued to guard the millions of dollars in treasure flowing out of the Dakota goldfields. Well financed by the Gilmer company, under the direction of Luke Voorhees, and led by the intrepid Scott Davis, the messenger service operated flawlessly throughout these years. A routine, scrupulously adhered to, was developed and proved highly successful.

A newspaper correspondent in 1882 interviewed one of the messengers, "a handsome, intelligent, and exceedingly jolly person" (not identified by name, unfortunately), who described the operation.

The messengers were making two trips a month, usually departing about the 3rd and the 17th, in the steel-lined "Monitor" coach. Passengers were not carried — only treasure and valuable express matter. Shipments ranged in value from $150,000 to $350,000.[28] Experience had taught that the heavy "salamander safe" guaranteed no safety, and its use had been discontinued, resulting in a reduction in weight and allowing for the addition of more bullion. The gold in 150-pound bricks was simply stacked in the coach with entire dependence on the messengers for its safe passage to Sidney, "a distance of 285 miles of howling wilderness in which desperadoes once ranged in large numbers." Those guardians of the gold at this time were five in number: Scott Davis, Jesse Brown, William Sample, Ross Davis, and John Cochran. In their demeanor these fellows exhibited, said the newsman with fine alliteration, "nothing that savors of borderism, bravado, or a penchant for bluff, bluster or blood." In their dress, conversation, and action when not engaged in their profession, they were "perfect gentlemen." But as they prepared for one of their trips they presented a "decidedly formidable" appearance, each man "armed with two improved self-cocking revolvers of largest caliber, a double barreled shot gun, and . . . supplied with 160 rounds of ammunition, while six improved Winchester rifles are conveniently placed within the coach."

Trips were planned so that passage through the most dangerous locations along the road was made during daylight hours. When crossing notorious "bad spots" like Buffalo Gap and Lame Johnny Creek, broken and rocky country ideal for road agent ambush, heavily armed and mounted guards scouted several hundred yards ahead before signaling the coach to advance.

"The outfit moves with great speed, the team of six great sleek horses dashing from station to station on a dead run; the team changed in less that five minutes, the run resumed, and thus the entire distance is covered in several hours less time than is usually consumed by the regular passenger coach." Thus guarded, more than $12,000,000 in gold had been transported from Deadwood to Sidney during the past three years without interruption by road agents or any loss whatever.[29]

Following the completion of the Chicago & Northwestern Railroad to Pierre in October 1880 the route from the Black Hills to this Missouri River town became increasingly more attractive for the stage line operators. In the latter years of the decade most treasure-bearing coaches with their vigilant guards traveled this route. Then in late 1890 the Fremont, Elkhorn, & Missouri Valley Railroad (later the Chicago & Northwestern) reached Deadwood after pushing its twin bands of steel up the route of the old Sidney stage run.[30]

From that time on passengers to and from the Black Hills traveled by rail, gold from the mines went out in cars, and the turbulent, fascinating era of the Deadwood stage was over.

— II —

TRAIL'S END

The stage hold-up has become a memory in the Black Hills, and that only with people who have populated the region for a quarter of a century. It was one of the incidents of travel that became less and less frequent with the advent of civilization and was completely abolished before the present mode of travel began here. So complete has the evolution been that those who ride into the Black Hills on plush [seats] fail in appreciation of the discomforts and perils that beset the traveler of an earlier period.

— Seth Bullock in the *Black Hills Daily Pioneer-Times*,
May 3, 1902

Following the turbulent days of the assaults on the Deadwood stage and the battle to suppress the Black Hills road agents, the lives of the remarkable characters who played prominent roles in that drama and survived continued on, of course.

In 1883 Gilmer and Salisbury sold their company to Russell Thorp, who maintained it until the arrival of the railroads delegated the Deadwood stagecoach lines to romantic history. The departure of the famous stage from Cheyenne on its last run to Deadwood on February 19, 1887, was a historic occasion witnessed by a large crowd, including a reporter for the *Cheyenne Daily Tribune* who wrote: "It was like bidding adieu to an old and cherished friend, as attested by the hundreds of people this morning who filled the streets in the neighborhood."[1]

The men who had formed that memorable stagecoach enterprise, Jack Gilmer, Monroe Salisbury, and Mathewson Patrick, went on to prosperous careers.

Gilmer went on to become a major investor in mining and stagecoach enterprises from the Dakotas to California while fathering eleven children, eight sons and three daughters. When he died in 1892 he was survived by his widow and six of the children.[2]

Salisbury partnered Gilmer in establishing mail contracts in states and territories across the West. Together they purchased interests in mines near Deadwood and Lead, Dakota. Salisbury later settled in San Francisco, and devoted his energies to breeding racehorses. In the spring of 1907 he traveled across the continent to New York, seeking treatment for cancer. He died there of the disease on May 9, 1907.[3]

After terminating his interest in the Cheyenne and Black Hills Stage operation in 1878, Mathewson T. Patrick and his brother Al opened up a stage line from the Union Pacific Railroad to Fort McKinney, Fort Custer, and the Yellowstone River. He also invested in Montana mining developments. During a mining boom in northern Wyoming he and his brother ran a stage line to the diggings from Laramie. In 1881 he married Eliza Burdette, daughter of the author and critic Charles Burdette. Patrick died in 1899 at the age of sixty-five.[4]

After exemplary service as superintendent of the Cheyenne and Black Hills Stage Company, Luke Voorhees left in 1883 to establish a large cattle ranch in Wyoming. On March 9, 1888, he was appointed territorial treasurer, a position he held for more than two years. He also served as treasurer of Laramie County for four years. President Woodrow Wilson appointed him receiver of public moneys and disbursing agent of the U.S. land office at Cheyenne in 1913, and he held that office until 1922. He died in Cheyenne at the age of eighty-nine on January 16, 1925.[5]

Many of the lawmen who pursued the Black Hills road agents went on to distinguished careers.

Sheriff Nathaniel K. Boswell, who led the posse that made the big outlaw haul near Rock Creek, served four terms as top law officer of Albany County, Wyoming. During those years he was a prominent member of General David Cook's Rocky Mountain Detective Association. Among his other accomplishments, Boswell was the first to appoint women to petit and grand juries. After completion of his last term as Albany County sheriff in 1882, he bought a ranch thirty-five miles from Laramie on the Colorado border and moved there with his wife and daughter. The following year the Wyoming Stock Growers Association made him chief of detectives. He died on October 12, 1921, a few weeks short of his eighty-fifth birthday.[6]

Seth Bullock, the first sheriff of Lawrence County, Dakota Territory, and the man who chased "Reddy" McKimie all the way to Ohio, concentrated on his Black Hills business enterprises after leaving office in 1878. In addition to his hardware stores in Deadwood and Rapid City, he had a ranch on the Belle Fourche River where he raised cattle and trotting horses. In 1884 he met Theodore Roosevelt, a bespectacled young New York aristocrat who had come to a ranch in the West for his health and was enthralled by the country and the pioneer types who inhabited it. Bullock and Roosevelt took an immediate liking to each other, and the friendship formed would stand the Deadwood entrepreneur in good stead in future years. Bullock could not have imagined, however, that the likeness of his friend would one day be carved on a Black Hills mountain together with those of American greats Washington, Jefferson, and Lincoln.

In 1895 Bullock at an expenditure of $40,000 built the Bullock, a three-story, sixty-room, steam-heated hotel in Deadwood that still stands today. Probably through the influence of Roosevelt, whose meteoric political rise was well under way, Bullock in 1900 received appointment as forest supervisor for the Black Hills, said to be the first position of its kind in the country. Roosevelt, elected vice president of the United States on a ticket headed by William McKinley in 1900, moved into the White House following McKinley's assassination in 1901. He proved to be very popular and was reelected in 1904. In a nationally publicized event Seth Bullock led a delegation of cowboys to Washington in 1905 to ride in the inaugural parade. Roosevelt remembered his friend by appointing him U.S. marshal for South Dakota, a position Bullock held for several years. In 1919 Bullock was the leader in a successful campaign to change the name of a peak in the Black Hills to "Mount Roosevelt" and erect a thirty-five-foot tower to honor his old friend. That same year both men died, Roosevelt on January 6 at the age of sixty, and Bullock, seventy, on September 29.[7]

T. J. Carr of Laramie County was in his third term as sheriff during the days of battle with the Black Hills road agents. It was he who brought outlaw Charley Ross back from Eureka, Nevada, to stand trial. In addition to his service as Laramie County sheriff, Carr, during a long career as a lawman, held positions as city marshal of Cheyenne, superintendent of the Rocky Mountain Detective Association, chief of detectives for the Union Pacific Railroad, warden of the Wyoming Territorial Penitentiary, and U.S. marshal for Wyoming. In all he put in nine years as federal marshal and deputy marshal under two presidents. Married and the father of three children, he died at San Antonio, Texas, on May 11, 1916, a month before he reached the age of seventy-four.[8]

John W. Dykins, sheriff of Sweetwater County, Wyoming, whose office played a leading role in the apprehension of a number of road agents, including Bill Bevins and Dutch Charlie, turned to cattle ranching after leaving the sheriff's office. In 1884 he helped organize the Farnsworth Post of the Grand Army of the Republic in Evanston. Later he owned a large ranch near Woodruff, Utah. In 1909 he was back in Wyoming, where he was elected mayor of Evanston and held office until 1913. He then moved to California, where he died in 1921.[9]

William Henry Harrison Llewellyn, the special agent of the Department of Justice who was involved with Boone May in the "Curly" Grimes killing, went to New Mexico in 1881 to assume the position of agent for the Mescalero Apaches. The next year he took the same post at the Jicarilla Apache reservation. He began a private law practice at Las Cruces, New Mexico, in 1885 and became more involved in politics, leading to multiple elections to the New Mexico territorial and state legislatures. During the Spanish-American War, he captained Troop G of Teddy Roosevelt's Rough Rider Regiment. After ascending to the presidency Roosevelt rewarded him with appointment to the office of U.S. attorney for New Mexico. Llewellyn was seventy-five years old when he died at El Paso, Texas, in 1927.[10]

John B. Furay, the Post Office inspector who also was instrumental in bringing the power and influence of the federal government into the battle against the road agents, had a distinguished thirteen-year career in the department during which he ran down criminals from Nebraska to the Pacific coast. He served on the Omaha city council, was a member of the board of public works of that city, and, until his death in 1907 at the age of sixty-six, remained prominent in Republican political circles.[11]

The railroad detective known as "Whispering" Smith, who was a principal figure in "Lame Johnny's" demise and the convoluted story of the Sydney gold heist, continued his colorful career. In 1881 he joined Llewellyn in New Mexico as chief stock herder and chief of Indian Police at the Mescalero reservation. By 1884 he had returned north to accept employment with the Wyoming Stock Growers Association as "roving" range inspector, or detective. Leaving the association in 1888, he took up his old occupation as railroad detective, hiring on with the Denver & Rio Grande line, and later was employed as security officer for the Pleasant Valley Coal Company in Utah. As the century turned the owners and editors of the *Denver Post*, who were feuding with the celebrated gunfighter and sportsman William B. ("Bat") Masterson, sent for Smith, whose reputation as a gun wielder rivaled Masterson's, and paid him to drive Bat out of town or dispose of him in some other manner. Masterson did indeed leave town for a time soon thereafter, but he was a man who traveled a great deal, and whether his departure on this occasion was prompted by Smith's menacing presence has never been determined. Over the next years Smith became increasingly addicted to drink, and on August 26, 1914, broke, bedraggled, and dispirited, he found himself in the drunk tank of the Arapahoe County jail in Denver. Somehow he managed to obtain a quantity of lye, swallowed it, and died an agonizing death.[12]

Little is known of the later life of John Manning, who succeeded Seth Bullock as sheriff of Lawrence County, Dakota Territory, and was reelected to a two-year term in 1878. According to Black Hills historian John S. McClintock, Manning died on September 15, 1911, at the age of seventy.[13]

Daniel Nottage, sheriff of Albany County, Wyoming, assisted Dykins in the capture of Bill Bevins. After his term as sheriff he moved to Texas and by 1891 was living in Jonesboro, Arkansas, where he was employed as assistant superintendent for the Arkansas & Texas Railway, a position he held for many years.[14]

After serving as a deputy sheriff under Seth Bullock and as a deputy U.S. marshal at Deadwood, A. M. ("Cap") Willard moved to Custer, Dakota Territory, where he was elected sheriff. He homesteaded the

Slim Buttes country north of Belle Fourche with his son, Boone, named after "Cap's" pal and fellow fighting man, D. Boone May. Over the years the Willards, father and son, ranged large cattle herds over their extensive ranch land. In 1924 "Cap" Willard collaborated with Jesse Brown on *The Black Hills Trails*, an important history of the region. He died on July 22, 1921, at the age of seventy-four and was buried in Deadwood's Mount Moriah Cemetery near many other Black Hills pioneers, including "Wild Bill" Hickok and "Calamity Jane."[15]

It is noteworthy that almost all of these badge-toters, after years of hard and dangerous work on the frontier, managed to hold other responsible positions, prosper financially in their business endeavors, and survive well into their seventies and eighties. They were indeed a hardy breed.

The survival record of the legendary shotgun messengers, who, together with the tough federal agents and lawmen of Wyoming and Dakota, were responsible for bringing road agency in the Black Hills to a halt, was not as positive. A January 1899 newspaper article summarizing the messengers' later careers focused on eight: Jesse and Jim Brown, Scott and Ross Davis, Boone and Bill May, Billy Sample, and Gale Hill.

After twenty years, said the report, only Jesse Brown remained in the Hills; the others had all sought other climes.[16] After the stagecoach robbers were killed, jailed, or scattered and the messenger service was discontinued, Brown went to Sturgis in Meade County, where he opened a business, served four terms as sheriff, was elected county commissioner, and worked with his old friend "Cap" Willard in producing *The Black Hills Trails*. He lived to the ripe old age of eighty-seven, dying in 1932.[17]

According to the newspaper story, Jesse Brown and Gale Hill "never looked for trouble . . . , avoided it so far as consistent, but when it came they would stand up and shoot and be shot at without flinching."[18]

Gale Hill, it will be remembered, was the shotgun messenger severely wounded at the Canyon Springs gunfight in September 1878. He had recovered sufficiently from his wounds by 1880 to serve as a town constable at Deadwood and deputy under Sheriff Manning,[19] but reportedly died from the effects of his wounds several years later.[20]

Jesse Brown (left) and Scott Davis, famed members of the Deadwood stage treasure guards, in later life. Courtesy Wyoming State Museum.

Another messenger who met an untimely and violent death while in the service was William Rafferty, "an extra" who was killed at Deadwood on January 22, 1879, while unloading a coach. His pistol slipped from his holster, fell to the ground, and exploded. The bullet struck him, and he died from the wound.[21]

Jim Brown, who, according to the 1899 article, was even "quicker on the trigger" than Scott ("Quick Shot") Davis, died in Arizona. Bill May also breathed his last in Arizona, shot down in Tucson by a "tough" with whom he had a dispute dating back to the stagecoach troubles in Sidney, Nebraska. Ross Davis was thought to be sheep ranching in Nebraska. Only Billy Sample still worked as a messenger, employed by Wells, Fargo for a Mexican railroad.[22] "Billy Sample and Ross Davis never smelt powder during their term of service with the Cheyenne and Black Hills Stage Co., but would have stood fire."[23]

The writer of the piece had little knowledge of what became of Scott Davis and Boone May, the most celebrated of the Black Hills shotgun messengers. Davis, "the captain and bulldog fighter," was said to be traveling for a Utah commission house, and May, "a small blonde, mild-mannered and speechy [who] was on the shoot with or without provocation," had died of malaria in South America.[24]

Actually, much more is known about these two notable characters.

While at Deadwood in 1881 Scott ("Quick Shot") Davis married a twenty-one-year-old woman from Missouri named Celia Jeanette Bryant, who, like her husband, preferred her middle name better than her first, and went by Jeanette or Jennie. With the passing of the messenger service Davis and his bride moved to Salt Lake City, where he took that job with the commission house. In 1886 he went to work for the Union Pacific Railroad. His title was "general live stock agent," but actually he was "something of a free lance. One day he would be designing the construction of a stock yards on the Pacific coast and the next day he would be enroute to Texas to secure the routing on a dozen train loads of cattle."[25] He also acted as a detective and special guard for the Union Pacific when the company encountered major criminal activity on its network of roads. On assignment in this capacity he reportedly led a posse that recovered loot stolen from the railroad by an outlaw gang headed by "Red Head Mike."[26]

As a cattle war heated up in Johnson County, Wyoming, in 1890 prominent rancher William C. Irvine received death threats from "rustlers" and hired Scott Davis as his personal bodyguard.[27] He also arranged an appointment for the noted man hunter and gunman as a detective-inspector for the Wyoming Stock Growers Association. Two years later, as one of the association's chief fighting men, Davis played a prominent role in the exploding cattle war. He was a member of the "invaders" who marched on Johnson County in April 1892 with the avowed purpose of killing or driving out all the "rustlers" the association leaders believed were preying on the herds of the big ranchers. Together with other gun-handy employees of the cattlemen's association and a couple dozen imported fighting mercenaries from Texas, he participated in the remarkable daylong gun battle with rustling suspect Nate Champion in which Champion and his pal Nick Ray were both killed. Later, Davis and his comrades-in-arms were besieged at the TA Ranch and subjected to a barrage of gunfire by an aroused citizenry. Rescued by the intervention of the U.S. Army, the "invaders" were kept under arrest for several months, charged with murder, but finally gained release when Johnson County ran out of funds to continue prosecution.[28]

With their only child, a girl named Irma, born in Nebraska in 1887, Scott and Jennie Davis made their home in Salt Lake City and later Denver, where he spent the rest of his life working for the Union Pacific. He died at the age of seventy-five on April 2, 1927, and was buried at Denver.[29]

When a thirty-eight-year-old Civil War veteran named Ambrose Bierce took over as general agent of the Black Hills Placer Mining Company in the spring of 1880,[30] he employed Boone May as a messenger and a personal bodyguard. In a letter to S. B. Eaton, general counsel for the company, Bierce described May as "a man who has captured and killed more road agents and horse thieves than any man in the west; whose name is a terror to all evil-doers in the [district]; whose fidelity and trustworthiness are as famous as his courage."[31] At the time May, along with Llewellyn, was facing a murder charge for the "Curly" Grimes killing, but this did not seem to bother Bierce at all. With the macabre humor for which he would later become renowned, he added the name of his new employee on the company roster as "Boone May, murderer." Bierce, a man of great physical courage whose senses were heightened by personal danger, admired those whom he recognized as having the same attributes. He "became much attached to this placid gunman, who calmly, without boast or swagger, went about his favorite occupation of potting road agents. If [Boone May] would rather shoot somebody than not, all had to admit that his corpses were invariably those of undesirable citizens, never of the law-abiding."[32]

In an article entitled "A Sole Survivor" Bierce described seeing May in action. The two men were transporting $30,000 in gold from Deadwood to Rockerville one stormy night. Bierce was at the reins of a wagon, and May, his guard, sat beside him with his rifle in a leather scabbard on his lap. Suddenly a mounted form loomed out of the night with the highwayman's time-honored order, "Hands up!"

"With an involuntary jerk at the reins I brought my team to its haunches and reached for my revolver," Bierce said. "Quite needless: with the quickest movement that I had ever seen in anything but a cat—almost before the words were out of the horseman's mouth— May had thrown himself backward across the back of the seat, face upward, and the muzzle of his rifle was within a yard of the fellow's breast!" Bierce coyly left the rest of the story to his reader's imagination, adding only that as he wrote these lines Boone May had long since been dead and "what further occurred among the three of us there in the gloom of the forest has, I fancy, never been related [but] I am the Sole Survivor."[33] How much of this tale is based on an actual occurrence and how much has been embellished by the author's propensity for fiction is anyone's guess, but it is clear that Bierce had the greatest respect for Boone May as a fearless and expert wielder of weapons.

His superiors, however, unconvinced that the company should have a notorious gunman and accused murderer on the payroll, and dubious about Bierce's managerial judgment, sent Marcus Walker, the secretary and treasurer, to the Black Hills to investigate. Walker was dismayed by May's reputation, if not his demeanor, and so reported back to headquarters. In his own reports, Bierce vigorously defended May:

He, Walker, objected to my employing Boone May . . . , who on Tuesday last had guarded us and our coming from Rapid, whom I need almost daily to protect the company's property and claims, and carry important papers, and *shall* need to carry gold and guard it. . . . Mr. May . . . is employed by me as messenger in a kind of service in which I have not the time to risk my own life instead of his. Every mining company has to employ such men, and detective besides. . . .[34]

The man [May] whom Mr. Walker calls my "guard" he knows to be my "messenger." [He] has *never* acted as a guard except in escorting currency through a country infested with robbers and cutthroats. Mr. Walker was a little afraid of him, but he is really quite harmless if tenderly handled.[35]

Outraged by Walker's criticism of his efforts on behalf of the company, Bierce tendered his resignation on September 24, 1880.[36]

Boone May, of course, lost his job also.

Late in 1880, following his acquittal in the matter of "Curly" Grimes's death, May led a hunting expedition into the wild country on the Little Missouri River, and it proved to be a memorable experience. Among those accompanying him were Fred Willard, H. O. Alexander, and Frank Howard. Fred's brother, "Cap," joined the group later. Game was plentiful. Fred Willard and Alexander downed fifteen deer in one day. May, an experienced buffalo hunter, using his heavy 45-120 Sharps rifle, killed twenty-three of the big beasts in a stand at a place called Chalk Buttes, and before the hunt was over the party had garnered 800 buffalo hides that they sold at Stoneville (now Alzada), Montana. Later Boone May, Fred Willard, and two hunters they picked up in Stoneville, George Owens and Will Gowdy, trapped beaver in the Long Pine Hills.[37]

That spring Agent Valentine McGillycuddy of the Pine Ridge Indian Agency posted a notice in a Deadwood paper: "Chief Young Man Afraid leaves here today with a party of one hundred Oglalas for a buffalo hunt north of the Hills. He is our best chief, and I bespeak kind treatment for him and his party."[38] Seeing this, some Deadwood citizens, termed "troublesome whites" by McGillycuddy, sent a message to Boone May and his friends who were happily engaged in hunting and trapping in the same area near the Little Missouri, warning them that the agent had issued warrants for their arrest and that the Indian party was out to serve them.[39] An inflammatory dispatch from Deadwood appearing in the *Cheyenne Daily Leader* of April 4 said that the Indian party in passing Fort Meade boasted "they would take Boone May dead or alive" and reported that "a party has gone out from this city to reinforce May, who is noted as a fighter of Indians and road agents. There is a probability of trouble."[40]

That was followed six days later by a story in the *Cheyenne Daily Sun* corroborating the report that McGillycuddy had issued a warrant to be served on May by the Indians: "May has a party of seventy encamped on the north bank of the Little Missouri river and is determined to resist to death. The Indians, under Young-man-afraid-of-his horses, numbering 100, are on the south bank, having driven every white man from their side of the river. They declare they will capture May if they have to kill every one of his companions. Much feeling exists here, and a number of May's friends started out on Sunday to help him out of the trouble which will undoubtedly occur."[41]

A later dispatch said that

> the Indians turned loose by Agent McGillycuddy at Pine Ridge have got as far north as the Little Missouri River and cleaned out the camps of several hunting and trapping parties. The hunters in that country have organized into a band comprising seventy members and purpose making red angels of some of the agency pets. The agent had a warrant sworn out for the arrest of Boone May and one of the liveliest fights ever seen in the West is predicted if the Indians attempt to carry out the order. The reds have done enough harm already to justify the boys in cleaning them out and Major McGillycuddy had better recall his pets or they may be hurt.[42]

According to Agent McGillycuddy, who denied issuing arrest warrants for May or his fellow hunters,[43] "the hunting parties of Boone May and Young Man Afraid did not meet. Neither was looking for the other, and . . . the Indians returned to the Agency, having interfered with no one. . . . But for weeks the frontier was in a state of agitation."[44]

However, "Cap" Willard, who was with the Boone May party, said they were indeed attacked by a band of Indians. Although taken by surprise, the barking of a camp dog being their only warning, the hunters thoroughly defeated the Indians. At least that was the way they told the story back in Deadwood:

> One Indian charged up to where Boone was standing with a shell jammed in his rifle and he dropped his rifle, pulled his six-

shooter and the Indian fell dead near the fire. Fred Willard fired a few rounds and then ran out and caught a couple of ponies that had been used for packing and hurried them over a bank out of the firing line and returned to the fight. By this time the Indians had killed all the white men's horses excepting the two rescued by Willard . . . , but none of the hunters were injured. The Indians decided to quit the fight and withdrew carrying with them their wounded men. They left behind them six dead and one wounded Indian close up to the fire whom Boone May soon put out of his misery with a knife. There were also twenty-two dead Indian ponies on the field. May was a fatalist and after the fight was over commented on his favorite subject, stating that "A man will not die until his time comes," and in order to prove his argument said to Fred Willard, "Now that Indian shot at me twice when my gun was jammed. Now what would you call that?" Fred Willard replied, "I would call that damn poor shooting," and that ended the argument.[45]

May and party "packed up and struck out for the Hills on foot, arriving at Crook City in good order."[46]

Soon after this adventure Boone May left the Black Hills. When next heard from by his Deadwood friends he was involved in mining ventures in South America. Never far from violent action, he was said to have shot and killed an army officer, then became a hunted fugitive, but escaped, only to fall victim and die of a tropical disease.[47]

Without a doubt the later career of Wyatt Earp, who purportedly acted as shotgun messenger on a single run from Deadwood to Cheyenne in the spring of 1877, has been publicized more than any law officer, stagecoach guard, or road agent of the Deadwood stage era. His adventures as a peace officer in Dodge City, Kansas, and Tombstone, Arizona, and his later activity as a gambler, sportsman, prize-fight referee, saloon-keeper, and speculator in the western states and territories have been narrated in countless books, motion pictures, and television dramas. Earp died at Los Angeles on January 13, 1929. He was eighty years old.[48]

Paul Blum, who worked the Bismarck route, was said to have replaced one stage career with another: "After being held up on two successive runs in exactly the same place, he decided that fate and the road agents were unreasonable and betook himself to a stage from which he faced footlights and a friendly audience instead of guns and masked men."[49]

John Cochran later became a deputy sheriff at Deadwood.[50]

Gene Decker moved to Billings, Montana, where he opened a curio shop and became a newspaperman.[51]

Eugene Smith took employment on the Union Pacific Railroad as a brakeman.[52]

Clark Bigelow Stocking returned to the southwest territories of New Mexico and Arizona. While serving as a deputy sheriff and jailer of Pinal County, Arizona, in 1889, he struck an obstreperous prisoner over the head with an iron bar, fracturing his skull and nearly killing him. Arrested and charged with assault with a deadly weapon, he was convicted but pardoned by Governor John N. Irwin.[53] He spent twenty years, off and on, in the National Home for Disabled Volunteer Soldiers at Sawtelle, Los Angeles County, California, where he wrote poetry and was made poet laureate of the Los Angeles County Pioneer Society. He died on June 2, 1934, at Los Angeles. He was ninety-four years old.[54]

Other young men who undertook the dangerous and arduous task of guarding passengers, mail, and treasure from the Black Hill mines—Dick Bullock, Charley Hayes, John Lafferty, Bill Linn, Robert McReynolds, M. M. Moore, and C. A. Skinner—faded from the annals and lived their later lives in obscurity.

And what of the outlaws, the road agents who plagued the Deadwood stage for those few eventful years?

Many were killed. Bob Castello,[55] "Lame Johnny" Donahue, "Curly" Grimes, Billy Mansfield, Archie McLaughlin, Frank Towle, "Dutch Charley," Frank McBride, "Big Nose George" Parrott, and others unnamed all departed this life, either dangling from the ends of vigilante lynch ropes or from bullet wounds inflicted by messengers or lawmen.

There was a large footnote to the "Big Nose George" Parrott story, however. After the outlaw was hanged at Rawlins, a young railroad physician, Dr. John E. Osborne, took possession of the body. He removed the top of the head, examined the brain, and then replaced it and made a death mask of Parrott. He gave the skullcap to his assistant, Dr. Lillian Heath, as a memento. Taking some skin from the thighs and chest of the cadaver, he tanned it, and made the resulting leather into a pair of shoes and decorative pieces for his medical bag. Osborne was elected governor of Wyoming in 1892, and, it is said, when he took the oath of office he was wearing those shoes and standing on top of "Big Nose George."[56] The rest of Parrott's body Dr. Osborne had stuffed into a whiskey barrel and buried near his office. In 1950 workers digging a new foundation in the Rawlins business district found a barrel with a skeleton inside that lacked the top of the skull. Dr. Heath came forward with the skullcap Osborne had given her and she was using as a doorstop. It fit the skull in the barrel perfectly. As one Wyoming historian has observed, "Big Nose George Parrotte [sic] was not a man easily forgotten."[57]

Many other road agents went to prison. John Babcock, Bill Bevins, Dunc Blackburn, Joseph Boyd, "Kid" Condon, George Duncan, Frank Harris, "Laughing Sam" Hartman, John Irwin, "Reddy" Mc-Kimie, Clark Pelton, Tom Price, Charley Ross, Albert Spears, and James Wall all spent time behind bars. Although prosecuting attorneys chose to drop highway robbery charges against John H. Brown and Charles Henry Borris, these self-confessed road agents languished for seven months in the Laramie prison before finally gaining their release.

The later history of a few of the highwaymen is known.

Bill Bevins served five years and seven months of his eight-year sentence.[58] Frank Grouard saw him again at Buffalo, Wyoming, in 1886. Bevins was walking to the Black Hills and refused to take a horse or ride the stage, saying he did not want anyone to know he was coming. Evidently he was dying, for, according to Grouard, only two weeks later the one-time high-rolling gambler cashed in his chips in a Spearfish, Wyoming, hotel.[59]

The story of Bevins's old sidekick, Clark Pelton, had a less sad ending. Pelton was a model prisoner in the penitentiary at Laramie, where he served his sentence for the killing of Adolph Cuny, and on April 29, 1882, Wyoming governor John W. Hoyt pardoned him.[60] Having learned the carpenter's trade in prison, Pelton, with the help of friends, started a contracting business in Laramie. One of his first contracts, it is said, was the rebuilding of the prison's security fence. Reformed completely, the former road agent, murderer, and convict had a successful business career as contractor, merchant, rancher, and lumberman. He was seventy-one years old when he died on June 30, 1930, while fishing in his favorite creek.[61]

Samuel S. ("Laughing Sam") Hartman, who had been arrested and jailed with Pelton but was separately tried and convicted in federal court, served a little more than three years of his nine-year, eight-month sentence. After reading letters requesting a pardon for the convict submitted by the judge who had sentenced him, the district attorney who had prosecuted him, and the prison superintendent who had confined him, President Chester A. Arthur on February 3, 1882, approved that pardon, and a week later Hartman walked out of the Detroit House of Corrections a free man.[62] No more is known of his life, but perhaps he finally learned how to laugh.

Robert McKimie, "Little Reddy from Texas," who avoided being tried in Wyoming for banditry and the murder of Johnny Slaughter by taking a prison sentence for assorted crimes in his native state of Ohio, was released from the state penitentiary on May 17, 1890, returned to Highland County for a short visit, and then disappeared from the historical record.[63]

Unquestionably the outlaws who made the biggest splash after leaving the Black Hills were the members of the Joel Collins gang and especially Collins's lieutenant, Sam Bass. Because of their own ineptitude as stage robbers and the furor over the murder of Johnny Slaughter, Collins and his remaining followers — Bass, Jim Berry, Jack Davis, Tom Nixon, and Bill Potts — in the late summer of 1877 determined to depart the Black Hills. Leaving by different routes, they rendezvoused at Ogallala, Nebraska, a cow town on the South Platte River and the line of the Union Pacific Railroad. There they plotted to rob a train. On the night of September 18, 1877, they took over the office of the station agent at Big Springs, Nebraska, destroyed his telegraph equipment, and ordered him to flag down the eastbound flier. Masked and heavily armed, the six bandits boarded the train as it ground to a stop. They emptied the way safe and relieved passengers of their money and valuables. They also discovered in the express car three heavy ironclad boxes. Ripping them open with axes, they found $60,000 in brand new twenty-dollar gold eagles that was being shipped from the San Francisco mint to Wells, Fargo & Company and a bank in New York City. Delighted with their haul,[64] the bandits rode off with their loot, but Collins, despite his mask, had been recognized by several of his victims, and an intensive manhunt was soon on for the train robbers. The gang split up, heading in different directions. Cornered at Buffalo Station, Kansas, by a party of civilians and U.S. Army cavalrymen, on September 25 Collins and Potts shot it out and were both killed. On October 14 officers mortally wounded Jim Berry near Mexico, Missouri, and he died two days later. Tom Nixon evidently returned to his native Canada, and disappeared. Sam Bass and Jack Davis made it safely back to Texas, where Bass organized a new gang and made headlines and a legendary name for himself with a series of sensational stagecoach and train robberies. Texas Rangers finally waylaid him at Round Rock and mortally wounded him in a shootout. He died on July 21, 1878, his twenty-seventh birthday.[65]

Millard F. Leech, the diminutive detective and bounty hunter, spent months in pursuit of the Collins gang after the Big Springs railroad robbery, but always seemed to be one step behind and never collected any of the large rewards offered for the members. His fame as a relentless man hunter did grow apace, however. Trading on that celebrity, he ran for the office of sheriff of Keith County, Nebraska, and was elected, but served only a few months. He resigned before his term expired.[66] In 1893 he narrowly escaped death when the Chicago Limited train bound for Boston on which he was a passenger crashed crossing a bridge near Chester, Massachusetts. Fourteen passengers were killed and more than twenty severely injured, including Leech. He and his wife, Emily, had married in 1880. In later years they and their six children settled in Boulder, Colorado.[67]

The outlaw "Persimmon Bill" Chambers vanished from the Black Hills, and his later history is shrouded in mystery. One chronicler wrote erroneously that Chambers attempted a stage holdup and "failed to recognize Boone May sitting among the coach passengers and Mr. May, as the saying is, 'blew a window in him.'"[68] There is another story that one of his own gang shot Bill, and he died in Red Canyon.[69] Wyoming sheriff Malcolm Campbell believed Bill returned to his haunts in Tennessee, where he was arrested, charged with an old murder, and hung after a short trial.[70] But A. M. ("Cap") Willard believed that Chambers, "after accumulating a good deal of gold, just quit the road and went back to his old home, where he took back his real name, married, and settled down to lead a respectable life."[71]

Jack Watkins was another road agent whose later life is beclouded. In late 1879, according to the *Laramie Daily Sentinel*, he was freighting between Leadville and Gunnison in Colorado.[72] In a book published in 1890 a former inmate of the Kansas and Missouri state penitentiaries averred that he had served time with "a notorious horse thief named John Watkins," who, after putting in a three-year stretch in the Missouri pen, got another ten-year sentence in the Kansas penitentiary.[73] Whether this John Watkins was the Andrew J. ("Jack") Watkins of Wyoming notoriety is not known. The *Laramie Daily Sentinel* in 1894 reported that Watkins was by then "a well-to-do ranchman in Mexico" who had settled down and become a reputable citizen.[74]

Other than women passengers who were robbery victims, there are few feminine roles in the saga of the dangerous Black Hills stagecoach days. But stories remain of a few females whose names have been attached to some of the legendary road agents.

Maude, the mistress of Joel Collins, departed the Black Hills with her lover by one of the stagecoaches upon which the gang had been preying. Collins left her to her own devices at Sidney while he went to rejoin his gang at Ogallala and plan further criminal enterprises.[75] Maude never saw him again, for within a month he was dead. The woman reportedly returned to Texas, where she became an inmate of a Dallas brothel.[76] She may have taken the name of her former paramour, for a "Maude Collins," twenty-two years old, occupation "prostitute," was enumerated in the 1880 U.S. Census at Denton County, Texas. Two seventeen-year-old girls, also prostitutes, were listed as boarders in the dwelling. If this was indeed the "gay girl" who had bedded Joel Collins in Deadwood, she, too, had only been in her teens at the time.[77]

Much better remembered was the woman called "Calamity Jane," whose wildly unfeminine behavior and catchy moniker caught the attention of writers of late-nineteenth-century dime novelists. With the help of sensation-seeking journalists and later motion picture and television producers, they made the name "Calamity Jane" recognizable in every American household and enshrined her in the pantheon of legendary western heroes and heroines. She married multiple times and gave birth to at least one child. A sometime muleskinner, bullwhacker, camp follower, and prostitute, she performed in vaudeville shows and was featured at the 1901 Pan-American Exposition at Buffalo, New York, but her propensity to drink hard liquor and shoot up her surroundings invariably resulted in her dismissal. She died at Deadwood on August 1, 1903, of "inflammation of the bowels," and was buried at her request beside the grave of "Wild Bill" Hickok. A historian summed up her life thusly: "Jane was a coarse woman, aged early by her wild and careless life. . . . Much fiction under the guise of fact has been written about her; she was a harlot, but considerably above that calling on several counts; an alcoholic, but a genial, if rambunctious one; unruly, but not particularly lawless; filled with deviltry, but not evil. She was one of the characters who made the west the West."[78]

The life of the woman known in Deadwood as Lurline Monte Verde following the death of her lover, Archie McLaughlin, was short and tragic. When she heard that McLaughlin had been hanged, she attempted suicide by swallowing poison. She did recover, but was never the same. No longer did she captivate men with her coquettish charm. She took to the bottle and the opium pipe. Leaving Deadwood, she began an aimless tour of western boom camps. In October 1881 San Francisco police, making a routine raid on a Chinese opium den, picked her up. Near death from the ravages of drugs and alcohol, she was placed in a hospital ward. There her mind cleared for a time, and she related her story, the strange tale of Belle Siddons-Mrs. Hallett-Madame Vestal-Lurline Monte Verde. She was only forty years old when she died.[79]

After the demise of the various stage lines to Deadwood, a number of the famous coaches ended up in museums. When Agnes Wright Spring published her seminal history, *The Cheyenne and Black Hills Stage and Express Routes*, in 1948, she could account for eight in museums: five in Wyoming; one in Deadwood; one in Tacoma, Washington; and one in the Smithsonian Museum at Washington, D.C. Some of them still had pink traces of the brilliant red paint that had once distinguished the carriages and contrasted nicely with the big yellow-spoked wheels. The one in Lusk, Wyoming, was a smaller, four-horse model that had been shipped from New Hampshire around Cape

Horn and worked in California and Nevada before seeing service in the Black Hills. Bullet holes from two robberies were still visible in the Rock River, Wyoming, coach.[80]

One of the coaches was resurrected in 1893 to become a major attraction at the Columbian Exposition held at Chicago. Constructed thirty years earlier by the Abbott, Downing & Company of Concord, New Hampshire, it had been one of thirty-two coaches ordered by Louis McLane, president of the Pioneer Stage Company of California and transported from Boston by the clipper ship *General Grant* around Cape Horn, a distance of 19,000 miles. Later it was purchased by the Gilmer company for the Deadwood run. "Its battered sides, its paintless panels, its missing boot, its rusty iron, are eloquent of hard knocks," a newspaper commented. "The vicissitudes of its career are marvelous. In the day of its prosperity, glistening with new paint and varnish, bedecked with gold leaf, every strap new and shining, it traversed the most deadly mail route in the West, from Cheyenne to Deadwood via Laramie, and through a country alive with the banditti of the plains." At the Fourth of July celebration at Concord, New Hampshire, in 1895 this coach was exhibited with a sign on its side: "1863 Home Again 1895."[81]

But the Deadwood stage with the most celebrated history was the one that ended up in the nation's capital. In 1883 William F. Cody, who was organizing what would soon become famous as "Buffalo Bill's Wild West," contacted Luke Voorhees, saying he would like to purchase a stagecoach that had made the Deadwood run to use in his presentation. Voorhees found a battered old model that he offered to sell for $1,800. When Cody balked at the price, Voorhees closed the deal by assuring him this was the very same vehicle in which the famous scout had ridden not long after killing Yellow Hair. Cody bought the coach, refurbished it, and used it in a highlighted feature of his production. The "Attack on the Deadwood Stage," with painted Indians on galloping ponies charging the six-horse stagecoach as it careened around the arena amid war whoops and thundering gunfire, became a high point of the Buffalo Bill show, exciting audiences throughout the United States.[82] The feature proved as popular with European audiences when Cody took his show across the Atlantic. The showman used it to parade many heads of state and members of royal families. Among the dignitaries who rode in the

William F. ("Buffalo Bill") Cody and the Deadwood stage, a featured attraction of "Buffalo Bill's Wild West." Courtesy Denver Public Library, Western History Collection.

coach were the president of France, the child king of Spain, the German emperor, and Pope Leo XIII.[83]

A story, perhaps apocryphal as it has been reported as happening at different places on different occasions, attached to Cody and this famous coach.

In one version of the tale the mock attack was presented in a command performance at Queen Victoria's Jubilee Celebration in 1886, and riding in the coach with Cody were the ruling monarchs of Belgium, Denmark, Greece, and Saxony, as well as the English Prince of Wales, the future King Edward VII. At the completion of the performance the prince, aware of Cody's reputation for prowess as a poker player, jokingly remarked, "Colonel, you've never held four kings like these." To which Cody is said to have responded, "I've held four kings, but four kings and the Prince of Wales makes a royal flush such as no man has ever held before."[84]

In a newspaper account some years later Cody, while performing his show in Berlin, conducted into the coach Emperor Wilhelm and three kings who were visiting Germany at the time. At the completion of their ride, the emperor is reported to have remarked: "Colonel Cody, I do not suppose that this is the first time you have ever held four kings."

"No, Your Majesty," returned the quick-witted scout, "but this is the first time I ever held four kings and a royal joker at the same time."[85]

Cody almost lost possession of the coach when he and his original partner in the Wild West show, the celebrated marksman Dr. W. F. Carver, agreed to go separate ways. The division of the show property was decided, item by item, by the flip of a coin. When it came to the Deadwood stage, Cody won.[86]

The Deadwood stage survived a disaster in 1885 when Cody hired a steamboat to convey his Wild West show to New Orleans to appear in the World's Industrial and Cotton Exposition scheduled for that winter. Near Rodney Landing, Mississippi, the showboat collided with another river vessel and sank within an hour. Much equipment was lost, but the coach was saved.[87]

This famous coach with its many-faceted history is still on exhibit at the Smithsonian Museum in Washington, D.C. All the remarkable figures who made the short history of the Deadwood stage so interesting have long been gone, but this tangible remnant of that remarkable period remains for all to see.[88]

Notes

CHAPTER 1

1. Leish, *American Heritage Pictorial History of the Presidents of the United States*, 1:192–94.

2. Sabin, *Wild Men of the Wild West*, 205; *Black Hills Daily Pioneer-Times* (Deadwood), May 3, 1902.

3. Klock, *All Roads Lead to Deadwood*, 147.

4. "Bismarck to Deadwood Stage Trail," http://www.waymarking.com/waymarks/WMHG; Brown and Willard, *Black Hills Trails*, 60–61. Memorable stagecoach drivers on these routes included "Hank" Williams, "Red" Raymond, Ben Gee, George Dean, Jack Matlock, James Callahan, Frank ("Kid") Ellis, "Stuttering Dick," W. L. Bronson, and Jim Levelle, the last of whom was considered by many the best of the lot (Brown and Willard, *Black Hills Trails*, 446; Klock, *All Roads Lead to Deadwood*, 111).

5. *Black Hills Daily Pioneer-Times* (Deadwood), May 3, 1902.

6. Ibid.

7. Parker, *Gold in the Black Hills*, 46.

8. Moody, *Stagecoach West*, 302.

9. Ibid. Eleven years later, at the same pickup location, in the same month of February, the last stagecoach from Cheyenne to the Black Hills departed (Spring, *Cheyenne and Black Hills Stage and Express Routes*, 81–82).

10. Howard, *"Doc" Howard's Memoirs*, 21.

11. Spring, *Cheyenne and Black Hills Stage and Express Routes*, 82.

12. Deadwood historian Watson Parker, in his book *Gold in the Black Hills* (118–19), is in error when he asserts that the "Brown" who partnered with Frank Yates in establishing the first stagecoach route out of Cheyenne into the Black Hills was the same "Brown" who represented the Gilmer, Salisbury, and Patrick concern in the buyout.

13. Spring, *Cheyenne and Black Hills Stage and Express Routes*, 83. "Doc" Howard, who had been driving for Yates, was one who took an instant dislike to "Stuttering" Brown. He had returned from his last trip, Howard said, when "a big red-faced man walked up to the front of the stage, got up on the wagon seat and informed me that he was Brown, the new owner. I didn't like him. So I quit" (Howard, *"Doc" Howard's Memoirs*, 21).

14. Spring, *Cheyenne and Black Hills Stage and Express Routes*, 345; Moody, *Stagecoach West*, 300–301; Woods, *Wyoming Biographies*, 92–93.

15. Spring, *Cheyenne and Black Hills Stage and Express Routes*, 346.

16. Ibid., 352–53.

17. Woods, *Wyoming Biographies*, 149–50.

18. Ibid., 190–91; Voorhees, *Personal Recollections*, 23–24.

19. Voorhees, *Personal Recollections*, 23–24; Moody, *Stagecoach West*, 301–303; Spring, *Cheyenne and Black Hills Stage and Express Routes*, 359; Fifer, *Bad Boys of the Black Hills*, 6–7.

20. Fifer, *Bad Boys of the Black Hills*, 6–7.

21. Klock, *All Roads Lead to Deadwood*, 28–29.

22. Voorhees, *Personal Recollections*, 33.

23. Parker, *Gold in the Black Hills*, 114.

24. Fifer, *Bad Boys of the Black Hills*, 6; Thorp, "Cheyenne to Deadwood Stage," 25.

25. Fred W. Schwartze was the operator of the Pole Creek Ranch, which provided "meals at all hours" and a two-story "hotel" with lodging arrangements for travelers. He was assisted by his daughter, Minna, who later went into show business. In 1904 Minna married a young newspaperman named Franklin P. Adams, who became a well-known columnist, member of the famous Algonquin Round Table, and radio personality (Spring, *Cheyenne and Black Hills Stage and Express Routes*, 98–99).

26. In June 1876 the company moved its station from Chug Springs to Bordeaux, John Hunton's ranch (Spring, *Cheyenne and Black Hills Stage and Express Routes*, 107).

27. Ibid., 98–110. The stagecoach stop at Three-Mile was originally a "hog ranch" featuring "sporting women" kept by the manager, John Owens, for the entertainment of soldiers from nearby Fort Laramie, cowboys, and freighters. Owens, slender, handsome, and always well groomed and tailored, was a deadly gunman and professional gambler who later held a number of law enforcement posts, including the office of Weston County, Wyoming, sheriff (DeArment, *Deadly Dozen*, Vol. 2, 71–93).

28. Spring, *Cheyenne and Black Hills Stage and Express Routes*, 114–22.

29. Taylor, "In the Days of the Deadwood Treasure Coach," 553.

30. Spring, *Cheyenne and Black Hills Stage and Express Routes*, 123. Bowman, a tough and courageous character, was often deputized to assist in the pursuit of the road agents who later plagued the stage line. In September 1879 he sold his Hat Creek property, including 200 acres of fine ranch under fence, buildings, corral, and four hundred head of cattle, for about $10,000 and moved with his bride to Gunnison, Colorado, where he was elected sheriff in 1883 (ibid.).

31. A man named McFarland and his wife, "Madam Bulldog," were the original owners of the Bulldog Ranch. The place got its name from the bulldogs she kept to prevent passing freighters from lassoing her chickens with their bullwhips. Legend has it that she once prepared a meal for a traveler who left a generous $20 piece in payment and later turned out to be the outlaw Sam Bass. The ranch was later run by another formidable female, a

large woman of explosive temperament named Madame Erb. She was said to weigh an eighth of a ton but set a good table for travelers. Once, when the redoubtable shotgun messenger and law officer Gale Hill attempted to arrest her on a charge of bigamy, she ran him off with a "three-foot six shooter" (Klock, *All Roads Lead to Leadville*, 132; Parker, *Deadwood*, 195–96).

32. Spring, *Cheyenne and Black Hills Stage and Express Routes*, 123–27.

33. Ibid., 128–29.

34. Moody, *Stagecoach West*, 303.

35. Mahnken, "Sidney–Black Hills Trail," 218.

36. Ibid.; Spring, *Cheyenne and Black Hills Stage and Express Routes*, 146.

37. Moody, *Stagecoach West*, 304–305.

38. Brown and Willard, *Black Hills Trails*, 460.

39. Spring, *Cheyenne and Black Hills Stage and Express Routes*, 157; Hedron, *Fort Laramie in 1876*, 140.

40. Spring, *Cheyenne and Black Hills Stage and Express Routes*, 161. That first coach carried nine passengers, eight men and one woman. Passengers in a second coach, arriving shortly afterward, included two women and a child (Klock, *All Roads Lead to Deadwood*, 28).

41. Parker, *Gold in the Black Hills*, 119.

42. Moody, *Stagecoach West*, 306; Spring, *Cheyenne and Black Hills Stage and Express Routes*, 195–96. The toll bridge across the bothersome North Platte was constructed by experienced bridge-builder Henry T. Clarke and opened for public use on May 10, 1876. About 2,000 feet in length, the sixty-one-span truss bridge "was a masterpiece of solid construction . . . , and it withstood heavy loads, ice, and floods for twenty-five years." Paradoxically, the first party to cross the bridge was a group of forty-five men not heading for the Hills, but returning in disgust from them (Mahnken, "Sidney–Black Hills Trail," 211, 214).

43. Mahnken, "Sidney–Black Hills Trail," 216–17.

44. *Laramie Daily Sentinel*, July 16, 1877. Oddly the company charged passengers $50 to travel from Cheyenne to Deadwood, and only $30 for the reverse trip (ibid., August 7, 1877).

45. Shippers of bullion to New York via the railroad were charged 1.5 percent, or $15 for every $1,000 of valuation. The stage company retained 1 percent and the Union Pacific Railroad the balance. In later years, when treasure shipments, routinely made twice a month, reached values as high as $2,000, the stage company grossed $200 a trip (Ingham, *Digging Gold among the Rockies*, 219).

46. Parker, *Deadwood*, 96.

47. Kellar, *Seth Bullock*, 160.

CHAPTER 2

1. Miller, *Sam Bass & Gang*, 35–36; Rosa and Kemp, *Rowdy Joe Lowe*, 104–106.

2. Hogg, *Authentic History of Sam Bass and His Gang*, 9–10.

3. Miller, *Sam Bass & Gang*, 42.

4. Ibid., 43.

5. Horan and Sann, *Pictorial History of the Wild West*, 87.

6. Sorenson, *Hands Up!* 48.

7. Martin, *Sketch of Sam Bass*, 15.

8. A "Maude Collins," twenty-two years old, occupation "prostitute," was enumerated in the 1880 U.S. Census at Denton County, Texas. Two seventeen-year-old girls, also prostitutes, were listed as boarders in her dwelling. If this was indeed the "gay girl" who had been the paramour of Joel Collins in Deadwood, she, too, had only been in her teens at the time (1880 U.S. Census, Denton County, Texas; Miller, *Sam Bass & Gang*, 319).

9. For some reason Ramon Adams, ordinarily a stickler for accuracy, insisted on spelling this name "McKemie" (*Six Guns and Saddle Leather*) or "McKemmie" (*Burs Under the Saddle* and *More Burs Under the Saddle*). The spelling here is that used by J. M. Bridwell in his 1878 sketch, *Life and Adventures of Robert McKimie*.

10. Bridwell, *Life and Adventures of Robert McKimie*, 3–5; *Laramie Daily Sentinel*, February 27, 1878.

11. Bridwell, *Life and Adventures of Robert McKimie*, 5. According to another writer, McKimie, before coming to Deadwood, had been involved in at least four fatal shooting scrapes in Texas and Utah (Carroll, "Clark Pelton," 18).

12. Fifer, *Bad Boys of the Black Hills*, 62.

13. Miller, *Sam Bass & Gang*, 50.

14. Reprinted in Horan and Sann, *Pictorial History of the Wild West*, 85.

15. *Cheyenne Daily Leader*, October 25, 1878; O'Neal, *Cheyenne*, 55.

16. *Cheyenne Daily Leader*, March 27, 1877; *Cheyenne Daily Sun*, March 27, 1877; *Laramie Daily Sentinel*, March 27, 1877. "It is the general opinion," the Laramie paper stated in a later edition (March 30, 1877), "that the men who fired on the Black Hills Stage near Deadwood were novices in the highway robbery line and probably tramps."

17. *Cheyenne Daily Leader*, March 27, 1877.

18. Miller, *Sam Bass & Gang*, 52.

19. *Cheyenne Daily Leader*, March 27, 1877.

20. Brown and Willard, *Black Hills Trails*, 247. Frank Towle would naturally come under suspicion as he was a rascal well known to Bullock and other law enforcement officers. A story about him was indicative of the man's character. When, "robbery bent," he had approached the Powder River ranch of John R. Smith, a man who had reputedly grown wealthy from beef sales to the military, Smith divined the outlaw's intent and put a bullet in him. Smith's wife nursed Towle to recovery, but when he could ride the bandit showed his gratitude by stealing Smith's horses (Flannery, *John Hunton's Diary*, 210). A "K. F. Towle" was a member of the Deadwood miners' court jury that acquitted Jack McCall for the murder of "Wild Bill" Hickok prior to McCall's conviction and execution in Yankton (Rosa, *They Called Him Wild Bill*, 315),

and some historians have suggested that this was Frank Towle, the notorious outlaw.

21. *Cheyenne Daily Sun*, April 5, 1877.

22. "Along the Cheyenne-Deadwood Stage Trail," http://userpages.aug.com/bdobson/deadwood.html; Spring, *Cheyenne and Black Hills Stage and Express Routes*, 191. No doubt the shock of Johnny's death contributed to the sudden passing of his mother, who died on April 29, only a month later, at the age of fifty-four (Spring, *Cheyenne and Black Hills Stage and Express Routes*, 191).

23. Edward Archibald Slack, born in 1842 at Oswego, New York, was a Civil War veteran who arrived in Wyoming in 1868, mined at South Pass, and ran a sawmill before going into the newspaper business. He published the *South Pass News* and the *Laramie Daily Independent* before taking control of the *Cheyenne Daily Sun* in 1875. Twenty years later he bought his competition paper, the *Cheyenne Daily Leader*. He died on March 23, 1907 (Woods, *Wyoming Biographies*, 171–72). It was reported that in Deadwood, "Luke Voorhees, manager of the line, nailed Johnny Slaughter's bullet-ridden [*sic*] vest to the door of the stage station and began to enroll vigilantes from among the hold-up victims" (Jahns, *Frontier World of Doc Holliday*, 81).

24. *Cheyenne Daily Sun*, April 5, 1877.

25. *Cheyenne Daily Leader*, June 3, 1877. This was an early robbery attempt by the newly formed Hat Creek gang led by Duncan Blackburn. See chapter 3.

26. *Galveston (Texas) Daily News*, July 24, 1878.

27. Hogg, *Authentic History of Sam Bass and His Gang*, 36–42.

CHAPTER 3

1. Root and Connelley, *Overland Stage to California*, 60.

2. Ayres, "After Big Game with Packs." The reference was to Joseph Alfred ("Jack") Slade, district superintendent of the Overland Stage Company more than a decade earlier, who by his fearlessness and cold-blooded efficiency intimidated the outlaw gangs preying on the line. Slade left a deep impression on all who ever knew him, including Mark Twain, who wrote a vivid description of him in *Roughing It*.

3. U.S. Census: Kinsman, Ohio, 1850, 1860, 1870; Fremont, Nebraska, 1860, 1870; Deadwood, Dakota, 1880; Salt Lake City, Utah, 1900; Denver, Colorado, 1910; Brown and Willard, *Black Hills Trails*, 522; McClintock, *Pioneer Days in the Black Hills*, 291; Spring, *Cheyenne and Black Hills Stage and Express Routes*, 344. Author Joe Koller, in his 1971 article "Saga of Quickshot Davis" (30), and several other sources give the year of Davis's birth as 1854, but the Census records consistently show he was born three years earlier. Jesse Brown and A. M. Willard knew Davis well, but were wrong in stating in their book *The Black Hills Trails* that Scott was only two when his father died and his mother then married R. W. Hazen and moved to Nebraska. James Davis, the father of Scott and Ross, was still alive at the age of seventy and

living at Kinsman, Ohio, with his wife, Sarah, and Ruben W. Hazen was living at Fremont, Nebraska, with his wife, Harriet, as late as 1870 (U.S. Census, 1860, 1870, 1880). Although John McClintock was one of the few writers correctly citing the year of Scott's birth, he erred in saying the family moved to Nebraska in 1858 and the lad left home at the age of fifteen, or in 1866 (*Pioneer Days in the Black Hills*, 291). In the U.S. Census of 1870 Scott Davis, eighteen years old, was enumerated at Fremont, Dodge County, Nebraska, working as a farmhand.

4. Census takers in 1860 enumerated the boys in both the James Davis Ohio household and the Nebraska home of Ruben Hazen.

5. U.S. Census, Lawrence County, Dakota Territory, 1880.

6. U.S. Census, Bourbon County, Kansas, 1860; Hockett, "Boone May."

7. Hansen, "Boone May," 19.

8. Johnson, *Happy as a Big Sunflower*, 163.

9. Root and Connelley, *Overland Stage to California*, 60.

10. Fifer, *Bad Boys of the Black Hills*, 54.

11. Reprinted in the *Lafayette (Louisiana) Advertiser*, June 4, 1890.

12. Spring, *Cheyenne and Black Hills Stage and Express Routes*, 342; Brown and Willard, *Black Hills Trails*, 15–20; McClintock, *Pioneer Days in the Black Hills*, 290–91.

13. Spring, *Cheyenne and Black Hills Stage and Express Routes*, 342.

14. Galen Elliott Hill was the son of Elizabeth May Hill, sister of the May boys' father, Samuel (Fred T. May to Sharon Cunningham, July 12, 2006).

15. Spring, *Cheyenne and Black Hills Stage and Express Routes*, 347; U.S. Census, Lawrence County, Dakota Territory, 1880; McClintock, *Pioneer Days in the Black Hills*, 297.

16. Brown and Willard, *Black Hills Trails*, 56–57.

17. Ibid., 48, 446; Bennett, *Old Deadwood Days*, 85–87; Spring, *Cheyenne and Black Hills Stage and Express Routes*, 188, 344; Casey, *Black Hills*, 237. Historians still debate whether Wyatt Earp, one of the most controversial characters of western history, did indeed serve as a shotgun messenger on a stagecoach run from Deadwood to Cheyenne in June 1877, as claimed by Stuart N. Lake in his hugely successful biography (*Wyatt Earp*, 162–63). Many students of the Deadwood period and Wyatt Earp's career have accepted this account, but Deadwood historian Watson Parker states emphatically that the story is "totally fallacious" (Parker, *Gold in the Black Hills*, 120). For an analysis of the dispute, see DeArment, "Another Wyatt Earp Tale— Myth or Fact?"

18. Brown and Willard, *Black Hills Trails*, 446.

19. Blum later became an actor. Bennett, *Old Deadwood Days*, 86.

20. *Colorado Banner* (Boulder), July 26, 1877.

21. *Cheyenne Daily Leader*, November 24, 1877. Another noted character on the wagon train taking Blackburn to Deadwood was Tom Mulqueen, a notorious gunman-gambler (ibid.).

22. Secrest, *I Buried Hickok*, 148.

23. *Cheyenne Daily Leader*, November 24, 1877; Wyoming Territorial Convict Register, 1873–1878, cited in Frye, *Atlas of Wyoming Outlaws*, 48–49.

24. Young, *Hard Knocks*, 206.

25. Bronson, *Red-Blooded*, 73. The nephew of famed abolitionist Henry Ward Beecher, Edgar Beecher Bronson (1856–1917) left his job as a reporter for the *New York Tribune* in 1877 to seek his fortune in the West. He ranched in Nebraska and west Texas but spent one year in Wyoming, where he met colorful stagecoach drivers and messengers like Gene Barnett, Boone May, and C. B. Stocking. In books he later authored (*The Red Blooded* [1910] and *The Vanguard* [1914]) he recounted some of the tales they told, embellishing them with details drawn from his own fertile imagination.

26. U.S. Census, Albany County, Wyoming Territory, taken June 30, 1870.

27. *Laramie Daily Sentinel*, November 27, 1871.

28. Ibid.

29. Burroughs, *Where the Old West Stayed Young*, 12.

30. *Hillsboro (Ohio) Gazette*, December 12, 1878, quoted in Bridwell, *Life and Adventures of Robert McKimie*, 53–54.

31. Yost, *Boss Cowman*, 48, 303. Age had warped Lemmon's memory a trifle; he remembered the name of the gunman as "Watson," but he clearly meant "Watkins."

32. Pence, *Boswell*, 90–92; Gorzalka, *Wyoming's Territorial Sheriffs*, 105–106. The historian Hubert Howe Bancroft, in his *History of Nevada, Colorado and Wyoming* (759), said that "Jack Watkins, a much dreaded desperado, was arrested by Boswell when no one else would attempt it."

33. *Laramie Daily Sentinel*, October 5, 1871.

34. Ibid.

35. Ibid., November 7, 14, 15, 1871; *Laramie Daily Independent*, September 14, 1872.

36. *Laramie Daily Sentinel*, November 27, 1871.

37. Quoted in Beery, *Sinners & Saints*, 34.

38. Frye, *Atlas of Wyoming Outlaws*, 28.

39. *Laramie Daily Sentinel*, May 24, 1875; Gorzalka, *Wyoming's Territorial Sheriffs*, 118–19; Pence, *Boswell*, 96–97.

40. *Laramie Daily Sentinel*, May 24, 1875; Pence, *Boswell*, 97. Thirty years later a black cowboy named Nat Love wrote a garbled account of the day's happenings. He said he and several companions rode into Laramie just as "the notorious Jack Watkins . . . , who was probably the most desperate criminal that was ever placed behind prison bars," escaped (Love, *Life and Adventures of Nat Love*).

41. *Laramie Daily Sentinel*, August 14, 1875; Frye, *Atlas of Wyoming Outlaws*, 28.

42. *Laramie Daily Sentinel*, May 24, 1875.

43. Ibid., September 1, 1875.

44. Ibid., September 5, 1875.

45. *Golden (Colorado) Weekly Globe*, August 19, 1876.

46. Frye, *Atlas of Wyoming Outlaws*, 43.

47. Quoted in DeBarthe, *Life and Adventures of Frank Grouard*, 60–61. The *Cheyenne Daily Leader* of July 10, 1877, said that once "a wealthy and honored citizen in Montana," Bevins was "led astray by wily gamblers [and] soon sunk from his high estate, and became a drunken, degraded ruffian."

48. Cody, *Life of Hon. William F. Cody*, 236–38.

49. Ibid., 241; Russell, *Lives and Legends of Buffalo Bill*, 117–18; *Colorado Banner* (Boulder), July 26, 1877.

50. This was the same Robert Foote who had a store in Buffalo, Wyoming, in 1892 at the time of the famous Johnson County War. He was a staunch supporter of the small ranchers in their fight with the big cattlemen, and his name allegedly appeared on the "death list" the invaders carried with them in their march on Buffalo (DeArment, *Alias Frank Canton*, 128–29).

51. DeBarthe, *Life and Adventures of Frank Grouard*, 60–61.

52. Frye, *Atlas of Wyoming Outlaws*, 34. Lessman served his full sentence. Several months after his release federal warrants were issued for his arrest on charges of stealing U.S. Army horses and mules from Fort McKinney, but he was never captured (ibid.).

53. *Laramie Daily Sentinel*, February 8, 1877.

54. Carroll, "Clark Pelton," 16.

55. Ibid.; *Cheyenne Daily Sun*, May 27, 1879.

56. *Laramie Daily Sentinel*; *Cheyenne Daily Sun*, April 5, 1877; Carroll, "Clark Pelton," 17.

57. *Laramie Daily Sentinel*, April 26, 1877.

58. *Cheyenne Daily Sun*, June 9, 1877.

59. Ibid., June 10, 1877; *Cheyenne Daily Leader*, June 10, 1877.

60. *Cheyenne Daily Leader*, June 15, 1877; *Cheyenne Daily Sun*, June 15, 1877; *Chicago Inter-Ocean*, June 15, 1877; *Laramie Daily Sentinel*, June 15, 1877. Although initial newspaper accounts of this robbery said the bandits got nothing for their trouble, a later edition of the *Laramie Daily Sentinel* (June 20, 1877) reported that the Cheyenne firm of Smith Brothers lost $300 in the holdup.

61. *Cheyenne Daily Sun*, June 15, 1877.

62. Traveling the road in June 1879 Rolf Johnson noted in his journal: "Paid a visit to the famous underground stables [that] used to be the head-quarters of Dunk [*sic*] Blackburn's gang of road agents and horse thieves." The "stable," he said, was "nothing but a cave dug in the bank of the creek and hidden by a thick growth of underbrush," but it was "a rendezvous of the outlaws" (Johnson, *Happy as a Big Sunflower*, 165).

63. Frye, *Atlas of Wyoming Outlaws*, 49.

64. Young, *Hard Knocks*, 198–200.

65. An example of the misinformation that filled the newspapers and confused readers as to the identity of the outlaws then and later is this piece from

the *Laramie Daily Sentinel* of August 25, 1877, quoting "Cherokee Bob," a supposedly knowledgeable frontiersman: "Webster's real name is Stewart. He came from Indiana to the mountains. When in New Mexico, he killed 'Coal Oil Jimmey' and another man for $1,000 reward. . . . When he did this, he was one of the gang himself. . . . [He] is lame in the right leg. Blackburn's real name is J. S. Pelton. He [has a] full red face and whiskers and looks in expression as though he would kill a man for a dollar."

66. *Cheyenne Daily Leader*, June 3, 1877.

67. Ibid., June 27, 28, 1877; *Cheyenne Daily Sun*, June 28, 1877; *Colorado Banner* (Boulder), July 26, 1877; *Fort Smith (Arkansas) Weekly Elevator*, August 8, 1877.

68. A story by "the Denver Correspondent of the *St. Louis Republican*," one of the passengers, was reprinted in the *Indianapolis Sentinel*, July 9, 1877.

69. *Black Hills Weekly Pioneer* (Deadwood), June 30, 1877.

70. *Indianapolis Daily Sentinel*, July 7, 1897.

71. Ibid. This "J. H. Holliday" was not the notorious gambler and gunman John Henry ("Doc") Holliday, who also spent some time in the Black Hills at this time, but Joseph H. Holliday, a salesman for a St. Louis firm (Tanner, *Doc Holliday*, 262; Silva, *Wyatt Earp*, 415).

72. *Colorado Banner* (Boulder), July 26, 1877.

73. *Indianapolis Sentinel*, July 9, 1877.

74. Ibid.

75. Ibid. The *Cheyenne Daily Leader* of June 28, 1877, estimated the "knights of the road" got away with about $12,000, $10,000 from the treasure box and $2,000 from the passengers.

76. *Indianapolis Sentinel*, July 9, 1877.

77. *Colorado Banner* (Boulder), July 26, 1877.

78. *Cheyenne Daily Leader*, July 8, 1877. Bill Bevins, according to this story, was the "captain of the Hat Creek gang" and the leader of the band that had killed Johnny Slaughter.

79. *Colorado Banner* (Boulder), July 26, 1877.

80. *Cheyenne Daily Leader*, June 28, 1877.

81. Flannery, *John Hunton's Diary*, 233.

82. *New Hampshire Sentinel* (Keene), August 9, 1877, quoting the *Omaha (Nebraska) Republican*.

83. *Laramie Daily Sentinel*, July 2, 1877; Carroll, "Clark Pelton," 18.

84. This sounds like the boasting of Bill Bevins, who was an experienced jail-breaker.

85. The *Cheyenne Daily Sun* (January 16, 1878) would later say "the booty obtained on that occasion was about $14,000 — the biggest haul made by the road agents at any time during the period when those highwaymen were intoxicated with frequent successes in their peculiar line of business."

86. *New Hampshire Sentinel* (Keene), August 9, 1877, quoting the *Omaha (Nebraska) Republican*. The assertion that his gang was divided into parts

working different sections of the road was nothing but Blackburn bombast. There were other road agent gangs at work in the Black Hills, but they were not affiliated.

87. *Cheyenne Daily Sun*, June 30, 1877.

88. *Cheyenne Daily Leader*, July 31, 1877.

89. *Trenton (New Jersey) State Gazette*, June 30, 1877.

90. *Laramie Daily Sentinel*, June 28, 1877.

91. *Cheyenne Daily Leader*, June 29, 1877.

92. Born in Hamburg, Germany, in 1840, Herman Glafcke came to the United States in 1857 and served in the Union army during the Civil War. In 1870 President Grant appointed him secretary of Wyoming Territory, a post he held for three years. He was postmaster at Cheyenne from 1873 to 1881. Concurrently with holding these positions, he published the *Cheyenne Daily Leader* from 1870 to 1881. At the time of his death, on March 25, 1912, he was deputy internal revenue collector for the district of Wyoming and Colorado (Woods, *Wyoming Biographies*, 93–94).

93. *Cheyenne Daily Leader*, July 1, 1877.

94. *Black Hills Weekly Pioneer* (Deadwood), June 30, 1877.

95. Fort Laramie Post Return, June 1877.

CHAPTER 4

1. *Cheyenne Daily Leader*, July 7, 1877.

2. Blackburn and Wall later claimed "that 'Reddy' and the woman robbed each of them of about $2,500 and took $6,000 from the other two men" (*Cheyenne Daily Sun*, January 16, 1878).

3. *Cheyenne Daily Leader*, January 30, 1878; Bridwell, *Life and Adventures of Robert McKimie*, 8; Carroll, "Clark Pelton," 19.

4. *Cheyenne Daily Sun*, July 10, 11, 15, 1877; *Cheyenne Daily Leader*, July 10, 15, 1877; *Laramie Daily Sentinel*, July 14, 1877.

5. *Cheyenne Daily Sun*, July 15, 1877; *Laramie Daily Sentinel*, July 12, 1877; Bancroft, *History of Nevada, Colorado and Wyoming*, 759; *Cheyenne Daily Leader*, July 15, 1877. Bevins's companions, Barker and Warmoth, after a six-mile chase and gun battle, were taken and held on a charge of resisting arrest (*Cheyenne Daily Sun*, July 11, 1877; Gorzalka, *Wyoming's Territorial Sheriffs*, 125–26).

6. The Lieninger Patent shackle, manufactured in Reno, Nevada, consisted of "two heavy pieces of polished steel fitted together so as to closely encircle the leg, locking in the most ingenious manner." This "stock" rested on a framework fastened to the prisoner's boot heel. "A man may walk in this shackle, but should he attempt to run, the 'stock' presses down upon the ankle, inflicting such intense pain as to throw the prisoner to the ground." This "curious piece of mechanism" was designed so that if the frame became broken, the sharpened metal would "fall upon the ankle joint, rendering locomotion absolutely impossible" (*Laramie Daily Sentinel*, July 14, 1877).

7. Frye, *Atlas of Wyoming Outlaws*, 43–44. On July 25 Bevins and another prisoner, J. C. ("Cayuse") Reynolds, "the Oregon horse thief," were thwarted by officers in an attempted jailbreak. "Extra precautions will now be taken. These desperadoes will be heavily manacled and an extra guard put on them from now till court term" (*Laramie Daily Sentinel*, July 26, 1877). In August District Court Judge Jacob B. Blair ordered him back to prison to serve out his sentence. The *Laramie Daily Sentinel* (August 6, 1877) observed that since breaking jail, Bevins had "amused himself in stage robbing" and had "declared he would die before he would go to the penitentiary, but he didn't."

8. The name of "Webster's" companion was given as "Duncan McDonald" rather than Blackburn in early reports (*Cheyenne Daily Sun*, July 24, 1877).

9. Fort Laramie Post Return, June 1877.

10. Report of Deputy Hayes to Sheriff Carr dated July 23, 1877, and reprinted in the *Cheyenne Daily Sun*, May 28, 1879. Jesse Brown and "Cap" Willard, who evidently had a low opinion of Hayes because of the botched arrest at the Six-Mile Ranch resulting in the death of their friend, Adolph Cuny, said that the outlaws had a "running fight" with the marshal, who "was obliged to flee and save himself" (Brown and Willard, *Black Hills Trails*, 260–61), but Hayes made no mention of this in his report.

11. *Cheyenne Daily Leader*, July 28, 1877; Engebretson, *Empty Saddles*, 59–60.

12. *Laramie Daily Sentinel*, August 22, 1877; *Cheyenne Daily Leader*, August 22, 1877; *Black Hills Daily Times* (Deadwood), August 20, 1877; Engebretson, *Empty Saddles*, 60; Carroll, "Clark Pelton," 20.

13. *Laramie Daily Sentinel*, August 27 1877; *Cheyenne Daily Leader*, August 23, 1877; *Helena (Montana) Independent*, August 28, 1877; *Trenton (New Jersey) State Gazette*, August 27, 1877; Brown and Willard, *Black Hills Trails*, 258–59.

14. Coursey, *Beautiful Black Hills*, 143–44.

15. *Cheyenne Daily Leader*, September 29, 1877.

16. Ibid. Carter P. Johnson, a sergeant stationed at Fort Laramie during this period, said that the two soldiers, members of F Company, Third U.S. Cavalry, were tried by court-martial, convicted, and sent to the penitentiary for their cowardice (Ricker, *Voices of the American West*, 244).

17. *Cheyenne Daily Sun*, September 28, 1877.

18. Ibid., September 29, 1877.

19. *Laramie Daily Sentinel*, October 5, 1877.

20. Ibid., October 18, 1877.

21. David, *Malcolm Campbell*, 57.

22. Dugan, *Making of Legends*, 108.

23. Ibid., 108–109.

24. Ibid., 110, quoting Sheffield Ingalls, *History of Atchison County* (Lawrence, Kans.: Standard Publishing, 1916).

25. *Cheyenne Daily Sun*, October 4, 1877; *Bismarck (Dakota) Tri-Weekly Tribune*, October 3, 1877; *Black Hills Daily Times* (Deadwood), October 8, 1878.

26. This Cyprian, also known as "Tit Bit," arrived in the Black Hills with the train that brought "Wild Bill" Hickok and a number of other delightfully named whores, including Big Dollie, Dirty Emma, Smooth Bore, and Sizzling Kate (Rosa, *They Called Him Wild Bill*, 286). "Tid Bit," or "Tit Bit," drew some attention when she paid $200 for a custom-made dress embroidered with the names of her regular customers, to the consternation, no doubt, of those who were married. "The brands and initials of her particular favorites cover the side of her neck and bosom," noted a newspaper, "and the brands, etc., of those occupying but an indifferent corner of her affections . . . are located so as to be frequently sat down upon (quoted in Secrest, *I Buried Hickok*, 114).

27. Secrest, *I Buried Hickok*, 102; Klock, *All Roads Lead to Deadwood*, 67.

28. Secrest, *I Buried Hickok*, 112.

29. *Cheyenne Daily Sun*, October 4, 1877; Dugan, *Making of Legends*, 111–14.

30. *Cheyenne Daily Sun*, October 4, 1877; *Black Hills Daily Times* (Deadwood), October 4, 1877; *Cheyenne Daily Leader*, October 4, 1877; *San Francisco Evening Bulletin*, October 4, 1877; *Omaha (Nebraska) Daily Bee*, November 28, 1877.

31. *Cheyenne Daily Leader*, October 9, 1877.

32. Spring, *Cheyenne and Black Hills Stage and Express Routes*, 220–21; *Omaha (Nebraska) Daily Bee*, November 28, 1877; *Black Hills Journal* (Rapid City, Dakota), November 23, 1878; Dugan, *Making of Legends*, 119–20; *Cheyenne Daily Leader*, January 19, 1878, quoting the *Black Hills Journal* of Rapid City. It is ironic that the *Journal* story incorrectly identified the jailed outlaw as "Samuel Young," the name used by Hartman's intended murderer in Deadwood.

33. *Omaha (Nebraska) Daily Herald*, January 6, 1878; Dugan, *Making of Legends*, 120–21.

34. *Cheyenne Daily Leader*, October 11, 1878; *Omaha (Nebraska) Daily Bee*, October 24, 1878.

35. *Cheyenne Daily Sun*, May 25, 1879; Frye, *Atlas of Wyoming Outlaws*, 75–76; Carroll, "Clark Pelton," 21.

36. *Cheyenne Daily Leader*, December 24, 1879. Pelton said he had been born in Cleveland, Ohio, and would not be twenty-three years old until January 29, 1880.

37. Ibid., December 25, 1879.

38. *Cheyenne Daily Sun*, October 10, 1877; *Laramie Daily Sentinel*, October 10, 1877.

39. Spring, *Cheyenne and Black Hills Stage and Express Routes*, 229–30.

40. *Cheyenne Daily Sun*, October 23, 1877; *Laramie Daily Sentinel*, October 24, 1877.

41. The *Laramie Daily Sentinel* of October 31, 1877, identified Sheriff Bullock's deputies as Ed Donahue, "Grasshopper Jim," and X. S. Burke.

42. *Cheyenne Daily Sun*, October 25, 1877.

43. In a newspaper interview after he was captured, Blackburn confirmed that Bullock had tried twice to trap him in October but had failed both times (*Cheyenne Daily Leader*, November 24, 1877).

44. *Cheyenne Daily Sun*, November 17, 1877.

45. The soldiers who did not continue with Davis were later court-martialed for neglect of duty (Thrapp, *Encyclopedia of Frontier Biography*, 3:382).

46. *Cheyenne Daily Leader*, November 22, 23, 1877; Spring, *Cheyenne and Black Hills Stage and Express Routes*, 234–36.

47. *Cheyenne Daily Sun*, November 23, 1877.

48. *Cheyenne Daily Leader*, November 23, 1877. A full account of the capture of the two outlaws was provided in this edition of the *Daily Leader* by a Green River correspondent identified only as "A Friend." He said that "too much credit can not be given Mr. Davis for his nerve and grit in following their trail for so long. Also to Charlie Brown and Pawnee Charlie for their sand in going out in search of them, not knowing their number, and without any offer of pay. They are good, solid boys, you bet."

49. *Cheyenne Daily Leader*, November 24, 1877; Spring, *Cheyenne and Black Hills Stage and Express Routes*, 236–37. Blackburn later showed the officers where his gun was hidden and made "Pawnee Charlie" a present of it (Spring, *Cheyenne and Black Hills Stage and Express Routes*, 237). A prime example of how stories like the pursuit and capture of Blackburn and Wall by Scott Davis have been distorted almost beyond recognition by old-timers is the account of Captain James Cooper Ayres, who was stationed at Fort Laramie during this period. In an 1899 magazine article he related how Davis, on learning that three unnamed men had stolen horses from a stage station, while still "wretched and feverish" from his unhealed bullet wound, "got up at once, mounted his horse, although every movement of his leg was agony, rode twenty miles, and overtook the thieves at a haystack." Single-handedly he attacked them, killing one as the others fled. "Exhausted, he slept soundly that night in the hay beside the dead robber." The next day he rode to Green River, "managed to get the drop on the two thieves in a saloon, and marched them both to jail." In addition to his other obvious errors in this recital, Ayres, perhaps intentionally, makes no mention of the army detail that initially accompanied Davis, but then left him to continue on his own (Ayres, "After Big Game With Packs").

50. *Cheyenne Daily Sun*, December 9, 1877; *Cheyenne Daily Leader*, December 9, 1877; Frye, *Atlas of Wyoming Outlaws*, 48–49.

51. *Cheyenne Daily Sun*, December 9, 1877.

52. *Cheyenne Daily Leader*, December 9, 1877. This same man, William J. Gidley, had killed one of his drivers in a "lamentable accident" only a little over a month earlier. While his stage was stopped at Cedar Creek on the

Custer route, Gidley and other passengers, armed with rifles against possible attack by road agents, began shooting at targets. Someone challenged Gidley to hit an outhouse some distance away, and the stage company executive aimed and fired, whereupon James Porter, the stage driver, who had been using the facility, emerged, exclaimed, "I am shot," and fell dead (*Iowa State Reporter*, October 31, 1877). The *Bismarck (Dakota) Tri-Weekly Tribune* of the same date reported Gidley's arrival back in town, but gave no details of the shooting other than James Porter had been killed "by a gun in the hand of another."

53. Klock, *All Roads Lead to Deadwood*, 150. Although the *Bismarck (Dakota) Tri-Weekly Tribune* of July 2, 1877, proclaimed that "the Bismarck line . . . seems remarkably exempt" from attack by road agents, only two weeks earlier, on June 18, a Northwestern Company stage from Deadwood had been stopped near Whitewood, Dakota Territory, reportedly by the "Dawson gang." Holdups continued in July with nine robbery attempts on the Deadwood-Bismarck coaches, actually one more than the assaults that month on the Deadwood-Cheyenne line (Cochran, *American West*, 128, 133). Responding to this upsurge in banditry against its line, the Northwestern Stage Company announced it would henceforth "put on out-riders, properly armed and equipped," to guard against road agents (*Bismarck [Dakota] Tri-Weekly Tribune*, August 3, 1877). But before that plan could be implemented another Northwestern coach was stopped near South Moreau by four high-waymen who, after searching the passengers and finding nothing of value, "expressed considerable disgust at capturing such a poverty stricken concern," and ordered them on. "The pony riders commence to-day and we shall probably hear no more of road agents," remarked the *Bismarck (Dakota) Tri-Weekly Tribune* (August 6, 1877). The line was relatively free of depredations by road agents for more than two years, but in late December 1879 one of the Northwestern coaches was stopped near Antelope Station. The bandits fired into the coach, killing the only passenger, a man named Cates, before riding off, reportedly with a treasure box (*Indianapolis Daily Sentinel*, January 5, 1880; *Stevens Point [Wisconsin] Daily Journal*, January 10, 1880).

54. *Cheyenne Daily Leader*, December 15, 1877.

55. Ibid., December 26, 1877; Spring, *Cheyenne and Black Hills Stage and Express Routes*, 238–397. The *Laramie Daily Sentinel* of August 10, 1878, reported that Blackburn was learning the saddle- and harness-making trade at Lincoln, and Wall was learning to make cigars.

56. Spring, *Cheyenne and Black Hills Stage and Express Routes*, 238.

57. *Cincinnati Daily Gazette*, January 15, 16, 1878; Bridwell, *Life and Adventures of Robert McKimie*, 3.

58. *New York Times*, February 24, 1895; Miller, *Sam Bass & Gang*, 321.

59. According to a long account of McKimie's career in the *Cheyenne Daily Leader* of January 30, 1878, a Hillsboro, Ohio, resident, suspicious of the free-spending McKimie, wrote to a friend of his, Millard F. Leech, in Ogallala, Nebraska, suggesting he check out the young man. Leech was indefatigable

in his efforts to bring road agents to justice. He had also trailed a suspect to Deadwood and had him arrested, only to find out that the man was innocent of any wrongdoing. The *Cheyenne Daily Sun* still praised his efforts: "His persistence in this affair is only equaled by his courage" (January 19, 1878).

60. *Cheyenne Daily Sun*, January 16, 1878.

61. Ibid.

62. *Cincinnati Daily Gazette*, January 15, 16, 17, 1878; *Cheyenne Daily Leader*, January 30, 1878; Bridwell, *Life and Adventures of Robert McKimie*, 9–10; Spring, *Cheyenne and Black Hills Stage and Express Routes*, 243.

63. *Laramie Daily Sentinel*, February 1, 1878.

64. Bridwell, *Life and Adventures of Robert McKimie*, 15–17. According to the account in the *Cheyenne Daily Sun* of February 20, 1878, "the two pistols with which Reddy effected his escape were furnished him by either his wife or the sheriff," the only ones who had access to McKimie's cell. McKimie would later say that he fired the first shot to scare the old man and the second went off accidentally (Bridwell, *Life and Adventures of Robert McKimie*, 20).

65. *Cheyenne Daily Sun*, February 20, 1878.

66. Bridwell, *Life and Adventures of Robert McKimie*, 22–23.

67. Ibid., 23–24.

68. *Hillsboro (Ohio) Gazette*, November 29, 1878.

69. Ibid.; *Cheyenne Daily Sun*, November 28, 29, 1878. On December 4, 1878, Sheriff Jeff Carr, at the behest of the Cheyenne stage company, telegraphed Sheriff Newell, requesting clarification of the McKimie situation and asking if a requisition was sent would Newell turn McKimie over to Laramie County officers, and on what terms. Newell wired back: "If the Governor don't revoke the requisition you can get him. The charges against him here are burglary, grand larceny, and shooting with intent to commit murder." The next day Newell followed up: "The Governor revoked the requisition. The costs and other expenses amount to four hundred and forty-three dollars. Will write you particulars." Carr found this very confusing until a later dispatch to the stage company officials explained that the requisition mentioned was the original one Seth Bullock had taken to Ohio months earlier, and a decision had been made to keep McKimie in Ohio and try him for his crimes there (*Cheyenne Daily Sun*, December 5, 1878).

70. Bridwell, *Life and Adventures of Robert McKimie*, 44–45, quoting the *Hillsboro (Ohio) Gazette*. Strangely, a recently published biography entitled *Seth Bullock: Black Hills Lawman* devotes only a single line to that officer's lengthy and determined effort to return McKimey (spelled "McKenna") to Deadwood for trial (Wolff, *Seth Bullock*, 53).

71. *Cheyenne Daily Leader*, January 14, 1879.

72. Engebretson, *Empty Saddles*, 161–62.

CHAPTER 5

1. Sabin, *Wild Men of the Wild West*, 207.

2. Brown and Willard, *Black Hills Trails*, 298.

3. *Sidney (Nebraska) Telegraph*, July 12, 1879.

4. Parker, *Gold in the Black Hills*, 180.

5. Engebretson, *Empty Saddles*, 92. Funded by a grant of $6 million from Stephen Girard, a French immigrant who was said to be the wealthiest man in America at the time of his death in 1831, the school opened in 1848 (ibid., 92, 103).

6. LaTelle, "Lame Johnny"; Rybolt, "Search for Whispering Smith."

7. *Black Hills Journal* (Rapid City, Dakota), July 5, 1879; *Sidney (Nebraska) Telegraph*, July 12, 1879.

8. Secrest, *I Buried Hickok*, 142–43.

9. *Black Hills Daily Times* (Deadwood), July 12, 1877.

10. *Cheyenne Daily Leader*, July 18, 1877, reprinted from the *Black Hills Champion* of Central City.

11. *Cheyenne Daily Leader*, July 29, 1877; *Cheyenne Daily Sun*, July 20, 1877. Some stagecoach passengers were more successful in concealing their valuables from the robbers. One was said to have hidden "a sizable roll of bills in the fat between his shoulder blades," which escaped detection. Another, Barney McVey, after selling a rich gold claim for $20,000, hid his money in a bag of oats at the rear of the coach. His pockets contained very little when he was stopped and searched by road agents. When they asked him why, he simply shrugged his shoulders and said he was a victim of hard luck (Klock, *All Roads Lead to Deadwood*, 72–73).

12. Spring, *Cheyenne and Black Hills Stage and Express Routes*, 218.

13. *Chicago Inter-Ocean*, July 26, 1877, quoting a special dispatch from Yankton, Dakota Territory, dated July 25. Basing his charge on nothing more than allegations by passengers, Editor Herman Glafcke of the *Cheyenne Daily Leader* accused Jim Sweeny, the driver of the Pierre stage, of complicity in this holdup and took the opportunity to disparage the operators of the Fort Pierre and Deadwood stage company, intimating that their operation was in collapse: "Some of the [company officials] are too poor to be useful and the others are too stingy to pay their debts. None of the drivers have been paid off, and the stock is very poorly fed and in miserable condition. Some of the partners have gobbled more than their share of the funds, and the company is badly involved in debt. The horses are being sold to pay the debts" (*Cheyenne Daily Leader*, July 31, 1877). Part of this may have been wishful thinking by one who had a personal stake in the continued success of Jack Gilmer's stage company operating out of Cheyenne, but it is true the Pierre outfit was poorly managed and never enjoyed the success of the Gilmer company.

14. Brown and Willard, *Black Hills Trails*, 258–59. These gestures of generosity on Blackburn's part, nor a perforated ear that had to be throbbing, did not deter Cook from organizing a posse the next day and starting in pursuit of the gang. He turned back only when he ran into a large band of hostile-appearing Indians (*Cheyenne Daily Leader*, August 24, 1877; *Helena [Montana] Independent*, August 28, 1877). Ed Cook was a tough character. In October 1876 during those first wild and wooly days at Deadwood, he had reportedly

killed a man named John Farrell in a brothel gunfight (Cochrane, *American West*, 121).

15. Brown and Willard, *Black Hills Trails*, 259. In a ghostwritten article under Wyatt Earp's name appearing in an 1896 edition of the *San Francisco Examiner*, the outlaw's shouted greeting to robbery victims was that he was "Lame Bradley, KNIGHT of the Road" (August 9, 1896).

16. Root and Connelley, in their notable *Overland Stage to California* (59), published in 1901, called him "Peg-Legged" Bradley. Charles Dawson, in his 1912 edition, *Pioneer Tales of the Oregon Trail*, listed "the most prominent of these highwaymen" and managed to mangle all four of the names: "Pegleg Bradley, Dunk Blackbird, Bill Price, and Charlie Grimes" (83).

17. Even the usually reliable Agnes Wright Spring made this mistake, saying that "Lame Johnny" Bradley was "taken care of by Vigilantes near Buffalo Gap," a fate that actually lay in store for Cornelius "Lame Johnny" Donahue (Spring, *Cheyenne and Black Hills Stage and Express Routes*, 296).

18. Dugan, *Making of Legends*, 117–18; Brown and Willard, *Black Hills Trails*, 259.

19. *Black Hills Daily Times* (Deadwood), January 20, 1878; *San Francisco Examiner*, August 9, 1896; Engebretson, *Empty Saddles*, 97; Dugan, *Making of Legends*, 120.

20. Richard C. Stirk interview in Ricker and Jensen, *Voices of the American West*, 283.

21. Sandoz, *Love Song to the Plains*, 212.

22. *Custer (Dakota) Chronicle*, February 12, 1881. In *Empty Saddles, Forgotten Names* (270), the historian Doug Engebretson expressed doubt that Fowler was a regular member of the "Lame Johnny" road agent gang, saying "nothing in my research has indicated that 'Fly Specked Billy' was a road agent, a category he had been placed in by some modern histories." Other sometime road agents suspected or accused of operating with the "Lame Johnny" gang were Jim McDonald and Fritz Stark (Klock, *All Roads Lead to Deadwood*, 70).

23. *Cheyenne Daily Leader*, October 4, 1877.

24. *Black Hills Daily Times* (Deadwood), February 10, 1880.

25. Bristow, *Whispering Smith*, 54.

26. Thrapp, *Encyclopedia of Frontier Biography*, 2:863; Hutton, *Doc Middleton*. A Texan named James M. Riley assumed the alias "Doc" Middleton when he turned to outlawry and made it famous in Nebraska (Hutton, *Doc Middleton*).

27. Hutton, *Doc Middleton*, 104–105.

28. Ibid., 105–38.

29. McGillycuddy, *Blood on the Moon*, 128.

30. DeArment, *Deadly Dozen*, Vol. 3.

31. Spring, "Who Robbed the Mail Coach?"

32. Rybolt, "Search for Whispering Smith," 5; Brown and Willard, *Black Hills Trails*, 300.

33. *Black Hills Journal* (Rapid City, Dakota), July 5, 1879; Engebretson, *Empty Saddles*, 97–98.

34. *Black Hills Daily Times* (Deadwood), July 8, 1879.

35. *Sidney (Nebraska) Telegraph*, July 12, 1879.

36. A man named Zack Sutley published a book in 1930 in which he stated that he was present at "Lame Johnny's" hanging but was not a member of the lynching party. His credibility is questionable, however, as he wrongly identified the officer in charge of Donahue as a deputy U.S. marshal named Frank Moulton, and the shotgun messenger someone named Walt Hunter. He also erroneously said that "Lame Johnny" had earlier been locked up in the Deadwood jail, but escaped (Sutley, *Last Frontier*, 247–54).

37. LaTelle, "Lame Johnny," 42.

38. "Whispering" Smith gave his version of the happenings that night in an interview for the *Black Hills Journal* (Rapid City, Dakota) of July 5, 1879. His story differed markedly from the recital of the affair written by Jesse Brown in the book he coauthored with A. M. Willard (*Black Hills Trails*, 300–301). Although other writers have inferred that Smith and the other men were guilty of failing to protect the prisoner, Irma H. Klock, in her *Black Hills Outlaws, Lawmen and Others* (8–9), charged that "Hawkbill," as she calls Smith, "never saw the necessity of taking a wrongdoer to jail when the miscreant could be hanged before then, with no further expense to the taxpayers." "Lame Johnny" knew Smith's reputation, she wrote, and before leaving Fort Robinson (which she calls "Red Cloud") told Harris (whom she calls "Rogers") that he did not expect to get to Rapid City alive. When the stage was stopped, she contended, "it was [Boone] May who opened the door and said, 'Get out, Johnny.' Smith gave him a push. Johnny begged to have his shackles removed but ended up tumbling out of the coach with Smith closely following him—and the stage drove on." A man who claimed to have witnessed the hanging and presumably was one of the lynchers told her many years later, she said, that it was Smith himself who "fixed the rope" around Johnny's neck and "suspended him into eternity" (ibid.).

39. John B. Furay to A. D. Hazen of the Post Office Department, January 8, 1880, quoted in Spring, "Who Robbed the Mail Coach?" 25.

40. Furay to D. B. Parker, chief inspector of the Post Office Department, July 7, 1880, quoted in ibid., 58. It has been alleged that Furay himself posted this bit of doggerel over the grave (Parker, *Gold in the Black Hills*, 180). Irma H. Klock said that the sign with its strange epitaph was placed on the grave by the Pete Oslund freighters who buried him. She added that in June 1889 some Buffalo Gap residents dug up "Lame Johnny" and removed the shackles from his bones. One set went to Fort Pierre, and the other to the Custer Museum (Klock, *Black Hills Outlaws, Lawmen and Others*, 7–9).

41. Engebretson, *Empty Saddles*, 102–103.

42. Ibid., 132.

43. Ibid., 132–33; Brown and Willard, *Black Hills Trails*, 274; *Cheyenne Daily Sun*, February 20, 1880.

44. *Black Hills Weekly Pioneer* (Deadwood), February 4, 1880, reprinted in the *Sioux County Herald* (Orange City, Iowa) February 19, 1880; *Las Vegas (New Mexico) Optic*, February 6, 1880; *Cheyenne Daily Sun*, March 5, 1880, quoting an interview with Llewellyn in the *Sioux City (Iowa) Journal*. As proof that he and May had no intention of killing Grimes, Llewellyn said in that interview that a $200 reward had been offered for the arrest and conviction of the outlaw. As a federal officer he could not have claimed it, but certainly Boone May could and would have, but there was no reward for a dead body.

45. *Cheyenne Daily Leader*, February 13, 1880.

46. Engebretson, *Empty Saddles*, 135.

47. *Cheyenne Daily Leader*, February 19, 1880.

48. *Omaha (Nebraska) Herald*, February 24, 1880.

49. *Cheyenne Daily Sun*, August 24, 1880, quoting the *Black Hills Daily Times* (Deadwood).

50. Engebretson, *Empty Saddles*, 137; Spring, *Cheyenne and Black Hills Stage and Express Routes*, 301; Brown and Willard, *Black Hills Trails*, 275. In her *Black Hills Outlaws, Lawmen and Others* (13), Irma H. Klock wrote that May and Llewellyn stood trial in September 1880 and were acquitted for killing another man at Pierre, but this is a confusion with the "Curly" Grimes murder trial. Ambrose Bierce, in a short story entitled "A Sole Survivor," indicates that Boone May, while awaiting trial in the Grimes murder case, killed another outlaw, but although Bierce knew Boone May well, this was fiction, and nothing in the contemporary records has been found to verify the tale.

CHAPTER 6

1. *Cheyenne Daily Sun*, July 26, 1877.

2. *Cheyenne Daily Leader*, July 25, 1877; Hockett, "Boone May," 1; Coursey, *Beautiful Black Hills*, 141–42.

3. *Cheyenne Daily Sun*, July 26, 1877.

4. *Cheyenne Daily Leader*, August 28, 1877; *Cheyenne Daily Sun*, August 28, September 2, 1877; *Laramie Weekly Sentinel*, August 27, September 3, 1877.

5. Hockett, "Boone May," 1; Spring, *Cheyenne and Black Hills Stage Routes*, 223.

6. *Cheyenne Daily Sun*, August 29, 1877.

7. Spring, *Cheyenne and Black Hills Stage Routes*, 223.

8. *Cheyenne Daily Sun*, August 29, 1877.

9. Ibid., August 31, 1877.

10. Ibid., September 2, 1877.

11. Ibid.

12. The *Laramie Daily Sentinel* of October 3, 1877, reported that Prescott Webb was an escaped murderer from Texas.

13. *Cheyenne Daily Sun*, September 2, 1877.

14. Ibid., December 19, 1877.

15. Ibid., December 21, 1877.

16. Ibid., December 29, 1877.

17. Ibid., January 1, 3, 1878.

18. Ibid., April 12, 1878.

19. Klock, *All Roads Lead to Deadwood*, 33.

20. *Cheyenne Daily Leader*, November 9, 1877, reprinted in newspapers as dispersed as the *Helena (Montana) Independent* (November 20, 1877) and the *San Francisco Chronicle* (November 8, 1877).

21. Ibid.

22. Frye, *Atlas of Wyoming Outlaws*, 22, 29.

23. Ibid., 46–47; Spring, *Cheyenne and Black Hills Stage Routes*, 232; Flannery, *John Hunton's Diary*, 263–64.

24. *Cheyenne Daily Sun*, November 9, 1877.

25. Ibid., October 5, 1877.

26. *Cheyenne Daily Leader*, October 5, 1877. The *Laramie Daily Sentinel* reprinted most of this editorial the next day and called it "Sound Talk."

27. *Cheyenne Daily Sun*, November 2, 1877.

28. Ibid. The story went out on the telegraph wires and was at first reported in newspapers across the country erroneously that the two men arrested were Blackburn and Wall, the notorious road agents still on the loose at the time (*San Francisco Bulletin*, November 2, 1877; *Wheeling [West Virginia] Daily Register*, November 2, 1877; *Indianapolis Sentinel*, November 2, 1877).

29. *Cheyenne Daily Sun*, November 14, 1877.

30. Frye, *Atlas of Wyoming Outlaws*, 47.

31. *Cheyenne Daily Sun*, November 16, 1877.

32. Ibid., November 20, 23, 1877.

33. Frye, *Atlas of Wyoming Outlaws*, 47; *Cheyenne Daily Sun*, November 25, 1877.

34. Frye, *Atlas of Wyoming Outlaws*, 47. The *Laramie Daily Sentinel* of June 21, 1878, reported the breakout attempt. "The injury is a severe but not dangerous flesh wound. If [Duncan] had been killed, nobody in this region would have gone into mourning for him. Warden A. J. House has a lot of guards there whom it is not worthwhile to fool with."

35. *Cheyenne Daily Sun*, February 17, 1879.

36. McLaughlin's sometime use of the name "Cummings" has led some writers of the period to confuse the Black Hills road agent with Jim Cummins, a Civil War Quantrill guerrilla and member of the Jesse James outlaw gang, but Archie McLaughlin, alias Cummings, died in 1878, and Jim Cummins, the last survivor of the James gang, lived on until 1929 (Browning, *Violence Was No Stranger*, 63–64).

37. McClintock, *Pioneer Days in the Black Hills*, 273.

38. *Cheyenne Daily Leader*, July 3, 1878; *Cheyenne Daily Sun*, July 3, 1878.

39. *Chicago Inter Ocean*, July 3, 1878; *Denison (Texas) Daily News*, July 6, 1878; *Argus and Patriot* (Montpelier, Vermont), July 11, 1878; *Racine (Wiscon-

sin) Argus, July 11, 1878. According to the *Laramie Daily Sentinel* of August 6, 1878, the heroics of Dan Finn were praised in an article in the *New York Graphic*. In a later edition the paper said Finn, no doubt trading on his new-found celebrity as a fighting man, had given up his trade as a train conductor and taken a position as an express guard on the Sidney–to–North Platte railroad run (August 14, 1878).

40. *Worcester* (Massachusetts) *Daily Spy*, July 6, 1878.

41. According to one account, in addition to the wounding of Brown, a road agent named Alex Caswell was killed and Archie McLaughlin slightly wounded in the shootout of July 2, 1878. The author's credibility is greatly damaged, however, by his reference to "Wells Fargo stagecoaches," and his assertion that the attempted robbery of the stage at Whoop Up Canyon was thwarted by "heavily armed Wells Fargo detectives" (Nash, *Encyclopedia of Western Lawmen & Outlaws*, 223). Although Wells, Fargo & Company played a significant role in the history of express shipments in the West, the company was not involved in the 1877–78 war with road agents on the Deadwood trails.

42. *Cheyenne Daily Leader*, October 5, 1878.

43. DeArment, *Knights of the Green Cloth*, 249–50.

44. Ibid.; Bryan, *Wildest of the Wild West*, 127.

45. The *Cheyenne Daily Sun* article, quoted in Spring, *Cheyenne and Black Hills Stage and Express Routes*, 282–84.

46. Ibid.

47. *Cheyenne Daily Sun*, January 11, 1879.

48. *Colorado Springs (Colorado) Gazette*, August 10, 1878, reprinted from the *Greeley (Colorado) Tribune*; Ingham, *Digging Gold among the Rockies*, 221–22.

49. When a deputy sheriff from Louisiana arrived in Colorado with a warrant and a governor's requisition for a dangerous gunman, he ran into a problem with the measure. "The posse comitatus act might do for the southern states," he said, "but it was not a success in Colorado. When I called on the military officer and begged for a few soldiers to assist me, he just laughed and read the posse comitatus act to me and said 'You southern folks passed the infamous law and I must obey it'" (*Cheyenne Daily Sun*, January 30, 1880).

50. *Cheyenne Daily Leader*, July 27, 1878.

51. Spring, *Cheyenne and Black Hills Stage and Express Routes*, 251–52.

52. Bancroft, *History of Nevada, Colorado and Wyoming*, 759.

53. *Cheyenne Daily Leader*, July 27, 1878; *Laramie Daily Sentinel*, July 29, 1878.

54. *Cheyenne Daily Leader*, September 14, 1878.

55. Ibid.

56. The *Laramie Daily Sentinel* of September 12, 1878, gave the name as James E. (Augustus) Johnson, but when arrested he insisted his name was William W. Johnson (*Laramie Daily Sentinel*, September 28, 1878).

57. Ingham, *Digging Gold among the Rockies*, 222.

58. Ibid., 223–24; *Cheyenne Daily Leader*, September 11, 1878.

59. *Cheyenne Daily Leader*, September 11, 1878.

60. Ibid., September 21, 1878.

61. *Laramie Daily Sentinel*, November 23, 1878.

62. *Cheyenne Daily Sun*, September 24, 1878.

63. Ibid., September 26, 1878.

64. Ibid., September 24, 1878; Cochrane, *American West*, 151.

65. *Cheyenne Daily Sun*, September 25, 1878.

66. Ibid., September 24, 1878.

CHAPTER 7

1. Engebretson, *Empty Saddles*, 87.

2. French for "machine gun."

3. Engebretson, *Empty Saddles*, 87–88.

4. Thrapp, *Encyclopedia of Frontier Biography*, 1:248.

5. *Laramie Daily Sentinel*, April 29, 1876.

6. David, *Malcolm Campbell*, 53.

7. Ibid., 54

8. Engebretson, *Empty Saddles*, 85.

9. *Golden (Colorado) Weekly Globe*, August 19, 1876.

10. Engebretson, *Empty Saddles*, 85–86.

11. *San Francisco Bulletin*, April 6, 1876.

12. Spring, *Cheyenne and Black Hills Stage and Express Routes*, 136–38; Raine, *Guns of the Frontier*, 112–13; David, *Malcolm Campbell*, 57; Cochrane, *American West*, 110.

13. *Cheyenne Daily Leader*, March 28, 1877.

14. Spring, *Cheyenne and Black Hills Stage and Express Routes*, 253.

15. Ibid., 252. Furay was not the only one to tie the names of Chambers and Jack Watkins together. A dispatch sent to the *Omaha (Nebraska) Daily Bee* from "Captain Jack" (J. W. Crawford) at Fort Fetterman asserted that "Persimmon Bill" was reported as hiding out with Sitting Bull. "He is a bad man and a coward too. . . . Jack Watkins is said to be with him. With such schemers as these two men, we would not be surprised to hear of some sharp movements on the part of the Redskins" (*Laramie Daily Sentinel*, August 10, 1876).

16. Spring, *Cheyenne and Black Hills Stage and Express Routes*, 252.

17. Jahns, *Frontier World of Doc Holliday*, 81.

18. Spring, *Cheyenne and Black Hills Stage and Express Routes*, 252–53.

19. Frye, *Atlas of Wyoming Outlaws*, 81. Apparently somewhere he had been tagged with the moniker "Big Nose George" because of his outsized beak, and he may have taken the alias "Parrott" as a sort of self-deprecatory joke.

20. Metz, *Encyclopedia of Lawmen, Outlaws, and Gunfighters*, 193.

21. Engebretson, *Empty Saddles*, 111, quoting the *Miles City (Montana) Press*, November 18, 1882.

22. *Cheyenne Daily Sun*, August 17, 1880.

23. A resident of Council Bluffs, Iowa, asserted that the man known as "Dutch Charley" in Wyoming had gone by the names of Lehman and Lander in that city before moving west. A native of southern Germany, he was "versed in all the German dialects." His criminal career began in Buffalo, New York, where he fleeced a fellow German out of $3,000. At St. Paul, Minnesota, in 1876 he reportedly stole a fine team and buggy. He gambled professionally at Council Bluffs and was believed to have skipped town after murdering a German butcher from Omaha (*Cheyenne Daily Sun*, January 16, 1879, quoting the *Council Bluffs [Iowa] Nonpareil*).

24. Spring, *Cheyenne and Black Hills Stage and Express Routes*, 254, 285. This writer, one of the earliest and most reliable chroniclers of Black Hills stagecoach history, followed local lore, affirming the belief that Frank James participated in Black Hills stagecoach robberies as "probably true." While admitting that "no positive proof" could be found to indicate that brother Jesse was guilty of any crime in Wyoming or Dakota Territory, Spring added that Jesse James "was known to have been working with [others] who were caught in connection with stage robberies" (ibid., 201).

One of the recurring myths in the saga of the Black Hills is the linking of the nationally famous James and Younger outlaw brothers to the Deadwood stagecoach robberies. Some respectable citizens, including Dr. John E. Osborne, later governor of Wyoming; pioneer Oliver P. Hanna; and Boone May, Dave Cook, Frank Grouard, and A. M. ("Cap") Willard, all highly respected law officers, contributed to this mythology. Dr. Osborne believed that "Sim Wan" was an alias employed by Frank James. He also thought Tom Reed was actually one of the Younger brothers (ibid., 285), ignoring the fact that all of the Youngers had been wounded and captured months before the first Deadwood stage robbery. Boone May said that at the time of the Old Woman's Fork holdup he recognized Tom Reed as Frank James (ibid., 262). Dave Cook of the Rocky Mountain Detective Association asserted erroneously that "Frank James, one of the James brothers, but who went by the name of McKinney [McKimie]," was a member of a Deadwood stage robbing gang (Cook, *Hands Up!* 156). Grouard, while scouting for the army at Fort McKinney, also held a deputy U.S. marshal appointment and received descriptions and photographs of Frank and Jesse James, who reportedly "had come up into the northern country." He said he "started out to arrest [Frank] James" but was unsuccessful (DeBarthe, *Life and Adventures of Frank Grouard*, 370–72). Hanna said Grouard told him at Fort McKinney there were seven bandits operating in that country, and the leaders were Frank James; Jim Cummins, longtime member of the James gang; and ""Big Nose George." He was asked to be on the lookout for them and report any sightings to Grouard or Detective Millard F. Leech. Once Hanna saw two men who answered the descriptions of Frank James and "Big Nose George" and noticed "what good shots they were; they would shoot a prairie chicken in the top of the trees a hundred yards away and never miss a one," but by the time he notified the officers the suspects had moved on (Hanna, *Old-Timer's Story*, 62). "Cap" Willard told Ed Lemmon that when he was a deputy under Sheriff Seth Bullock, he rode eighteen miles, shook hands with Frank James at his hideout near Belle Fourche, and rode back. Willard had to be "joshing" Lemmon; no mention of the James brothers or such an unbelievable incident appears in the book Willard coauthored with Jesse Brown. W. H. Taylor, who rode with posses in the final extermination of the road agent gangs, wrote in 1909 that one of them, an outlaw going by the name "MacDonald," was "probably Frank James" ("In the Days of the Deadwood Treasure Coach").

Mary Lou Pence, in her biography of Boswell, followed the lead of Agnes Wright Spring and repeated these allegations. She indicated that "Sim Wan" was in actuality Jesse James and brother Frank was "McKinney" (McKimie?), attributing this information to "Big Nose George" Parrott in his confession to Boswell (*Boswell*, 113, 140). She said that Boswell at one time had Jesse James locked up in his Laramie jail, but he escaped with the assistance of his cousin, a Mrs. Bramel, wife of the jailer. Boswell said he did not learn the true identity of his prisoner until later when he saw a reward poster for Jesse James (ibid., 100). This author went on to say that during the winter of 1879–80 the James brothers were "hiding under aliases and diving in and out of the Big Horns and Montana's isolated haunts" (ibid., 127).

William A. Settle addressed the question of the purported activities of the James brothers in the Black Hills in his ground-breaking biography of Jesse James published in 1966, and dismissed the reports with a few words: "Between 1876 and October of 1879 [the James boys'] reputations occasionally caused them to be suspected when a robbery occurred, and their names were then and later connected with some far-flung adventures, but no evidence points to them during this period. . . . In May of 1879 a telegraphed report to Eastern papers from Omaha told of Frank James encamped with a band of cowboys and deserters from the Army in the Wind River country of Wyoming. . . . The Liberty *Tribune* (May 30, 1879) branded this story, 'Humbug big!' And so the tales went" (*Jesse James Was His Name*, 101–102). Recent careful biographers of the James brothers have ignored the reports, saying simply that following the disastrous bank robbery attempt at Northfield, Minnesota, in September 1876 the brothers escaped to the friendly confines of Missouri, and later Tennessee, where they took up new names and lay low for years (Yeatman, *Frank and Jesse James*; Stiles, *Jesse James*). A Wyoming historian devoted an entire chapter in a book to the question of whether the James brothers were ever active in Wyoming and came to the conclusion that the Liberty, Missouri, newspaper was probably correct in branding the stories "Humbug Big!" (Beery, *Sinners & Saints*, 185–93).

25. *Black Hills Daily Times* (Deadwood), July 27, 1880.

26. Engebretson, *Empty Saddles*, 112.

27. *Cheyenne Daily Sun*, August 17, 1880.

28. Ibid., August 28, 1878.

29. Ibid., August 29, 1878.

30. Ingham, *Digging Gold among the Rockies*, 225.

31. *Cheyenne Daily Leader*, September 15, 1878; *Black Hills Daily Times* (Deadwood), September 14, 1878; *Laramie Daily Sentinel*, September 16, 1878; Sabin, *Wild Men of the Wild West*, 209–10. In *Red Blooded* (73–74), Edgar Beecher Bronson recounted a story of a Deadwood stage holdup and resulting gunfight involving messenger Boone May that, despite many inaccuracies of detail and exaggerations, must have been based on this affair. Bronson, who placed the time of the occurrence in February 1878 rather than September, claimed he was one of the passengers in the coach, which was driven by Gene Barnett and guarded by Boone May and C. B. Stocking (rather than Zimmerman). Entering the most dangerous zone, May and Stocking, he said, "shifted from the coach to the saddle [and] dropped back perhaps thirty yards behind us." When a road agent appeared in the road ahead, "threw a snap shot" over the head of Barnett, and ordered him to stop, Boone May dropped the bandit with a single shot, setting off "a quick interchange of shots." May yelled at Barnett to drive on and "away we flew at a pace materially improved by three or four shots the bandits sent singing past our ears and over the team!" Bronson said they later learned May and Stocking had killed four of the bandits before stampeding the others. This fantasy was repeated in Sabin, *Wild Men of the Wild West*, 209–12.

32. Engebretson, *Empty Saddles*, 140; Spring, *Cheyenne and Black Hills Stage and Express Routes*, 261–62.

33. Gorzalka, *Wyoming's Territorial Sheriffs*, 105–107; Pence, *Boswell*, passim. There has been some disagreement among writers regarding the officer or officers who arrested Jack McCall in Laramie. Pence (*Boswell*, 99) and Gorzalka (*Wyoming's Territorial Sheriffs*, 111) credit Boswell for the arrest. Joseph G. Rosa, the foremost authority on "Wild Bill" Hickok, in his biography of the famous gunfighter (*They Called Him Wild Bill*, 318), identified Deputy U.S. Marshal Balcombe as the arresting officer. The *Laramie Daily Sentinel* of August 30, 1876, reported simply that McCall had "been arrested by the authorities here" and "the officers of the law here deserve great credit."

34. In the posse were former Albany County sheriffs Thomas J. Dayton and Daniel Nottage, Jack T. Donahue, Morgan F. Knadler, Nicholas Thies, Thomas F. Dougan, Ed S. Kerns, Brad Fonce, John Metcalf, Jud F. Holcomb, Al LeRoy, Jack Fee, B. Halsted, Frank Brown, and J. English. Ex-sheriff Nottage was called back to Laramie "on urgent business" and did not take part in the arrests (*Laramie Daily Sentinel*, December 23, 1878; Pence, *Boswell*, 119).

35. The name is given as "Otto Oleson" in some newspaper accounts, for example, the *Laramie Daily Sentinel*, December 23, 1878.

36. *Cheyenne Daily Leader*, December 24, 1878; *Cheyenne Daily Sun*, December 24, 1878, January 2, 1879; *Cincinnati Daily Gazette*, December 24, 1878; *Omaha (Nebraska) World Herald*, December 25, 1878; Pence, *Boswell*, 117–22; Cook, *Hands Up!* 155–58; Spring, *Cheyenne and Black Hills Stage and Express Routes*, 285–86.

37. *Cheyenne Daily Leader*, December 28, 1878; Spring, *Cheyenne and Black Hills Stage and Express Routes*, 286. Rather than belonging to Boone May, the

coat in question may have been the "ulster overcoat" taken by the bandits from passenger Goldsworthy in the first robbery that night.

38. Vassar was arrested in Iowa by a deputy U.S. marshal on a charge of robbing the mails and brought back to Wyoming. The *Laramie Daily Sentinel* called him "one of the hardest of the lot," for whom officers in Wyoming, Dakota, and Iowa held warrants. "The authorities have positive evidence of his guilt, so that it is safe to predict that his criminal career is at an end for several years to come, at least" (*Laramie Daily Sentinel,* January 17, 1879).

39. *Cheyenne Daily Sun,* May 16, 1879.

40. *Cheyenne Daily Leader,* December 28, 1878; Hockett, "Boone May," 2. The names of those taken into custody differ somewhat in the various accounts. The story of the capture in the *Omaha (Nebraska) Herald* of December 25, 1878, identified the prisoners as "Frank Ruby [Frederick C. Robie], Hank Harrington, Joe Van Ness [Minuse], and a Swede whose name was not known." The dispatch from Cheyenne in the *Cincinnati Daily Gazette* of December 24, 1878, named them as "Harrington, Maruse [Minuse], Ruby [Robie], Howard, Sleson, and 'the Kid' [Condon]." Cook's account (*Hands Up!* 161) listed six arrestees: "Erwin [Irwin], Ruby [Robie], Condon, Harrington, Douglas, and Dutch Charley," omitting Joe Minuse. Pence (*Boswell,* 123) also enumerated six: Minuse, Harrington, Robie, Condon, Vassar, and Howard, omitting Irwin and "Dutch Charley," who were both arrested later. Spring's account (*Cheyenne and Black Hills Stage and Express Routes,* 286) listed "Dutch Charley," Minuse, Harrington, Robie, Douglas, and Condon as those captured at the camp and Irwin as a later arrestee. No account appears to be completely accurate.

41. *Laramie Daily Sentinel,* January 17, 1879.

42. Frye, *Atlas of Wyoming Outlaws,* 73–74; Pence, *Boswell,* 123–24. The brutal interrogation of Joe Minuse has been wrongly attributed to shotgun messengers Boone May and Billy Sample by some Deadwood historians. One wrote that May and Sample wore masks while terrorizing their prisoner, and when Sample's mask slipped down Minuse recognized him, whereupon May and Sample pulled their guns and "Joe was dispatched to plead his case before his Maker" (Klock, *All Roads Lead to Deadwood,* 32–33). In telling much the same story another writer said, "Evidently Minuse didn't know when to shut his mouth because he then threatened to kill Sample. It was at this point that Boone May lost his patience with Minuse and shot him" (Hansen, "Boone May," 42). Nothing of the kind ever happened, of course, for Minuse was not killed by his interrogators and, as evidenced by the court records, later went to prison. But the two messengers did not deny the story when it made the rounds. Boone May, in particular, made no effort to refute his growing reputation as a killer, evidently believing that it served as a deterrent for young men with stage-robbing aspirations.

43. *Cheyenne Daily Sun,* January 6, 1879. The detectives mentioned may well have been the ubiquitous man hunter Millard F. Leech and James L. ("Whispering") Smith, for both were mentioned in another account of the

arrest. Leech, noted the *Sun* in its January 3 edition, "was at Green River and had something to do with the arrest. The capture is regarded as important by Captain [James L. ("Whispering")] Smith and others who know of Charley's exploits."

44. A magazine writer stated that a $5,000 reward had been offered for Frank Towle, dead or alive, an extraordinary amount for the time (Hansen, "Boone May," 21), but contemporary published accounts mention only $1,000 rewards offered for members of the outlaw gang.

45. Quoted in Hockett, "Boone May," 2.

46. *Cheyenne Daily Sun*, May 2, 1879.

47. Ibid., January 3, 1879

48. Ibid., January 7, 1879.

49. *Laramie Daily Sentinel*, January 10, 1879.

50. Ibid., January 17, 1879.

51. Engebretson, *Empty Saddles*, 121.

52. *Cheyenne Daily Sun*, January 3, 1879.

53. Pence and Homsher, *Ghost Towns of Wyoming*, 59.

54. Wolfe, "Curtains for Big Nose George," 50.

55. *Cheyenne Daily Leader*, January 7, 1879; Engebretson, *Empty Saddles*, 121.

56. *Cheyenne Daily Sun*, January 30, 1879.

57. Cook, *Hands Up!* 164; Spring, *Cheyenne and Black Hills Stage and Express Routes*, 288. There appears to be some confusion here between the road agents Frank Howard and Henry Harrington, both reportedly killed at this time by a man named Smith. In any event these fellows disappeared from the scene and played no further role in the Deadwood coach story.

58. Frye, *Atlas of Wyoming Outlaws*, 64; Spring, *Cheyenne and Black Hills Stage and Express Routes*, 287.

59. Frye, *Atlas of Wyoming Outlaws*, 65.

60. Ibid., 65. John Vassar was no stranger to the court system. On September 22, 1878, near Fort Fetterman, he shot and killed Deputy Sheriff William Foy but was cleared on the age-old plea of self-defense (*Cheyenne Daily Sun*, September 24, 1878).

61. *Cheyenne Daily Sun*, January 31, 1879.

62. Frye, *Atlas of Wyoming Outlaws*, 63.

63. Ibid., 63–64.

64. *Laramie Daily Sentinel*, September 13, 1879.

65. Ibid., December 9, 1879, quoting the *Cheyenne Daily Leader;* Frye, *Atlas of Wyoming Outlaws*, 73–74.

66. *Black Hills Daily Times* (Deadwood), July 27, 1880; Engebretson, *Empty Saddles*, 118.

67. *Yellowstone Journal*, August 7, 1880.

68. Frye, *Atlas of Wyoming Outlaws*, 81, quoting *Reminiscences of Frontier Days*, the private diary of M. Wilson Rankin.

69. Ibid.

70. *Helena (Montana) Independent*, August 8, 1880.

71. Gorzalka, *Wyoming's Territorial Sheriffs*, 165.

72. *Springfield (Massachusetts) Republican*, December 16, 1880.

73. Van Pelt, *Dreamers & Schemers*, 108.

74. Gorzalka, *Wyoming's Territorial Sheriffs*, 165; Frye, *Atlas of Wyoming Outlaws*, 81; *Omaha (Nebraska) Daily Herald*, November 19, 1880; *Titusville (Pennsylvania) Herald*, March 24, 1881.

75. Interestingly, another inmate of the Rawlins jail at this time was James Averell, awaiting trial on a charge of murder. Later freed when witnesses against him could not be found, Averell made headlines eight years later when he and Ellen Watson, called "Cattle Kate" in press reports, were lynched as rustlers in the buildup to the infamous Johnson County War (Hufsmith, *Wyoming Lynching of Cattle Kate*, 76–78).

76. Gorzalka, *Wyoming's Territorial Sheriffs*, 171.

77. *Titusville (Pennsylvania) Herald*, March 24, 1881; *Alton (Illinois) Daily Telegraph*, March 24, 1881; Van Pelt, *Dreamers & Schemers*, 109. The leg irons, fashioned by Rawlins blacksmith James Candlish, are still on exhibit in the Union Pacific Railroad Museum. The Carbon County commissioners later presented Rosa Rankin with a fine gold watch as a reward for her quick action in preventing the escape of the dangerous desperado (Wolfe, "Curtains for Big Nose George," 50).

78. *Alton (Illinois) Daily Telegraph*, March 24, 1881.

79. Van Pelt, *Dreamers & Schemers*, 109.

80. *Lethbridge Herald* (Alberta, Canada), November 30, 1932.

CHAPTER 8

1. Mahnken, "Sidney–Black Hills Trail," 222.

2. Spring, *Cheyenne and Black Hills Stage and Express Routes*, 222; Klock, *All Roads Lead to Deadwood*, 70.

3. Spring, *Cheyenne and Black Hills Stage and Express Routes*, 248–49. The *Laramie Daily Sentinel* of September 21, 1878, announced that "A. D. Butler of Cheyenne has just finished building another iron-clad coach for the Cheyenne & Black Hills Stage Line."

4. Spring, "Canyon Springs Robbery," 6; *Bald Mountain News*, (Terry, South Dakota), January 6, 1899.

5. Spring, *Cheyenne and Black Hills Stage and Express Routes*, 270. According to Luke Voorhees, the treasure consisted of $37,000 in gold dust and gold bars, and $3,500 in currency (*Lusk [Wyoming] Herald*, March 2, 1950).

6. Taylor, "In the Days of the Deadwood Treasure Coach," 558.

7. McClintock, *Pioneer Days in the Black Hills*, 212. In a 1971 magazine article author Joe Koller ("Saga of Quickshot Davis," 32) added several more names to this list: Tim Harris, "Long Yank," and "Red" Laughlin ("Red Cloud" perhaps).

8. McClintock, *Pioneer Days in the Black Hills*, 213.

9. *Cheyenne Daily Leader*, October 19, 1878; *Lusk (Wyoming) Herald*, February 25, 1932; Spring, "Canyon Springs Robbery," 7.

10. Taylor, "In the Days of the Deadwood Treasure Coach," 558.

11. McClintock, *Pioneer Days in the Black Hills*, 213–14; Coursey, *Beautiful Black Hills*, 146–47; Spring, "Canyon Springs Robbery," 7.

12. W. H. Taylor, in his "Days of the Deadwood Treasure Coach" (558–59), said he related this story just as it was told to him by Gale Hill. In a 1959 magazine article a writer described the Canyon Springs robbery and gun battle and said, "Gail [*sic*] Hill" was dying when he saw an "outlaw lining up a rifle on Scott Davis. The last act of [Hill's] life was to put a bullet into the gunman, killing him" (Harrison, "Shotgun Messenger on Hell's Highway, 63). Of course neither Hill nor the robber he shot died that day.

13. In his account of the shooting Seth Bullock said Campbell "rolled out on the ground. He attempted to get to his feet when one of the robbers put a pistol to his head and killed him" (*Black Hills Daily Pioneer-Times* [Deadwood], May 3, 1902). Bullock, of course, was not at the scene. Scott Davis, who was, made no mention of such a brutal execution.

14. Spring, *Cheyenne and Black Hills Stage and Express Routes*, 267–68, quoting Davis's account in the *Lusk (Wyoming) Herald*, February 25, 1932. A magazine writer stated that "Davis saw Speer [*sic*] in the doorway of the barn and shot him down," killing him, for Davis later found his dead body (Koller, "Saga of Quickshot Davis," 32). This is erroneous. Al Spears was later captured, tried, convicted, and sentenced to prison.

15. *Black Hills Journal* (Rapid City, Dakota), October 5, 1878; *Black Hills Daily Pioneer-Times* (Deadwood), May 3, 1902.

16. In his 1899 article Captain James Cooper Ayres of Fort Laramie wrote another greatly distorted account of the Canyon Springs fight, saying that Scott Davis outfought the six robbers and held them at bay until assistance arrived ("After Big Game with Packs").

17. *Black Hills Daily Pioneer-Times* (Deadwood), May 3, 1902; Spring, *Cheyenne and Black Hills Stage and Express Routes*, 269–70.

18. *Cheyenne Daily Sun*, September 30, 1878; *Winnipeg Free Press*, October 9, 1878, quoting Jack Gilmer's account of the affair in the *Black Hills Daily Times* (Deadwood).

19. Because of its proximity to Cold Spring ranch, the assault has often been called the "Cold Springs Robbery" (Spring, *Cheyenne and Black Hills Stage and Express Routes*, 129). One wonders why Miner did not ride one of the stage horses to Cold Springs. Perhaps the robbers drove them off before departing. None of the witness accounts provide an answer.

20. *Black Hills Daily Pioneer-Times* (Deadwood), May 3, 1902.

21. Luke Voorhees, in recounting the story of the holdup thirty-six years later, said: "Davis walked backward for nearly a quarter of a mile, so he could see the road agents and not be shot openly without getting some of them. He made ten miles on foot in two hours to the next station where he

got horses and three messengers" (*Lincoln [Nebraska] Daily Star*, September 20, 1914). In another account Voorhees said messengers Boone May, Jesse Brown, and Jim Brown were waiting at the next station, together with coach driver Tom Cooper, "the best and coolest six-horse driver I ever knew [who] never shirked any danger" (*Lusk [Wyoming] Herald*, March 2, 1950).

22. Taylor, "In the Days of the Deadwood Treasure Coach," 560.

23. Early dispatches from Deadwood gave Gale Hill little hope of survival (*Salt Lake [Utah] Tribune*, September 28, 1878).

24. *Black Hills Daily Pioneer-Times* (Deadwood), May 3, 1902.

25. Spring, *Cheyenne and Black Hills Stage and Express Routes*, 270.

26. *Sioux County Independent* (Orange City, Iowa), October 16, 1878. W. H. Taylor said Campbell had "nine balls in his body" ("In the Days of the Deadwood Treasure Coach," 559).

27. *Black Hills Daily Pioneer-Times* (Deadwood), May 3, 1902.

28. Ibid., May 4, 1902.

29. Ibid.

30. Early dispatches reporting the robbery contained many errors. The *Laramie Daily Sentinel* of September 28, 1878, for example, stated that the road agents had opened fire, "wounding the driver and messenger, killing Campbell, the guard who was a soldier of the Third Cavalry." The misinformation about Campbell being a "guard" was repeated in the paper's edition as late as October 3, 1878.

CHAPTER 9

1. Even before the holdup and murder at Canyon Springs aroused the ire of citizens there were indications that folks were getting fed up with the depredations of the road agents. In its issue of September 16, 1878, ten days before the robbery, the *Laramie Daily Sentinel* noted: "There is some talk of organizing a company of fifty persons in Cheyenne to hunt the Stage robbers even to their dens in the mountains. Scott Davis says he will lead the party if desired."

2. *Cheyenne Daily Sun*, September 27, 1878.

3. *Cheyenne Daily Leader*, September 28, 1878; Spring, *Cheyenne and Black Hills Stage and Express Routes*, 260–61.

4. *Laramie Daily Sentinel*, September 30, 1878.

5. Spring, *Cheyenne and Black Hills Stage and Express Routes*, 270.

6. *Cheyenne Daily Sun*, September 30, 1878.

7. Ibid., October 7, 1878; *Cheyenne Daily Leader*, October 1, 1878; *Black Hills Daily Pioneer-Times* (Deadwood), May 4, 1902; Taylor, "In the Days of the Deadwood Treasure Coach."

8. *Cheyenne Daily Sun*, September 30, 1878.

9. Taylor, "In the Days of the Deadwood Treasure Coach"; *Cheyenne Daily Sun*, October 7, 1878.

10. About this time officers arrested the man calling himself "Tony Pastor" (George Howard) on suspicion of complicity in the Canyon Springs

robbery but later released him for lack of evidence (*Laramie Daily Sentinel*, October 17, 1878). Later a rumor spread that Pastor had been hanged by freighters on Crow Creek, ten or twelve miles south of Cheyenne (ibid., November 16, 1878).

11. *Cheyenne Daily Sun*, November 27, 1878; Frye, *Atlas of Wyoming Outlaws*, 57–58.

12. One author said that Davis chose to work alone in the outlaw hunt and trailed a party of three, "Tim Harris," "Long Yank," and "Red Laughlin," into Red Canyon. In a long-distance rifle duel he killed "Long Yank" and in a "running fight" wounded and captured Harris and Laughlin (Koller, "Saga of Quickshot Davis," 32–33). None of this was reported in the press or court records, and the tale seems to be simply fiction.

13. *Black Hills Daily Pioneer-Times* (Deadwood), May 6, 1902; Engebretson, *Empty Saddles*, 16; Taylor, "In the Days of the Deadwood Treasure Coach."

14. *Black Hills Daily Pioneer-Times* (Deadwood), May 9, 1902. The exploits of C. B. Stocking were sketched by a writer claiming "personal acquaintance of many years standing" with the noted frontiersman in the *Silver City (New Mexico) Enterprise* of December 26, 1884. A native of Michigan, Stocking is said to have gone to California in the gold rush of 1849, participated in the Pitt River Indian War, joined the ranks of the California Column in the Civil War, carried mail and guarded stagecoaches in New Mexico, scouted for the army in Wyoming, and single-handedly stood off a lynch mob, having his horse shot out from under him and receiving a bullet wound. He surveyed in Nevada and Utah, ran a business in California, and hunted, trapped, and traded with Indians in Montana before coming to the Black Hills.

15. *Black Hills Daily Pioneer-Times* (Deadwood), May 9, 1902; Spring, *Cheyenne and Black Hills Stage and Express Routes*, 271.

16. *Black Hills Daily Pioneer-Times* (Deadwood), May 6, 1902.

17. *Black Hills Journal* (Rapid City, Dakota), October 5, 1878.

18. *Cheyenne Daily Leader*, October 15, 1878. W. H. Taylor alleged that during the escape, McBride proved such a burden to his fellow bandits that Goodale suggested killing him, but Carey rejected that idea and, taking McBride, split off from the others (Taylor, "In the Days of the Deadwood Treasure Coach").

19. *Cheyenne Daily Leader*, November 16, 1878. Later a search made for this man's grave proved unsuccessful (*Black Hills Daily Times* [Deadwood], November 8, 1878).

20. *Black Hills Daily Times* (Deadwood), November 21, 1878.

21. Ibid., October 3, 1878.

22. *Black Hills Journal* (Rapid City, Dakota), October 12, 1878.

23. *Black Hills Daily Times* (Deadwood), October 3, 1878; *Black Hills Daily Pioneer-Times* (Deadwood), May 7, 1902.

24. *Black Hills Daily Pioneer-Times* (Deadwood), May 7, 1902.

25. *Black Hills Journal* (Rapid City, Dakota), October 12, 1878.

26. "The body of the wounded robber, or what was supposed to be his, was found some time afterwards by men driving stock through to Pierre. It was about half a mile from where they had left their wagon" (*Black Hills Daily Pioneer-Times* [Deadwood], May 8, 1902).

27. Ibid., May 7, 1902.

28. Ibid., May 9, 1902. A newspaper reported that the gold brick "weighed about 650 ounces and was valued between $10,000 and $20,000. Dr. Whitfield received a reward of $1,100" (*Black Hills Journal* [Rapid City, Dakota], October 12, 1878, quoted in Engebretson, *Empty Saddles*, 19). Wyoming historian Agnes Wright Spring, quoting an unidentified clipping found in a scrapbook, said the find was valued at $3,200, and Whitfield was given $1,100 (Spring, *Cheyenne and Black Hills Stage and Express Routes*, 273). The account of Major Brennan, who weighed the brick and paid the reward, would seem to be the more accurate.

29. *Black Hills Daily Times* (Deadwood), October 12, 1878.

30. Spring, "Canyon Springs Robbery," 8. Gouch reportedly was convicted of stealing the woman's pacer and served two years in prison (McClintock, *Pioneer Days in the Black Hills*, 215).

31. *Black Hills Pioneer* (Deadwood), October 18, 1878, reprinted in the *Cheyenne Daily Sun*, October 21, 1878.

32. Nothing is known of "Jack Smith," who is mentioned as a road agent and Tom Price gang member only by Jesse Brown. The name may have been an alias for another known gang member, possibly Dave Black.

33. Brown and Willard, *Black Hills Trails*, 302.

34. The *Laramie Daily Sentinel* of October 16, 1878, reported "Price was wounded four times, twice fatally."

35. *Black Hills Pioneer* (Deadwood), October 18, 1878, reprinted in the *Cheyenne Daily Sun*, October 21, 1878.

36. Boone May thought the escaped bandit was Dave Black, which may have been another name for the same individual. In any event "Jack Smith" or "Dave Black" after this shooting clash was not seen again in the Black Hills (*Cheyenne Daily Sun*, February 17, 1879).

37. Brown and Willard, *Black Hills Trails*, 303.

38. Ibid., 304.

39. Quoted in the *Laramie Daily Sentinel*, October 23, 1878.

40. *Cheyenne Daily Sun*, February 17, 1879.

41. Frye, *Atlas of Wyoming Outlaws*, 68.

42. *Cheyenne Daily Leader*, October 22, 1878.

43. Brown and Willard, *Black Hills Trails*, 304–305.

44. Spring, *Cheyenne and Black Hills Stage and Express Routes*, 278.

45. *Cheyenne Daily Sun*, November 4, 1878. The story went out on the wire services and was reported in the November 4 editions of the *Indianapolis Sentinel* and the *Chicago Inter-Ocean*, as well as other papers. Russell Thorp, Jr., whose father purchased the Cheyenne and Black Hills stage line from Gilmer and associates in 1883, wrote that he discussed this lynching with

Scott Davis in the 1930s, and Davis told him that since all parties to the affair were now dead he could reveal that "frontier justice had prevailed that day and was carried out by the shotgun messengers of the stage line under the direction of the management" (Thorp, "Cheyenne to Deadwood Stage," 50).

46. *Cheyenne Daily Sun*, October 17, 1878, quoting the *Council Bluffs (Iowa) Nonpareil*.

47. Ibid.; *Atlantic (Iowa) Telegraph*, October 16, 1878; *Chicago Inter-Ocean*, October 15, 1878.

48. *Atlantic (Iowa) Telegraph*, October 16, 1878.

49. Ibid., October 23, 1878.

50. Ibid., October 30, 1878; *Laramie Daily Sentinel*, October 26, 1878.

51. *Cheyenne Daily Sun*, October 24, 1878.

52. *Central City (Nebraska) Times*, October 31, 1878, quoted in Engebretson, *Empty Saddles*, 28.

53. Spring, *Cheyenne and Black Hills Stage and Express Routes*, 274; Engebretson, *Empty Saddles*, 29.

54. *Kearney (Nebraska) Press*, November 6, 1878, quoted in Engebretson, *Empty Saddles*, 28; Spring, *Cheyenne and Black Hills Stage and Express Routes*, 274.

55. Taylor, "In the Days of the Deadwood Treasure Coach."

56. *Laramie Daily Sentinel*, October 30, 1878.

57. Ibid., October 28, 1878.

58. *Cheyenne Daily Sun*, November 2, 1878.

59. *Laramie Daily Sentinel*, November 9, 1878.

60. Frye, *Atlas of Wyoming Outlaws*, 262; Spring, *Cheyenne and Black Hills Stage and Express Routes*, 279.

61. *Cheyenne Daily Sun*, November 2, 4, 1878.

62. *Laramie Daily Sentinel*, November 29, 1878; Frye, *Atlas of Wyoming Outlaws*, 262.

63. Frye, *Atlas of Wyoming Outlaws*, 262. In January 1878 the Wyoming Board of Penitentiary Commissioners, meeting in Cheyenne, approved a five-year contractual agreement with Nebraska to house Wyoming convicts at the Lincoln prison at a cost of 40 cents per day per prisoner (*Laramie Daily Sentinel*, January 21, 1878).

64. Quoted in the *Laramie Daily Sentinel*, October 18, 1878.

65. *Omaha (Nebraska) World Herald*, December 21, 1878.

66. It is clear that Charley Ross, alias Jack Campbell, and the "Jack Campbell" operating as a member of the "Big Nose George" Parrott gang in Montana as late as 1880 were not the same man. The use of another outlaw's name was a ploy often employed by western outlaws to confuse lawmen. Interestingly, the Jack Campbell of Montana sometimes went by "Carey," the name of the Canyon Springs stage robber who escaped the general roundup of road agents after that crime. The name exchange trick did confound law officers and the general citizenry at the time and has presented a problem for historians ever since.

67. It was the capture of Ross, following on the incarceration of Brown and Borris and the lynching of McLaughlin and Mansfield, that prompted Lurline Monte Verde to contact a reporter for the *Cheyenne Daily Sun* to tell her story about nursing the badly wounded Brown after the Whoop Up robbery.

68. *Cheyenne Daily Sun*, April 13, 1879.

69. Ibid.

70. Frye, *Atlas of Wyoming Outlaws*, 69; Spring, *Cheyenne and Black Hills Stage and Express Routes*, 281.

71. Frye, *Atlas of Wyoming Outlaws*, 57, 61; *Cheyenne Daily Sun*, November 27, 1878.

72. *Laramie Daily Sentinel*, November 9, 1878. In his account of the robbery and chase written many years later, Luke Voorhees said: "We recovered the greater part of the gold dust and gold bars, as my men were after the robbers so hot that they dropped most of the gold so they could make better time getting away." His memory beclouded somewhat by the passage of time, perhaps, Voorhees said that only four bandits were involved in the holdup. "My men caught two of them, two we never did get," he said, but hinted that after the Canyon Springs affair road agents often received hempen justice: "When the messengers caught any of them they were not known to do any stage robbing from that time on. . . . Lame Johnny and others disappeared" (*Lusk [Wyoming] Herald*, March 2, 1950).

73. *Lincoln (Nebraska) Daily Star*, September 20, 1914.

CHAPTER 10

1. *Cheyenne Daily Sun*, January 23, 1879.

2. Ibid., March 14, 1879.

3. Ibid., March 26, 1879.

4. Ibid., April 22, 1879.

5. Ingham, *Digging Gold among the Rockies*, 219, 227.

6. *New Hampshire Sentinel* (Keene), September 18, 1879.

7. Brown and Willard, *Black Hills Trails*, 269.

8. *Cheyenne Daily Sun*, August 22, 1877.

9. Quoted in Lee, *Wild Towns of Nebraska*, 78.

10. Rybolt, "Legend Becomes Reality," 33. This haul would amount to more than $3.5 million in 2009 dollars (Tom's Inflation Calculator).

11. Brown and Willard, *Black Hills Trails*, 270.

12. Sheriff "Con" McCarty was called "Dan McCarthy" by magazine writer Koller ("Saga of Quickshot Davis," 30), who said McCarthy, after promoting a bare-knuckle prize fight matching Davis with an opponent years earlier, had skipped out with the proceeds, thus engendering the distrust of Davis.

13. Brown and Willard, *Black Hills Trails*, 271.

14. Ibid.; *Cheyenne Daily Leader*, March 11, 1880; *Cheyenne Daily Sun*, March 12, 1880.

15. Brown and Willard, *Black Hills Trails*, 271–72.

16. Ibid., 272; Lee, *Wild Towns of Nebraska*, 90–91.

17. Brown and Willard, *Black Hills Trails*, 273; Bristow, *Whispering Smith*, 63.

18. *Cheyenne Daily Leader*, March 11, 1880; *Cheyenne Daily Sun*, March 11, 1880; *Reno (Nevada) Evening Gazette*, March 12, 1880; Rybolt, " 'Whispering Smith' Still a Mystery," 6.

19. Rybolt, " 'Whispering Smith' Still a Mystery," 6; Bristow, *Whispering Smith*, 64.

20. Bristow, *Whispering Smith*, 64.

21. *Sidney (Nebraska) Telegraph*, May 29, 1880; *Palo Alto (California) Reporter*, June 5, 1880.

22. Brown and Willard, *Black Hills Trails*, 274.

23. Rybolt, " 'Whispering Smith' Still a Mystery," 7.

24. Ibid.; Bristow, *Whispering Smith*, 66.

25. *Sidney (Nebraska) Telegraph*, January 8, 1881; Cochrane, *American West*, 177. Joe Koller, in his article extolling Scott Davis, credits his hero instead of Smith for shooting "Patsy" Walters and Dennis Flannigan (whom he calls "Finnegan") and says incorrectly that Davis was made marshal at Sidney ("Saga of Quickshot Davis," 55).

26. *Reno (Nevada) Evening Gazette*, April 2, 1881; Lee, *Wild Towns of Nebraska*, 91.

27. Brown and Willard, *Black Hills Trails*, 274.

28. Or from $4 million to $9.5 million in 2009 dollars (Tom's Inflation Calculator).

29. *Winnipeg Free Press*, March 27, 1882. This would represent more than a third of a billion in 2009 dollars (Tom's Inflation Calculator).

30. Kingsbury and Smith, *History of Dakota Territory*, 1329; Parker, *Deadwood*, 100; Mahnken, "Sidney–Black Hills Trail," 225.

CHAPTER 11

1. Quoted in Thorp, "Cheyenne to Deadwood Stage," 51.

2. Spring, *Cheyenne and Black Hills Stage and Express Routes*, 346.

3. Ibid., 352–53; *Idaho Statesman* (Boise), November 3, 1891; *Ohio Democrat* (New Philadelphia), October 4, 1894; *Stevens Point (Wisconsin) Daily Journal*, May 11, 1907.

4. Spring, *Cheyenne and Black Hills Stage and Express Routes*, 352; Woods, *Wyoming Biographies*, 150–51.

5. Voorhees, *Personal Recollections*, 9; Spring, *Cheyenne and Black Hills Stage and Express Routes*, 357; Woods, *Wyoming Biographies*, 191.

6. Pence, *Boswell*, passim; Gorzalka, *Wyoming's Territorial Sheriffs*, 105–13; Woods, *Wyoming Biographies*, 41.

7. Kellar, *Seth Bullock*, passim; Wolff, *Seth Bullock*, 162–63; Parker, *Deadwood*, 76; White, *Index of U.S. Marshals*, 11; Thrapp, *Encyclopedia of Frontier Biography*, 1:190.

8. Spring, *Cheyenne and Black Hills Stage and Express Routes*, 281; Gorzalka, *Wyoming's Territorial Sheriffs*, 37–42; White, *Index of U.S. Marshals*, 13.

9. Gorzalka, *Wyoming's Territorial Sheriffs*, 83–85.

10. Thrapp, *Encyclopedia of Frontier Biography*, 2:563–64.

11. *Omaha (Nebraska) World Herald*, January 17, 1907.

12. Bristow, *Whispering Smith*; DeArment, *Deadly Dozen, Vol. 3.*

13. McClintock, *Pioneer Days in the Black Hills*, 333.

14. Gorzalka, *Wyoming's Territorial Sheriffs*, 129.

15. McClintock, *Pioneer Days in the Black Hills*, 290; Brown and Willard, *Black Hills Trails*, 513–15.

16. *Bald Mountain News* (Terry, South Dakota), January 6, 1899.

17. McClintock, *Pioneer Days in the Black Hills*, 290–91.

18. *Bald Mountain News* (Terry, South Dakota), January 6, 1899.

19. U.S. Census, Lawrence County, Dakota Territory, 1880; McClintock, *Pioneer Days in the Black Hills*, 297; Spring, *Cheyenne and Black Hills Stage and Express Routes*, 347.

20. Bennett, *Old Deadwood Days*, 87–88; Fred T. May to Sharon Cunningham, July 12, 2006.

21. *Black Hills Daily Times* (Deadwood), January 22, 1879; Spring, *Cheyenne and Black Hills Stage and Express Routes*, 352.

22. Billy Sample, one of the last three Black Hills stagecoach messengers, together with Dick Bullock and Bill Linn, was reportedly later working as a messenger on the Mexican Central Railroad, with a run of 800 miles and twenty stations along the way (Bennett, *Old Deadwood Days*, 85–86).

23. *Bald Mountain News* (Terry, South Dakota), January 6, 1899.

24. Ibid.

25. Creagan, "He Knew the West in All Its Paces," 11.

26. *Lincoln (Nebraska) Daily Star*, September 20, 1914; *Billings (Montana) Gazette*, October 13, 1932; Spring, *Cheyenne and Black Hills Stage and Express Routes*, 344.

27. Frink, *Cow Country Cavalcade*, 94; Smith, *War on Powder River*, 188.

28. O'Neal, *Johnson County War*, passim; DeArment, *Alias Frank Canton*, 120–44.

29. U.S. Census: Salt Lake County, Utah, 1900; Denver County, Colorado, 1910; Creagan, "He Knew the West in All Its Paces," 11; Spring, *Cheyenne and Black Hills Stage and Express Routes*, 344.

30. The Black Hills Placer Mining Company was incorporated under the laws of New York and Dakota on December 8, 1879, and headquartered on Wall Street, New York City. The name of Cornelius Vanderbilt stood high on an impressive list of company trustees and important stockholders. Company counsel was Sherburne Blake Eaton, to whom Bierce reported at length, often defending his employment of Boone May, the celebrated gunman and accused murderer. The company secretary and treasurer was Marcus Walker, who came to Deadwood to check up on Bierce and made no secret of his distaste for May (Fatout, *Ambrose Bierce and the Black Hills*, 17–18).

31. Bierce to Eaton, September 2, 1880, quoted in ibid., 18.

32. Fatout, *Ambrose Bierce and the Black Hills*, 76–77.

33. Bierce, *Collected Works of Ambrose Bierce*.

34. Bierce to Eaton, September 2, 1880, quoted in Fatout, *Ambrose Bierce and the Black Hills*, 18.

35. Bierce to Eaton, September 14, 1880, quoted in ibid., 119–20.

36. Bierce, *Collected Works of Ambrose Bierce*, 122. Bierce went on to a notable career as a journalist and author; his short stories have been favorably compared with those of Edgar Allan Poe and Bret Harte. He disappeared in Mexico in 1913.

37. Bennett, *Old Deadwood Days*, 88; Brown and Willard, *Black Hills Trails*, 441–44; *Duluth (Minnesota) Daily Tribune*, June 17, 1881; Fred T. May to Sharon Cunningham, July 12, 2006.

38. McGillycuddy, *Blood on the Moon*, 148–49.

39. Ibid., 149.

40. *Cheyenne Daily Leader*, April 4, 1881.

41. *Cheyenne Daily Sun*, April 12, 1881. Variations of this story were picked up by the news services and disseminated with exaggerated embellishments to papers as distant as Bangor, Maine (*Bangor [Maine] Whig and Courier*, April 15, 1881).

42. Quoted in McGillycuddy, *Blood on the Moon*, 149.

43. *Cheyenne Daily Leader*, May 5, 1881.

44. McGillycuddy, *Blood on the Moon*, 149.

45. Brown and Willard, *Black Hills Trails*, 444.

46. Ibid.

47. Bennett, *Old Deadwood Days*, 88; Fatout, *Ambrose Bierce and the Black Hills*, 165; *Rocky Mountain News* (Denver), January 6, 1899. There are several versions of Boone May's Latin American adventures and misadventures. In one, Boone May and a relative named Fred May struck it rich with a gold mine in Peru, but got into trouble with government authorities over rights to their claim. In a heated argument a Peruvian military officer reportedly slapped Boone in the face, whereupon Boone drew a gun and shot the man dead. He and his partner fled into the wilderness, but Boone was "suddenly seized with a strange malady that seemed to dry up his blood and eat away his bones, [and] he died after two days."

Another story had Boone May striking it rich in Bolivia, but getting into trouble when he shot and killed an army officer over the affections of "a dark-eyed South American beauty." He hid out with Indians "near the head of the Amazon" until he could go to Rio de Janeiro, where he reportedly died of yellow fever.

A. M. Willard, who corresponded with Boone May up until May's death, merely said the old shotgun messenger died in Brazil, with providing details (Daryl May to Sharon Cunningham, July 17, 2006).

If, as was reported, he had cashed in his chips before the turn of the century, Boone May missed out on a sizable inheritance, for his brother Bill, having prospered in the mining business during the years following the stage-coach robbery excitement, died about 1900, leaving a considerable fortune. Brother Jim was dead, and there were no heirs other than the long-departed brother Boone.

Significantly, the major role played by Boone May in winning the war against the Deadwood trail bandits had not been forgotten more than two decades after he had left the Black Hills region. National newspapers reporting the death of William May lauded the one-time road agent nemesis: "Boone May was the most noted of all the messengers who accompanied the treasure coach on its trips out of the Black Hills. He was known for his fearlessness and for the deadly execution he exhibited in the numerous encounters with the road agents who infested the region" (*Omaha [Nebraska] World Herald*, January 30, 1903; *Dallas Morning News*, March 8, 1903).

48. In his huge volume, *Wyatt Earp: A Biography of the Legend*, vol. 1, *The Cowtown Years*, Lee A. Silva devoted almost three dozen pages (400–32) to a detailed analysis of whether Wyatt Earp actually acted as a shotgun messenger on the Deadwood stage, a question still hotly debated among Earpianics (as they are called). He finally concluded that the story is true — probably.

49. Bennett, *Old Deadwood Days*, 86.

50. Spring, *Cheyenne and Black Hills Stage and Express Routes*, 343.

51. Bennett, *Old Deadwood Days*, 87; Klock, *All Roads Lead to Deadwood*, 115.

52. *Winnipeg Free Press*, March 27, 1882.

53. *Arizona Weekly Journal* (Prescott), August 21, 1889; *Journals of the Seventeenth Assembly of the Territory of Arizona*, 41.

54. Ancestry.com Family Tree.

55. According to Edwin L. Sabin, road agent Bob Castello was "shot by a boy in a camp he had jumped" (*Wild Men of the Wild West*, 206).

56. *Cheyenne Daily Leader*, August 20, 1881; Gard, *Frontier Justice*, 209–10; Gorzalka, *Wyoming's Territorial Sheriffs*, 167.

57. Gorzalka, *Wyoming's Territorial Sheriffs*, 167. The shoes made from Parrott's skin were long on display at the Carbon County Museum in Rawlins and the skullcap at the Union Pacific Railroad Museum in Omaha (Browning, *Violence Was No Stranger*, 189).

58. Frye, *Atlas of Wyoming Outlaws*, 44–45.

59. DeBarthe, *Life and Adventures of Frank Grouard*, 64.

60. Frye, *Atlas of Wyoming Outlaws*, 76.

61. Carroll, "Clark Pelton," 21.

62. Dugan, *Making of Legends*, 123–26.

63. Engebretson, *Empty Saddles*, 161–62.

64. The outlaws had good reason to be delighted; $60,000 in 1877 would be equal to $1,685,000 in 2009 (Tom's Inflation Calculator).

65. The literature focusing on Sam Bass is abundant. In his introduction to the 1956 edition of *A Sketch of Sam Bass, the Bandit* by Charles L. Martin,

originally published in 1880, outlaw and lawman bibliophile Ramon Adams said that he had about 200 books in his personal library dealing with Bass. Since then a number of books examining the Sam Bass story have appeared, most notably Rick Miller's comprehensive 1999 volume, *Sam Bass & Gang*. Jack Davis, the last member of the Texas gang who had preyed on stage-coaches in the Black Hills, dropped from sight and was not heard of again. Detective Millard F. Leech suggested Davis may have been the mysterious Frank Jackson of the Bass gang in Texas, who also disappeared after the Round Rock shootout (Miller, *Sam Bass & Gang*, 266).

66. Nielsen, *Ogallala*, 22–23. For some reason, being sheriff of Keith County, Nebraska, was not a position many coveted during the cow town period. In less than five years Leech and five other men moved in and out of the office (Yost, *Call of the Range*, 61).

67. *Cranbury (New Jersey) Press*, September 8, 1893; *New York Times*, February 24, 1895; U.S. Census, Boulder County, Colorado, 1900.

68. Sabin, *Wild Men of the Wild West*, 207.

69. Engebretson, *Empty Saddles*, 90.

70. David, *Malcolm Campbell*, 57.

71. Yost, *Call of the Range*, 83.

72. *Laramie Daily Sentinel*, November 1, 1879.

73. Reynolds, *Twin Hells*, 209.

74. *Laramie Daily Sentinel*, May 24, 1894. If Jack Watkins survived to 1889 he might have been amused to find himself as a major figure in a dime novel published that year. Newspaperman Leander P. Richardson, who was in Deadwood in its salad days, later wrote a number of fictional stories about people and events in the Black Hills. A featured character in *The Road Agents: A Tale of Back Hills Life* was outlaw Jack Watkins, who vied for the affections of the heroine, only to be defeated by the hero, Oregon Bill (McDermott, *Gold Rush*, 80–81).

75. Sorenson, *Hands Up!* 49; Miller, *Sam Bass & Gang*, 63.

76. Martin, *Sketch of Sam Bass*, 15.

77. 1880 U.S. Census, Denton County, Texas; Miller, *Sam Bass & Gang*, 319.

78. Thrapp, *Encyclopedia of Frontier Biography*, 1:220. The life of "Calamity Jane" has been recounted in many books. The best by far is McLaird, *Calamity Jane: The Woman and the Legend*.

79. *Helena (Montana) Independent*, November 3, 1881, reprinted from the *San Francisco Examiner*; DeArment, *Knights of the Green Cloth*, 251–52.

80. Spring, *Cheyenne and Black Hills Stage and Express Routes*, 359.

81. Root and Connelley, *Overland Stage to California*, 58–59, 62.

82. Spring, *Cheyenne and Black Hills Stage and Express Routes*, 359, 363; *New York Times*, September 2, 1890, reprinted from the *Chicago Tribune*; Fifer, *Bad Boys of the Black Hills*, 10–11.

83. Root and Connelley, *Overland Stage to California*, 64.

84. Fifer, *Bad Boys of the Black Hills*, 11.

85. *Sheridan (Wyoming) Press*, December 29, 1900.

86. Fifer, *Bad Boys of the Black Hills*, 10–11.

87. Russell, *Lives and Legends of Buffalo Bill*, 309.

88. This particular coach was reportedly built in 1873 and was not, as has often been asserted, the famous ironclad "Monitor" (Greene, *900 Miles on the Butterfield Trail*, 29).

Bibliography

GOVERNMENT DOCUMENTS
Fort Laramie Post Return, June 1877. Microcopy No. 617, Roll 597, National Archives and Records Service, Washington, D.C.
Journals of the Seventeenth Assembly of the Territory of Arizona. 1893.

U.S. CENSUS
Colorado: Boulder County, 1900; Denver County, 1910
Dakota Territory: Lawrence County, 1880
Kansas: Bourbon County, 1860
Ohio: Trumbull County, 1850, 1860, 1870
Nebraska: Dodge County, 1860, 1870
Texas: Denton County, 1880
Utah: Salt Lake County, 1900
Wyoming: Albany County, 1870

MANUSCRIPTS
Browning, James A. "The Western Reader's Guide," Vol. 2.

LETTERS AND E-MAILS
Daryl May to Sharon Cunningham, July 17, 2006
Fred T. May to Sharon Cunningham, July 12, 13, 2006
Barbara McCallister to Sharon Cunningham, July 22, 2006

NEWSPAPERS
Alton (Illinois) Daily Telegraph, March 24, 1881
Argus and Patriot (Montpelier, Vermont), July 11, 1878
Atlantic (Iowa) Telegraph, October 16, 23, 30, 1878
Arizona Weekly Journal (Prescott), August 21, 1889
Bald Mountain News (Terry, South Dakota), January 6, 1899
Bangor (Maine) Daily Whig and Courier, April 15, 1881
Bismarck (Dakota) Tri-Weekly Herald, July 20, 1877
Bismarck (Dakota) Tri-Weekly Tribune, July 2, August 3, 6, October 3, 31, 1877
Black Hills Daily Pioneer-Times (Deadwood), May 3–9, 1902
Black Hills Daily Times (Deadwood), July 12, August 20, September 29,

October 4, 1877; January 20, September 14, October 3, 8, November 8,
21, 1878; January 22, July 3, 1879; February 10, July 27, 1880

Black Hills Journal (Rapid City, Dakota), October 5, 12, 1878; July 5, 1879

Black Hills Weekly Pioneer (Deadwood), June 26, 1876; June 30, 1877;
October 18, 1878

Cheyenne Daily Leader, January 1877–May 1879; February 13, March 11,
1880; August 20, 1881

Cheyenne Daily Sun, March 1876–May 1879; February 20, March 5, 11, 12,
August 17, 24, 1880

Chicago Inter-Ocean, June 15, July 26, 1877; July 3, October 15, November 4,
1878

Cincinnati Daily Gazette, January 15, 16, 17, December 24, 1878

Colorado Banner (Boulder), July 26, 1877

Colorado Springs Gazette, August 10, 1878

Cranbury (New Jersey) Press, September 8, 1893

Custer (Dakota) Chronicle, February 12, 1881

Dallas Morning News, March 8, 1903

Denison (Texas) Daily News, July 6, 1878

Denver Times, July 16, 1877

Duluth (Minnesota) Daily Tribune, June 17, 1881

Fort Smith (Arkansas) Weekly Elevator, August 8, 1877

Galveston (Texas) Daily News, July 24, 1878

Golden (Colorado) Weekly Globe, August 19, 1876

Helena (Montana) Independent, August 28, November 20, 1877; August 7,
1880; November 3, 1881

Hillsboro (Ohio) Gazette, November 29, December 12, 1878

Idaho Daily Statesman (Boise), November 3, 1891

Indianapolis Daily Sentinel, July 7, 9, November 2, 1877; November 4, 1878;
January 5, 1880

Iowa State Reporter (Waterloo), October 31, 1877

Lafayette (Louisiana) Advertiser, January 4, 1890

Laramie Daily Independent, September 14, 1872

Laramie Daily Sentinel, October–November, 1871; May 24, August 14,
September 1, 5, 1875; April 1876–April 1881; May 24, 1894

Laramie Weekly Sentinel, August 27, September 3, 1877

Las Vegas (New Mexico) Optic, February 6, 1880

Lethbridge Herald (Alberta, Canada), November 30, 1932

Lincoln (Nebraska) Daily Star, September 20, 1914

Lusk (Wyoming) Herald, February 25, 1932; March 2, 1950

New Hampshire Sentinel (Keene), August 9, 1877; September 18, 1879

New York Times, September 27, 1881; September 2, 1890; February 24, 1895

Ohio Democrat (New Philadelphia), October 4, 1894

Omaha (Nebraska) Daily Bee, November 27, 1877; October 24, 1878

Omaha (Nebraska) Daily Herald, January 6, 1878

Omaha (Nebraska) Republican, September 23, 1881

Omaha (Nebraska) World Herald, December 21, 25, 1878; February 24, November 19, 1880; January 30, 1903; January 17, 1907
Palo Alto (California) Reporter, June 5, 1880
Philadelphia Inquirer, March 24, 1901
Racine (Wisconsin) Argus, July 11, 1878
Reno (Nevada) Evening Gazette, March 12, 1880; April 2, 1881
Rocky Mountain News (Denver), January 6, 1899
Salt Lake (Utah) Tribune, September 28, 1878
San Francisco Chronicle, November 8, 1877
San Francisco Evening Bulletin, October 4, November 2, 1877
San Francisco Examiner, August 9, 1896
Sheridan (Wyoming) Press, December 29, 1900
Sidney (Nebraska) Telegraph, July 12, 1879; May 29, 1880; January 8, 1881
Silver City (New Mexico) Enterprise, December 26, 1884
Sioux County Herald (Orange City, Iowa), February 19, 1880
Sioux County Independent (Orange City, Iowa), October 16, 1878
Springfield (Massachusetts) Republican, December 16, 1880
Stevens Point (Wisconsin) Daily Journal, January 10, 1880; May 11, 1907
Titusville (Pennsylvania) Herald, March 24, 1881
Trenton (New Jersey) State Gazette, June 30, August 27, 1877
Wheeling (West Virginia) Daily Register, November 2, 1877
Winnipeg Free Press, October 9, 1878; March 27, 1882
Worcester (Massachusetts) Daily Spy, July 6, 27, 1878
Yellowstone Journal (Miles City, Montana), August 7, 1880

ARTICLES

Anonymous. "Along the Cheyenne-Deadwood Trail." http://userpages .aug.com/bdobson/deadwood.html.

Anonymous. "Bismarck to Deadwood Stage Trail." http://www.waymarking .com/waymarks/WMHG.

Ayres, Captain James Cooper. "After Big Game with Packs." *Century Magazine*, May–October 1899.

Carroll, Murray L. "Clark Pelton: The Stage-Robbing Kid." *True West*, August 1990, 16–21.

Carson, John. "Iron Man Llewellyn." *Frontier Times*, January 1972, 21–21, 58–60.

Creagan, Leo F. "He Knew the West in All Its Paces." *Union Pacific Magazine*, October 1927, 11, 19.

DeArment, R. K. "Another Wyatt Earp Tale — Myth or Fact?" *Wild West History Association Journal* 3, no. 6 (December 2010).

Hansen, John. "Boone May: Shotgun Messenger." *Great West*, December 1974, 18–21, 42.

Harrison, C. William. "Shotgun Messenger on Hell's Highway." *True Western Adventures*, April 1959, 16–17, 62–64.

Hockett, William M. "Boone May—Gunfighter of the Black Hills." http://www.bar-w.com/boonemay.html.

Koller, Joe. "Saga of Quickshot Davis." *The West*, March 1971, 30–33, 53–56.

LaTelle, G. H. "Lame Johnny." *True West*, November–December 1963, 41–42.

Lawton, R. T. "Necktie Party Ended Lame Outlaw's Career." http://www.deadwoodmagazine.com/archivedsite/Archives/LameJohnny.

Mahnken, Norbert R. "The Sidney–Black Hills Trail." *Nebraska History* (1949): 203–25.

Rybolt, Robert. "Legend Becomes Reality—Whispering Smith Is Real!" *True West*, February 1984, 32–36.

———. " 'Whispering Smith' Still a Mystery." *Quarterly of the National Association for Outlaw and Lawman History* (Spring 1985): 2–8.

Spring, Agnes Wright. "Who Robbed the Mail Coach?" *Frontier Times*, September 1967, 25.

———. "The Canyon Springs Robbery." *Frontier Times*, January 1968, 6–11, 52–56.

Taylor, W. H. "In the Days of the Deadwood Treasure Coach: A Chapter from the Recollections of W. H. Taylor." *Pacific Monthly* (June 1909): 553–63.

Thorp, Russell, Jr. "Cheyenne to Deadwood Stage." *True West*, June 1966, 23–25, 49–51.

Vaughn, J. W. "The Fort Laramie Hog Ranches." *New York Posse Brand Book of the Westerners*, No. 2, 1966, 39–41.

Wolfe, George D. "Curtains for Big Nose George." *True West*, March–April 1961, 18–19, 50–52.

BOOKS AND PAMPHLETS

Adams, Ramon F. *Burs Under the Saddle: A Second Look at Books and Histories of the West*. Norman: University of Oklahoma Press, 1964.

———. *Six-Guns and Saddle Leather: A Bibliography of Books and Pamphlets on Western Outlaws and Gunmen*. Norman: University of Oklahoma Press, 1969.

———. *More Burs under the Saddle: Books and Histories of the West*. Norman: University of Oklahoma Press, 1979.

Allen, Frederick. *A Decent Orderly Lynching: The Montana Vigilantes*. Norman: University of Oklahoma Press, 2004.

Anonymous. *Journals of the Seventeenth Assembly of the Territory of Arizona*. Phoenix: Herald Book and Job Office, 1893.

Bancroft, Hubert Howe. *History of Nevada, Colorado and Wyoming. 1540–1888*. San Francisco: Historical Co., 1890.

Beery, Gladys B. *Sinners & Saints: Tales of Old Laramie City*. Glendo, Wyo.: High Plains Press, 1994.

Bennett, Estelline. *Old Deadwood Days*. New York: Charles Scribner's Sons, 1935.

Bierce, Ambrose. *The Collected Works of Ambrose Bierce, Vol. 1*. Bel Air, Calif.: Dodo Press, 2008.

Bragg, William F. *Wyoming: Rugged but Right*. Boulder, Colo.: Pruett Publishing, 1979.

Bridwell, J. W. *The Life and Adventures of Robert McKimie, Alias "Little Reddy," from Texas*. Hillsboro, Ohio: Hillsboro Gazette Office, 1878. Reprint, Houston: Frontier Press of Texas, 1955.

Bristow, Allen P. *Whispering Smith: His Life and Misadventures*. Santa Fe, N.Mex.: Sunstone Press, 2007.

Bronson, Edgar Beecher. *The Red-Blooded*. Chicago: A. C. McClurg, 1910.

——. *The Vanguard*. New York: George H. Doran, 1914.

Brown, Jesse, and A. M. Willard. *The Black Hills Trails*. Rapid City, S.Dak.: Rapid City Journal, 1924.

Brown, Larry K. *The Hog Ranches of Wyoming*. Glendo, Wyo.: High Plains Press, 1995.

——. *Coyotes and Canaries: Characters Who Made the Wild West Wild . . . and Wonderful!* Glendo, Wyo.: High Plains Press, 2002.

Browning, James A. *The Western Reader's Guide: A Selected Bibliography of Nonfiction Magazines, 1953–91*. Stillwater, Okla.: Barbed Wire Press, 1992.

——. *Violence Was No Stranger: A Guide to the Grave Sites of Famous Westerners*. Stillwater, Okla.: Barbed Wire Press, 1993.

Bryan, Howard. *Wildest of the Wild West: True Tales of a Frontier Town on the Santa Fe Trail*. Santa Fe, N.Mex.: Clear Light, 1988.

Burroughs, John Rolfe. *Where the Old West Stayed Young*. New York: William Morrow, 1962.

Casey, Robert J. *The Black Hills and Their Incredible Characters*. Indianapolis, Ind.: Bobbs-Merrill, 1949.

Cochrane, Keith. *American West: A Historical Chronology*. Rapid City, S.Dak.: Cochrane, 1992.

Cody, William F. *The Life of Hon. William F. Cody, Known as Buffalo Bill, the Famous Hunter, Scout and Guide: An Autobiography*. Hartford, Conn.: Frank E. Bliss, 1879.

Collier, William Ross, and Edwin Victor Westrate. *Dave Cook of the Rockies*. New York: Rufus Rockwell Wilson, 1936.

Cook, D. J. *Hands Up! or Twenty Years of Detective Life in the Mountains and on the Plains*. Norman: University of Oklahoma Press, 1958.

Coursey, G. W. *Beautiful Black Hills*. Mitchell, S.Dak.: Educator Supply, 1926.

Cowan, Bud. *Range Rider*. Garden City, N.Y.: Doubleday, Doran, 1930.

David, Robert B. *Malcolm Campbell, Sheriff*. Casper, Wyo.: S. E. Boyer, 1932.

Dawson, Charles. *Pioneer Tales of the Oregon Trail and of Jefferson County*. Topeka, Kans.: Crane, 1912.

DeArment, Robert K. *Knights of the Green Cloth: The Saga of the Frontier Gamblers*. Norman: University of Oklahoma Press, 1982.

——. *Alias Frank Canton*. Norman: University of Oklahoma Press, 1996.

——. *Deadly Dozen, Vol. 3*. Norman: University of Oklahoma Press, 2009.

DeBarthe, Joe. *The Life and Adventures of Frank Grouard, Chief of Scouts, U.S.A.* St. Joseph, Mo.: Combe Printing, 1894.

Dimsdale, Thomas J. *The Vigilantes of Montana, or Popular Justice in the Rocky Mountains*. Alexandria, Va.: Time-Life Books, 1980.

Drago, Harry Sinclair. *Road Agents and Train Robbers*. New York: Dodd, Mead, 1973.

Dugan, Mark. *The Making of Legends: More True Stories of Frontier America*. Athens: Swallow Press/Ohio University Press, 1997.

Engebretson, Doug. *Empty Saddles: Forgotten Names: Outlaws of the Black Hills and Wyoming*. Aberdeen, S.Dak.: North Plains Press, 1982.

Erwin, Richard E. *The Truth about Wyatt Earp*. Carpinteria, Calif.: O. K. Press, 1992.

Fatout, Paul. *Ambrose Bierce and the Black Hills*. Norman: University of Oklahoma Press, 1956.

Fattig, Timothy W. *Wyatt Earp: The Biography*. Honolulu, Hawaii: Talei Publishers, 2002.

Fifer, Barbara. *Bad Boys of the Black Hills . . . And Some Wild Women Too*. Helena, Mont.: Far Country Press, 2008.

Flanagan, Mike. *The Old West: Day by Day*. New York: Facts on File, 1995.

Flannery, L. G. ("Pat"). *John Hunton's Diary*. Vol. 2, *1876–'77*. Lingle, Wyo.: Guide-Review, 1958.

Frink, Maurice. *Cow Country Cavalcade: Eighty Years of the Wyoming Stock Growers Association*. Denver: Old West, 1954.

Frye, Elnora L. *Atlas of Wyoming Outlaws at the Territorial Penitentiary*. Laramie, Wyo.: Jelm Mountain Publications, 1990.

Fuller, Clark. *Pioneer Paths*. Broken Bow, Neb.: Purcells, n.d.

Gard, Wayne. *Frontier Justice*. Norman: University of Oklahoma Press, 1949.

Gorzalka, Ann. *Wyoming's Territorial Sheriffs*. Glendo, Wyo.: High Plains Press, 1998.

Greene, A. C. *900 Miles on the Butterfield Trail*. Denton: University of North Texas Press, 2006.

Hanna, Oliver Perry. *An Old-Timer's Story of the Old Wild West*. Casper, Wyo.: Hawks Book, 1984.

Hardy, William P. *A Chronology of the Old West*. New York: Vantage Press, 1988.

Hogg, Thomas E. *Authentic History of Sam Bass and His Gang*. Bandera, Tex.: Frontier Times, 1932.

Horan, James D., and Paul Sann. *A Pictorial History of the Wild West*. New York: Crown, 1954.

Howard, James W. *"Doc" Howard's Memoirs*. N.p.: n.d. (ca. 1930).

Hufsmith, George W. *The Wyoming Lynching of Cattle Kate, 1889*. Glendo, Wyo.: High Plains Press, 1993.

Hughes, Richard B. *Pioneer Years in the Black Hills*. Glendale, Calif.: Arthur H. Clark, 1957.

Hutton, Harold. *Doc Middleton: Life and Legends of the Notorious Plains Outlaw*. Chicago: Swallow Press, 1974.

Ingham, G. Thomas. *Digging Gold among the Rockies*. Lake City, Colo.: Western Reflections, 2008.

Jahns, Pat. *The Frontier World of Doc Holliday: Faro Dealer from Dallas to Deadwood*. New York: Hastings House, 1957.

Johnson, Rolf. *Happy as a Big Sunflower: Adventures in the West, 1876–1880*. Lincoln: University of Nebraska Press, 2000.

Kellar, Kenneth C. *Seth Bullock: Frontier Marshal*. Aberdeen, S.Dak.: North Plains Press, 1972.

Kelly, Charles. *The Outlaw Trail: The Story of Butch Cassidy and the "Wild Bunch."* New York: Bonanza Books, 1938.

Kingsbury, George Washington, and George Martin Smith. *History of Dakota Territory*. Cincinnati: S. J. Clarke, 1915.

Klock, Irma H. *All Roads Lead to Deadwood*. Lead, S.Dak.: Irma H. Klock, 1979.
———. *Black Hills Outlaws, Lawmen and Others*. Deadwood, S.Dak.: Dakota Graphics, 1981.

Lake, Stuart. *Wyatt Earp: Frontier Marshal*. Boston: Houghton Mifflin, 1931.

Langford, Nathaniel Pitt. *Vigilante Days and Ways: The Pioneers of the Rockies*. New York: A. L. Burt, 1912.

Lee, Wayne C. *Wild Towns of Nebraska*. Caldwell, Idaho: Caxton Printers, 1988.

Leish, Kenneth W., ed. *The American Heritage Pictorial History of the Presidents of the United States, Vol. 1*. New York: Simon and Schuster, 1968.

Love, Nat. *The Life and Adventures of Nat Love*. Los Angeles: Wayside Press, 1907.

Martin, Charles L. *A Sketch of Sam Bass, the Bandit*. Norman: University of Oklahoma Press, 1956.

May, Robin. *The Gold Rushes: From California to the Klondike*. London: William Luscombe, 1977.

McClintock, John S. *Pioneer Days in the Black Hills*. Norman: University of Oklahoma Press, 2000.

McDermott, John D. *Gold Rush: The Black Hills Story*. Pierre: South Dakota Historical Society Press, 2001.

McGillycuddy, Julia B. *Blood on the Moon: Valentine McGillycuddy and the Sioux*. Lincoln: University of Nebraska Press, 1990.

McLaird, James D. *Calamity Jane: The Woman and the Legend*. Norman: University of Oklahoma Press, 2005.

McLoughlin, Denis. *Wild & Woolly: An Encyclopedia of the Old West*. Garden City, N.Y.: Doubleday, 1975.

Metz, Leon Claire. *The Encyclopedia of Lawmen, Outlaws, and Gunfighters*. New York: Checkmark Books, 2003.

Miller, Rick. *Sam Bass & Gang*. Austin, Tex.: State House Press, 1999.

Moody, Ralph. *Stagecoach West.* New York: Thomas Y. Crowell, 1967.

Moses, George. *Those Good Old Days in the Black Hills.* Rapid City, S.Dak.: Rapid City Journal, 1991.

Nash, Jay Robert. *Encyclopedia of Western Lawmen & Outlaws.* New York: Paragon House, 1992.

Nielsen, Elaine. *Ogallala: A Century on the Trail.* Ogallala, Neb.: Keith County Historical Society, 1984.

O'Neal, Bill. *The Johnson County War.* Austin, Tex.: Eakin Press, 2004.

———. *Cheyenne: A Biography of the "Magic City" of the Old West, 1867–1903.* Austin, Tex.: Eakin Press, 2006.

Parker, Watson. *Gold in the Black Hills.* Lincoln: University of Nebraska Press, 1966.

———. *Deadwood: The Golden Years.* Lincoln: University of Nebraska Press, 1981.

Pence, Mary Lou. *Boswell: The Story of a Frontier Lawman.* Cheyenne, Wyo.: Pioneer Printing & Stationery, 1978.

Pence, Mary Lou, and Lola M. Homsher. *The Ghost Towns of Wyoming.* New York: Hastings House, 1956.

Quiett, Glenn Chesney. *Pay Dirt: A Panorama of American Gold Rushes.* New York: D. Appleton-Century, 1936.

Raine, William MacLeod. *Guns of the Frontier.* New York: Houghton Mifflin, 1940.

Reynolds, John N. *The Twin Hells.* Chicago: Bee Publishing, 1890.

Ricker, Eli S., and Richard E. Jensen. *Voices of the American West, The Settler and Soldier: Interviews of Eli S. Ricker, 1903–1919.* Lincoln: University of Nebraska Press, 2005.

Root, Frank A., and William Elsey Connelley. *Overland Stage to California.* Topeka, Kans.: Crane, 1901.

Rosa, Joseph G. *They Called Him Wild Bill: The Life and Adventures of James Butler Hickok.* Norman: University of Oklahoma Press, 1964.

Rosa, Joseph G., and Waldo E. Koop. *Rowdy Joe Lowe: Gambler with a Gun.* Norman: University of Oklahoma Press, 1989.

Russell, Don. *The Lives and Legends of Buffalo Bill.* Norman: University of Oklahoma Press, 1960.

Sabin, Edwin L. *Wild Men of the Wild West.* New York: Thomas Y. Crowell, 1929.

Sandoz, Mari. *Love Song to the Plains.* Lincoln: University of Nebraska Press, 1966.

Secrest, William B., ed. *I Buried Hickok: The Memoirs of White Eye Anderson.* College Station, Tex.: Creative Publishing, 1980.

Settle, William A., Jr. *Jesse James Was His Name: Or Fact and Fiction concerning the Careers of the Notorious James Brothers of Missouri.* Columbia: University of Missouri Press, 1966.

Silva, Lee A. *Wyatt Earp: A Biography of the Legend.* Vol. 1, *The Cowtown Years.* Santa Ana, Calif.: Graphic Publishers, 2002.

Smith, Helen Huntington. *The War on Powder River*. New York: McGraw-Hill, 1966.

Sorenson, Al. *Hands Up! The History of a Crime*. 1877. Reprint, College Station, Tex.: Creative Publishing, 1982.

Spring, Agnes Wright. *The Cheyenne and Black Hills Stage and Express Routes*. Glendale, Calif.: Arthur H. Clark, 1949.

Stephens, John Richard, ed. *Wyatt Earp Speaks! Cambria, Calif.: Fern Canyon Press, 1998*.

Stiles, T. J. *Jesse James: Last Rebel of the Civil War*. New York: Alfred A. Knopf, 2002.

Sutley, Zack T. *The Last Frontier*. New York: Macmillan, 1930.

Tallent, Annie D. *The Black Hills: Or the Last Hunting Grounds of the Dakotahs*. Sioux Falls, S.Dak.: Brevet Press, 1974.

Tanner, Karen Holliday. *Doc Holliday: A Family Portrait*. Norman: University of Oklahoma Press, 1998.

Tefertiller, Casey. *Wyatt Earp: The Life behind the Legend*. New York: John Wiley & Sons, 1997.

Thompson, George A. *Throw Down the Box! Treasure Tales from Gilmer & Salisbury the Western Stagecoach King*. Salt Lake City, Utah: Dream Garden Press, 1989.

Thrapp, Dan L. *Encyclopedia of Frontier Biography in Three Volumes*. Glendale, Calif.: Arthur H. Clark, 1988.

Turner, Alford E., ed. *The Earps Talk*. College Station, Tex.: Creative Publishing, 1980.

Van Pelt, Lori. *Dreamers & Schemers*. Glendo, Wyo.: High Plains Press, 1999.

Voorhees, Luke. *Personal Recollections of Pioneer Life on the Mountains and Plains of the Great West*. N.p., 1920.

White, Virgil D. *Index of U.S. Marshals, 1789–1960*. Waynesboro, Tenn.: National Historical Publishing, 1988.

Wilson, R. Michael. *Great Stagecoach Robberies of the Old West*. Guilford, Conn.: Twodot, 2007.

Wolff, David A. *Seth Bullock: Black Hills Lawman*. Pierre: South Dakota State Historical Society Press, 2009.

Woods, Lawrence M. *Wyoming Biographies*. Worland, Wyo.: High Plains Publishing, 1991.

Yeatman, Ted. P. *Frank and Jesse James: The Story behind the Legend*. Nashville, Tenn.: Cumberland House Publishing, 2000.

Yost, Nellie Snyder. *The Call of the Range: The Story of the Nebraska Stock Growers Association*. Denver: Sage Books, 1966.

———, ed. *Boss Cowman: The Recollections of Ed Lemmon, 1857–1946*. Lincoln: University of Nebraska Press, 1969.

Young, Harry ("Sam"). *Hard Knocks: A Life Story of the Vanishing West*. Pierre: South Dakota State Historical Society Press, 2005.

Index

Prince of Wales (King Edward VII), 214
Promontory Summit, Utah, 8, 12
Prussia, 117

Quantrill, William C., 234n36
Queen Victoria's Jubilee Celebration,
  214

Rafferty, William, 36, 200
Railroads: Arkansas & Texas, 197; Cen-
  tral Pacific, 8, 23; Chicago and North-
  western, 192; Denver & Rio Grande,
  197; Fremont, Elkhorn and Missouri
  Valley, 192; Mexican Central, 250n22;
  Nashville and Lebanon, 84; Northern
  Pacific, 148; Union Pacific, 7, 8, 25,
  37, 39, 69, 77, 82, 84, 97, 98, 117, 136,
  140, 141, 144, 146, 148, 182, 184, 185,
  186, 188–90, 194, 196, 200, 201, 206,
  208, 217n45; Utah Northern, 148
Raines (Reins), Fonce ("Lorenzo"). See
  Duncan, George F.
Rainsboro, Ohio, 23, 83, 84, 87
Raleigh, N.C., 87
Ranches: Alkali, 76; Ben Eager, 157;
  Boggs, 44; Bull Dog, 102, 216n31;
  Cold Springs, 156, 243n16; Hager,
  133; Owens, 132; Six-Mile, 63–64, 72,
  79; TA, 201, 225n10; Ten-Mile, 168
Randall, Charles. See "Dutch Charley"
Randall, Todd, 8
Rankin, James G. ("Jim"), 148–49
Rankin, Joseph, 149
Rankin, Robert ("Bob"), 149–50
Rankin, Rosa, 150, 242n77
Rapid City, Dak., 17, 71, 72, 98, 100,
  164, 165, 167, 195, 202, 232n38
Rawlins, Wyo., 136, 144, 145, 148, 149,
  207, 242n75, 242n77, 252n57
Ray, Nick, 201
Raymond, John B., 71
Raymond, "Red," 215n4
Reconstruction Period, 123
Red Canyon, 14, 48, 125, 209, 245n12
"Red Head Mike," 200
Reed, F. B., 52
Reed, Thomas, 133–35, 137, 138, 141,
  146, 179, 237n24
Reed, William, 114

Remington Company, 3
Reno, Nev., 224n6
Republican Party, 3, 4, 197
Reynolds, Bainbridge, 60
Reynolds, J. C. ("Cayuse"), 225n7
Richards, Charles, 23
Richardson, C. W., 7
Richardson, Leander P., 253n74
Richardson (blacksmith), 183
Richmond, Va., 87
Rifles, Henry, 66, 68; Sharp's, 52, 53,
  106, 203; Spencer, 52; Winchester, 63,
  68, 122, 155, 165, 169, 192
Riley, James M. See Middleton, David
  Charles ("Doc")
Rio de Janeiro, 251n47
Rivers: Amazon, 251n47; Belle Fourche,
  195; Big Dry, 5; Cheyenne, 15, 32, 33,
  51, 52, 55, 56, 66, 126, 133; Dry Chey-
  enne, 137; Little Big Horn, 4; Little
  Laramie, 39; Little Missouri, 203, 204;
  Missouri, 7, 65, 71, 167, 192;
  Niobrara, 14, 17; North Platte, 8,
  217n42; Platte, 17; Powder, 218n20;
  South Platte, 43, 44, 208; Wind,
  238n24; Yellowstone, 148, 194
Robbers' Roost, 15, 33, 105, 106, 123,
  164
Roberts (shotgun messenger), 52–54
Robie, Frederick C., 140, 147, 179, 240n40
Rochester, N.Y., 128
Rock Creek, Wyo., 139–41, 194
Rock Creek-Fort Fetterman Stage Line,
  141
Rockerville, Dak. 202
Rock River, Wyo., 212
Rockville, Dak. 202
Rodney Landing, Miss., 214
Rogers, Richard, 40
Roosevelt, Theodore, 195, 196
Root, Frank, 32
Rosa, Joseph G., 239n33
Ross, Charles, 116, 119, 121–22, 122,
  133–35, 137, 147, 148, 177–78, 196,
  207, 247n66, 248n67
Round Rock, Tex., 209, 253n65
Ruby, Frank. See Robie, Frederick C.
Rusten, Harry, 82
Ryan, Duncan. See Duncan, George F.
Ryan, Thomas, 189

Wyoming Territorial Penitentiary, 79, 82, 115, *163*, 163–64, 176, 177, 196, 207

Yale lock, 151
Yankton, Dak., 5, 71, 94, 182, 218n20, 230n13
Yates, F. D. & Company, 9, 10, 13
Yates, Frank D., 8, 9, 215n12, 215n13
Yellow Hair, 5, 212

Yellowstone National Park, 64
Young, Harry ("Sam"), 49–50, 70
Young, Samuel. *See* Hartman, Samuel
Younger brothers, 5, 237n24
Young Man Afraid (Indian chief), 203–204

Zimmerman, John, 138, 142, 147, 239n31